Mac®
SECRETS

Mark Hattersley

WILEY

Wiley Publishing, Inc.

ACQUISITIONS EDITOR: Aaron Black

PROJECT EDITOR: Jennifer Lynn

TECHNICAL EDITOR: Dennis Cohen

PRODUCTION EDITOR: Rebecca Anderson

COPY EDITOR: Kitty Wilson

EDITORIAL DIRECTOR: Robyn B. Siesky

EDITORIAL MANAGER: Mary Beth Wakefield

FREELANCER EDITORIAL MANAGER: Rosemarie Graham

ASSOCIATE DIRECTOR OF MARKETING: David Mayhew

PRODUCTION MANAGER: Tim Tate

VICE PRESIDENT AND EXECUTIVE GROUP PUBLISHER: Richard Swadley

VICE PRESIDENT AND EXECUTIVE PUBLISHER: Barry Pruett

ASSOCIATE PUBLISHER: Jim Minatel

PROJECT COORDINATOR, COVER: Katie Crocker

COMPOSITOR: Chris Gillespie, Happenstance Type-O-Rama

PROOFREADER: Jen Larsen, Word One NY

INDEXER: Johnna VanHoose Dinse

COVER DESIGNER: Ryan Sneed

COVER IMAGE: © Chad Baker / Lifesize / Getty Images

I'd like to dedicate this book to my two girls: my wife, Rosemary, and Amber the cat. Neither can resist the allure of shiny Macs either. In my wife's case, she hides it well as Associate Editor of PC Advisor. Amber, my kitten, definitely loves the Mac and has spent much of the last few months trying to help me out by tapping the keyboard while I work and getting her claws stuck. Any typos are hers.

—Mark Hattersley

About the Author

Mark Hattersley is an avid Mac enthusiast who has been working with Macs since he first came across a Macintosh at college and was hooked on its beauty and simplicity.

He is now editor in chief of *Macworld UK*, and runs a number of Mac-related titles, including *Macworld*, MacVideo.tv, *iPad & iPhone User*, and a design publication called *Digital Arts*.

He also develops apps for the iPhone, writes books (like this one) and is training to run his first marathon. He rides an electric bike to work called a GoCycle, the most Apple-like non-Apple product he owns.

Mark lives in London with his wife Rosemary and his cat Amber, and frequents the Greenwich Meantime Brewery, which he maintains is the finest bar in the world.

Mark can be found on Twitter (@markhattersley) and is happy to chat about Macs all day long.

About the Technical Editor

Dennis R. Cohen has been, among other things, a poker dealer, restauranteur, teacher, programmer, editor, and author...the latter three occupying his time for the past three decades plus. He is the author, co-author, or contributing author of more than 30 books and has been the technical editor of over 300 titles, including this and every previous edition of *Mac Secrets*. He lives in Spokane, WA with his wife, three dogs, and three cats in close proximity to nine grandchildren (and their parents) and three great-grandkids.

Acknowledgments

You never write a book like this completely on your own, and I'd like to thank everyone who helped me: Jennifer Lynn, whose infallible project editing skills kept me from straying too far off track (sorry for writing far too much at first); Dennis Cohen, the Technical Editor, whose searing insights and breadth of Apple knowledge astonished and humbled me on more than one occasion; Kitty Wilson and Rebecca Anderson for impeccable copy editing and production editing, respectively. Finally, thanks to Aaron Black for hiring me in the first place.

Contents at a Glance

Contents

Read This First

Back in 1997, I was doing the first job I'd every truly loved: I was a writer for a technology magazine. I was two years into the job, and my beloved Macintosh—an amazing Performa 580—was the heart and soul of my work, and my life. And I worked hard—all day long and most of the night. I really loved that job. And I loved that Mac!

That same year, one of Apple's biggest rivals, Michael Dell (founder and chairman of Dell, Inc.) was asked what he'd do if he was in charge of Apple. "What would I do?" he replied. "I'd shut it down and give all the money back to the shareholders."

"Huh?" I thought. "What about all of us in the office? All these people who love Apple? How can this company possibly be in trouble?"

But Dell had hit the nail on the head: Apple was in trouble. Serious trouble. Steve Jobs later revealed in 2010, after he returned to the company in the winter of 1996, that he had less than 90 days to turn it around or face bankruptcy.

Here we are, just over a decade later, and Apple isn't just a big company—it's the biggest tech company in the world with a market capitalization worth of $287 billion. By the time you read this, it may not be just the biggest tech company by market share, but also the biggest company in the world.

Many people think that this is all thanks to the iPod, iPhone, and more recently, the iPad. And while these devices are great products, and they've undoubtedly been big successes, they mask the massive spike in popularity of the Apple Mac and Mac OS X: the computer and operating system double-combo that has been the heart of Apple for more than a decade. Apple sells around 14 million Macs every year, and the number goes up each quarter with more and more Mac users. The Mac is—in short—big business.

Apple started fighting back in 1998 with the classic iMac, and followed it with a range of sumptuous, stylish and, above all, stunning products that continue to this day. Since that infamous comment by Dell, Apple has consistently produced machines that outperformed, out-styled, and eventually overpowered everything else on the market. Nothing comes close to today's Apple Mac.

Which is why Apple is getting millions of new customers every year. And they're not just the old guard picking up a new machine; these are new customers, new to

Macs and typically coming from the world of Microsoft Windows. Apple calls these individuals *switchers*, and they are most welcome to the world of Apple Mac, which is—let's face it—a heck of a lot more fun than Windows.

Modern operating systems have developed over the years, and they are big and complex beasts. Even ones like Mac OS X, which are beautifully simple to use, have a level of complexity that you don't find in other products. And as Mac OS X has evolved, so has its audience, gradually learning the nuances of new features as they go about deftly operating the computer system.

But what about the newcomers? What about those millions of new Mac fans who don't remember the introduction of Mac OS X in 2001? Don't remember the gradual release of new features such as Exposé, Dashboard, Spotlight, Time Machine, or Quick Look? Where should they learn all that info that tried-and-true Mac users have gained in a decade's work?

The answer is, of course, this book: *Mac Secrets*. I wanted to put in everything I knew about Macs and Mac OS X—every little trick and tidbit I've picked up in the last 10 years—and let the new guys learn the all the best tricks. Mac OS X has thousands of features. Each bundled application and utility has hundreds of hidden functions, and Mac fans like me have tweaked and transformed regular programs beyond all recognition.

I really want to share that knowledge with other people. So it doesn't matter if you've just gotten your first Mac or if you've had one for years. This book is for anybody who wants to get more out of a Mac, anybody who wants to tweak, change, and transform their Mac.

Mac Secrets is for Mac fans: young or old.

Who This Book Is For

Have you ever been to an Apple Store? I'm guessing you probably have, at least once. Probably when you bought the Mac.

You've seen the Apple Genius, yeah? The guy or the girl working at the Apple store in the cool t-shirt who knows all the inside moves for Mac OS X. They'll help you set up a Mac, fix it if it's broken, and pass on insider tips and tricks.

This book is for those people who want to be the Genius they see at the Apple Store.

What This Book Covers

Mac Secrets is mainly about Mac OS X, although I also look into Mac hardware—both the machine that you buy and the hardware you can attach to it.

Apple transformed the Mac in 2006 by switching from the older Power-PC based processors to Intel chips. And in 2009 it completed this process by releasing Mac OS X 10.6 Snow Leopard, an update completely rewritten from scratch to work only on Intel Macs and to get the most out of those machines. I recommend that any Mac user run an Intel Mac and upgrade to Mac OS X 10.6 Snow Leopard, if you aren't running it already (it's only a $29 upgrade). Those are the technologies that this book is really all about.

Of course, you can run an older Mac if you want, and you can run an older version of the operating system. You'll still get plenty out of this book. But computing is all about being in the present and looking to the future. And if you want to be that Apple Genius, you need to be on top of things.

How This Book Is Structured

I've divided this book into four sections, each one designed to guide you on your way from Mac newbie to Apple Genius.

The first part, "Becoming a Mac Setup Pro," is all about buying and setting up a Mac. Even if you already have a Mac you'll get a lot from this first part. I look at how to get great deals, how to switch from Windows to a Mac, and how to manage Mac OS X networks and disks.

Next, in Part II, "Getting More Out of a Mac," I look at making the most of your Mac. This includes everything from upgrading to speeding up your system to personalizing and protecting Mac OS X from intrusion.

The third part, "Becoming a Digital Genius," is all about, well, becoming a digital genius. Music, movies, and digital images are so important these days, and I share my thoughts on how you can be amazing with the media you have on your Mac. I also look at the iPad, iPhone, and iPod touch and how you can transform your Mac experience with one of these handheld devices.

Finally—and here's the doozy—we look at turning you from a Mac expert to a Mac Genius in Part IV, "Training Up as a Mac Genius." This final section is all about cloud computing, UNIX, troubleshooting, and computer programming. It's tough stuff, but once you've read the final part, you'll be legitimately able to refer to yourself as an Apple Genius.

What You Need to Use This Book

To use this book, you'll need a Mac (preferably an Intel-based Mac) and a copy of Mac OS X 10.6 Snow Leopard. If you aren't yet running Snow Leopard, I recommend that you upgrade now.

I also recommend that you have a high-speed Internet connection while you work, because many of the secrets described in this book hook into the Internet. I frequently offer Web links so that you can download files or find extra information online.

Features and Icons Used in This Book

The following features and icons are used in this book to help draw your attention to some of the most important or useful information in the book, some of the most valuable tips, insights, and advice that can help you unlock the secrets of Mac OS X.

▶ Watch for margin notes like this one that highlight some key piece of information or that discuss some poorly documented or hard to find technique or approach.

SIDEBARS

Sidebars like this one feature additional information about topics related to the nearby text.

TIP The Tip icon indicates a helpful trick or technique.

NOTE The Note icon points out or expands on items of importance or interest.

CROSSREF The Cross-Reference icon points to chapters where additional information can be found.

WARNING The Warning icon warns you about possible negative side effects or precautions you should take before making a change.

Are you ready? Let's get started. It's going to be a fun ride.

PART I

BECOMING A MAC SETUP PRO

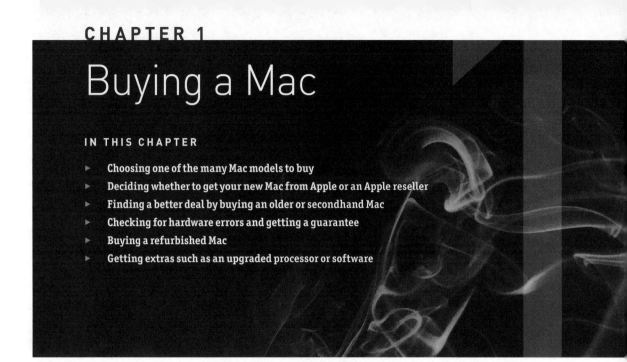

Congratulations, you are—or are about to be—the proud owner of an Apple Macintosh computer, or Mac. Even if you're a seasoned "Machead," this chapter will give you advice for picking up your next model. This chapter covers what you need to know about getting a Mac: everything from choosing which model to buy, to deciding where to buy a Mac, to getting a good deal on older, secondhand, or refurbished models. This chapter also describes the optional extras Apple offers with its new Macs, plus accessories you should consider for a Mac. But first you must choose which Mac is right for you.

CHOOSING WHICH MAC TO BUY

If you don't have a Mac already, which one should you get? That's a conundrum that only you can answer. The good news, however, is that there are no bad Mac computers. Unlike the free-for-all bazaar that makes up the rest of the PC market, Apple makes just a few models, and it makes sure all of them arrive at your desk in peak condition. Each model is markedly different from the others, but the differences are based on your needs, not quality.

Every new model is typically ahead of the technology curve, is well designed, and has the kind of build quality you'd expect from a premium manufacturer such as BMW or Mercedes. This quality comes with a premium price tag, but with a bit of savvy shopping, you may be able to get a better deal than you originally thought.

▶ That's not to say there haven't ever been any bad Macs. The G4 Cube and Twentieth Anniversary Macs were generally considered flops. But Apple has had far more hits than misses.

FOUR MYTHS ABOUT MACS

When you're in the process of buying a Mac, especially if you're moving from a PC to a Mac, you may have some misconceptions. Although Macs have become much more popular recently, a lot of people who've never started up a Mac have plenty to say about them as computers, usually based on nonsense they've heard from other non-Mac users.

Here are four of the biggest myths about using Macs:

- ▶ **Macs aren't compatible with Windows PC:** Almost every type of file that you can open on a PC (Microsoft Office documents, movies, and so on) can be opened on a Mac. You can make changes to these files on a Mac and share them with Windows users. You can even run Windows inside Mac OS X.

- ▶ **Macs can't run Microsoft Office:** Wrong! Macs have been able to run Microsoft Office since 1989, and Microsoft Word first appeared on the Mac way back in 1984.

- ▶ **Macs can't reuse PC peripherals:** Macs use the same connections that most PC peripherals use (most notably USB), and they are largely made using the same type of physical internal components (hard drives, RAM, and so on). Digital cameras, camcorders, printers, and other devices work as well on a Mac as they do on a PC.

> ▶ **Macs don't have any software:** More than 12,000 applications are available
> for Macs, covering about every kind of computing task you can imagine.
> Just about every major program (Microsoft Office, Adobe Creative Suite,
> FileMaker, and so on) is available for Mac.
>
> If you hear any negative talk along these lines, you can be sure that it's a com-
> plete myth.

When choosing a Mac, the model you pick largely depends on the features you
require. Macs are available in six different models, and each one is aimed at a particular kind of user.

Mac Pro

The Mac Pro, as shown in Figure 1-1, is the most powerful Mac on the market. (Often
it's the most powerful home computer on the market.) It's also the most upgradable
Mac, offering a level of internal access denied on models such as the iMac.

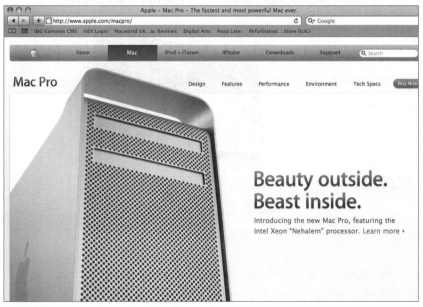

FIGURE 1-1: The Mac Pro model is the most upgradable Mac, with an internal structure
that makes adding and replacing components easy.

CROSSREF Chapter 10 has more information on upgrading options for Macs.

Most home users find the Mac Pro overkill. Unless you have a specific requirement for a Mac Pro feature, such as RAID to perform Mac OS X Server functions, or if you require high-end computing function (video editors, scientists, and 3-D graphic designers typically fall into this category), you should consider Apple's consumer model, the iMac, instead.

iMac

The iMac is perhaps the computer for which Apple is most famous. The iMac started out as a classic colorful unit that Apple used to re-launch itself into the computing market. It has since evolved into a svelte aluminum widescreen unit, as shown in Figure 1-2.

FIGURE 1-2: The iMac is Apple's all-in-one desktop computer, aimed at home users.

One of the biggest advantages of purchasing an iMac over other Mac models is the large high-quality widescreen display that makes up the bulk of the computer, including the hard drive. The minimalist design of the iMac also makes it a superb space-saving option.

When you purchase a new iMac, you get an Apple Wireless Keyboard and Magic Mouse by default. However, you can opt for a wired Apple Keyboard and/or a wired

Apple Mouse. New Mac Pro computers come with the older wired mouse and keyboard, but you can pay extra to upgrade to the newer Magic Mouse and wireless keyboard.

CHOOSING A BIGGER DISPLAY

Designers and video editors aren't the only ones who benefit from a large display. In 2005, Pfeiffer Consulting tested the Apple 30-inch Cinema HD display against a 17-inch display in a number of tasks. The report found that working on a 30-inch display doubled productivity when using applications such as word processing or spreadsheet editing; it tripled productivity when using design programs such as Adobe Photoshop. If you consider how much you're paid per hour, spending the extra money on a large display can pay for itself. To read the report, see `http://images.apple.com/pro/pdf/Cin_Disp30_report.pdf`.

Mac mini

The Mac mini is Apple's lowest-cost model. It was originally targeted specifically at Windows switchers (people who used Windows PCs but wanted to move to Mac). As its name suggests, the Mac mini is an exceptionally small unit, as shown in Figure 1-3. What the Mac mini lacks in stature, it certainly doesn't lack in performance, offering much the same specification as the MacBook.

FIGURE 1-3: The Mac mini is Apple's best-value machine, and its small stature makes it a great choice for PC owners looking to put a Mac on their desk.

Its small size and low power consumption have endeared the Mac mini to Apple enthusiasts who've found a range of uses for the device beyond that originally envisioned by Apple. For example, it's possible to attach a Mac mini to a television set to create a great media center. Many people also use the Mac mini as a server for a home office or other small office, and Apple recently created a special edition called the Mac mini Server that comes with two internal hard drives (but no optical drive) and is packaged with Apple's Mac OS X Server software.

MacBook

The MacBook is one of the most popular computers Apple has ever produced. First introduced in 2006, the MacBook is Apple's entry-level notebook.

The MacBook sports a 13-inch display, and the keyboard is made from square plastic keys (often referred to as the "chiclet" design because the keys resemble pieces of Chiclets chewing gum), as shown in Figure 1-4. It also houses Apple's large glass multi-touch trackpad to control the on-screen mouse and perform gestures.

▶ Apple always refers to its laptops as notebooks. It's just Apple's term for the same thing though.

FIGURE 1-4: The MacBook, the most popular computer Apple has ever made, is Apple's entry-level notebook and offers a lot of power for a reasonable price.

CROSSREF Chapter 14 has more information on multi-touch trackpad gestures.

The white MacBook is the only model not to feature a backlit keyboard that lights up automatically when the ambient lighting fades. With the exception of the Mac mini, the MacBook is the highest-value-for-the-money Mac. It's no surprise that the MacBook is Apple's best-selling Mac of all time.

WHAT'S A UNIBODY?

All of Apple's notebook models feature a unibody casing. In a unibody casing, the external frame of the case houses the internal components. Although this may sound commonplace, it's actually quite rare. Most devices are created using an internal frame, with external parts attached to it. The unibody design enables Apple notebooks to be lighter and stronger than rival models.

MacBook Pro

Like the MacBook, the MacBook Pro is a portable notebook. As the "Pro" moniker suggests, the MacBook Pro has higher specifications and a wider range of features.

The two most instantly noticeable differences between the MacBook and the MacBook Pro are the silver aluminum casing and the larger display, as shown in Figure 1-5. As well as the 13-inch screen on the MacBook, the MacBook Pro has 15- and 17-inch display options. These larger screen options also have more powerful innards, most noticeably the presence of a discrete graphics card. A discrete graphics card has its own memory, unlike the integrated graphics option used on the MacBook, which shares its memory with the main system. This ensures that the MacBook Pro is a much more powerful unit, especially for graphics-intensive tasks such as digital image and video editing, or for running games or programs that use 3-D graphics.

▶ The current MacBook Pro switches seamlessly between an energy-efficient graphics card and a powerful discrete graphics card for 3-D performance.

The MacBook Pro also features a backlit keyboard. When the light in your environment fades, the keys light up, enabling you to easily continue typing.

FIGURE 1-5: A range of MacBook Pro notebook models offer advanced components and larger display options than the MacBook.

MacBook Air

First introduced in 2007, the MacBook Air is a unique model that some Mac users consider a slightly odd purchase. The MacBook Air is similar to the 13-inch MacBook Pro, except it is shrunk down to an ultrathin case that measures just 0.76 inches thick, as shown in Figure 1-6. As the name suggests, the MacBook Air is all about being lightweight. It weighs in at just 3 pounds, almost 2 pounds less than the MacBook.

FIGURE 1-6: The MacBook Air's lightweight structure makes it a popular choice for users who spend a lot of time carrying around a notebook.

The screen remains the full 13-inch size, and it has the same full-sized backlit keyboard as the MacBook Pro. Although it lacks the glass trackpad from the MacBook and MacBook Pro, it does have multi-touch capability. Another omission is the optical drive, which you can purchase separately and attach via USB. Apple has a feature called Disc Sharing that enables a MacBook Air to "borrow" the optical drive from another Mac or PC computer.

The reason the MacBook Air is considered an odd purchase is because, on paper, the specs don't add up. Despite costing considerably more than other MacBooks, the MacBook Air has much lower specifications. However, by shaving two pounds off the weight of a MacBook, without compromising on the screen or keyboard, Apple has made a notebook that's incredibly popular among users who carry around a notebook all day long.

▶ I own a MacBook Air and swear by it. When walking around all day with a notebook, the extremely low weight is worth every penny.

FOUR REASONS PEOPLE BUY MACS

I asked the Apple experts why people buy Macs over PCs, and they gave me four main reasons:

▶ **Security:** Macs are more resistant to viruses, malware, and hacking than Windows-based computers. Although several thoughts exist about why this is true, the fact remains that you are less likely to suffer certain Internet-based problems when running a Mac.

▶ **Reliability:** Macs are, by and large, more reliable than Windows computers. This is partly because the Mac OS X software is better coded and works with a more limited set of hardware. Also, Apple creates both the software and the hardware, so the two are designed to work together without trouble.

▶ **Ease of use:** Apple is obsessed with making computers and software easy to use. Nobody in the world designs a software interface as well as Apple.

▶ **Style:** Sometimes it just matters.

So there are four reasons so many people buy Macs. They're secure, reliable, easy to use, and amazing looking. Why on Earth would anybody want to use anything else?

DECIDING WHERE TO GET YOUR MAC

Once you've decided which Mac to buy, the next obvious task is to get one. Because Apple tightly controls distribution, you are less likely to get a better deal by shopping around for a Mac than you are when buying a PC. Having said that, there are deals out there, and there are reasons for buying a Mac from a store other than Apple. But let's start with going straight to the horse's mouth.

Buying a Mac Directly from Apple

Apple makes computers and sells them directly to its customers. Typically, you can purchase a Mac from Apple in one of two ways:

▶ **Apple Online Store:** Apple offers a comprehensive online store at www.apple .com/store. You can also select a range of configuration options and customize your selection to a granular level, as shown in Figure 1-7.

▶ **Apple Retail Store:** Apple has a network of 300 worldwide stores. Apple stores operate in most major cities in the United States and Europe, as well as in Japan; Apple even has a store in China. You can find a complete list of Apple Retail Stores at www.apple.com/retail/storelist. The key advantage to visiting a physical store is that all Macs are on display, enabling you to get hands-on experience before deciding on a purchase. Apple also has a range of specialists on hand in each Apple Retail Store to answer your questions.

FIGURE 1-7: Apple's online store is an increasingly popular way to customize a Mac and have it delivered directly to your door.

Buying a Mac from an Apple Reseller

As well as buying a Mac directly from Apple, you can also purchase one from an Apple Authorized Reseller. These resellers are stores (both online and physical) that specialize in selling Macs and have passed stringent quality control from Apple, in offering both knowledgeable service and after-sales support.

Although fierce price-cutting isn't as predominant within the Mac retail community as it is in PC stores, Apple Resellers do sometimes run special offers, such as free hardware or software with new Mac purchases. You can find an Apple Reseller near you online at www.apple.com/buy/locator.

Apple also has Online Authorized Resellers that sell Macs online. These websites are worth checking out before making a purchase, just in case you can find a better deal than you can get from Apple. Apple has a list of Authorized Online Resellers operating in the United States online at http://solutionprofessionals.apple.com/catalog.

One high-profile exception is eBay. The sellers on eBay are unlikely to be Apple Authorized and, you may want to be careful about purchasing a Mac on eBay. Having said that, Apple warranties are valid with Apple regardless of where you purchased your Mac, and Apple uses an online system to track products via serial numbers and authorize products for repair.

> ▶ Resellers sometimes offer longer warranties, in a bid to lure customers away from official Apple Stores.

CROSSREF Chapter 21 has more information on troubleshooting a Mac.

GETTING A BETTER DEAL ON A MAC

One of the most common—and, to be fair, in some cases justified—reasons against purchasing a Mac over a PC is cost: Apple makes premium computers and charges a premium cost.

At this writing, the lowest-priced Apple notebook—the MacBook—is priced at $999; Dell offers a superficially similar laptop for $550. Upon closer inspection, the Dell computer offers a far lower spec, and I would argue a lower build quality than the MacBook.

I won't get too far into a Mac-versus-Windows PC debate. However, you should be aware of several good arguments for paying the premium Apple charges: superior build quality, integrated hardware and OS, more security against malware and virus

> ▶ When you compare the costs of Apple computers to those of PCs with similar specifications, the price is in the same ballpark. It's just that all Apple computers are high spec.

threats, industry standard software such as Final Cut Pro that is unavailable on a PC, and superior home software such as iPhoto and GarageBand that is Mac-only. None of these arguments, however, means much if your budget simply won't stretch.

So what can you do if you really want to own a Mac but simply can't stretch to the amount that Apple charges? Fear not. There are some secret tricks that can get you a great Mac on a budget.

GETTING A COLLEGE DISCOUNT

Apple has a discount scheme for college students. The good news is that to qualify, you can also be a college or K–12 teacher, administrator, staff member, or board member at any level in an educational establishment. Go to www.apple .com/education for more information about getting up to 10 percent off the price of a new Mac. You can also get up to 10 percent off the price of a new Mac by joining the Apple Developer Connection (http://developer.apple.com). For an annual membership fee, the Developer Connection gives developers access to the latest software development tools. A student with an active membership in the Apple Developer Connection can use both discounts simultaneously.

Buying an Older Model

As mentioned earlier in this chapter, one of the joys of buying a brand-new Mac is that typically Apple sources high-spec components that are designed to outperform other computers on the market. Apple is often the first to market with new computer processors, and Macs are typically stuffed to the brim with the fastest components.

This high-end performance is great news for new owners, who can be sure their Mac has a healthy life span. (The typical Mac lasts up to five years before technology demands require an upgrade.) But it's even better news for bargain hunters because it means that even last year's Mac is technically better than most of this year's Windows-based PC models. Get an older-model Mac, and you'll get a healthy discount on a great computer.

Because Apple is so secretive regarding new launches, the Apple Resellers may have plenty of old models in stock when a new model is launched. You can shave one-third of the price off a Mac by buying a previous-generation model.

▶ To get an older model with a healthy life span, stick with Intel Macs (avoid models with old G5 processors) and choose a machine from the last two years.

TIP Make sure to buy a machine powerful enough to handle your tasks. Two websites are useful if you're buying an older model: Low End Mac has a complete list of all profiles from older Macs (`www.lowendmac.com/profiles.htm`). Also useful is *Macworld's* Speedmark testing (`www.macworld.com/info/speedmark`). *Macworld's* reviews contain comprehensive Speedmark testing for all current and older models.

Buying a Secondhand Mac

Another great way to pick up a Mac for less money is to get a secondhand model, as shown in Figure 1-8. Apple has a lot of power users and aficionados who are always after the latest models and are more than happy to sell you an old one. As with buying an older model, picking up a secondhand model doesn't necessarily mean that you are buying an obsolete Mac. Macs have a healthy life span, and even a model from a couple years ago will still function admirably.

▶ Apple also sells secondhand refurbished models. There's more on this later in the chapter.

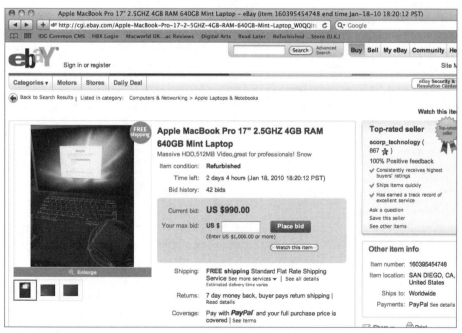

FIGURE 1-8: Buying a secondhand Mac or an older model is a great way to pay less than the premium that Apple charges on brand-new computers.

You need to check that the machine you are picking up is powerful enough to meet your needs. Aside from this, the main considerations with picking up a sec-ondhand model are ensuring that the device is in good working order, determining whether it has warranty still available, and making sure you pay a reasonable price.

GETTING INFORMATION ABOUT A SECONDHAND MAC

Because you are unlikely to buy a secondhand Mac from a store, you may want to check that the advertised Mac matches the description. You might also be able to get a lot of information about the Mac that even the seller might not be aware of.

You can get information about a Mac via a Mac OS X application called System Profiler, as shown in Figure 1-9. If you are inspecting a Mac in person, you can use System Profiler to check the Mac. To access System Profiler choose Apple ➜ About This Mac from the menu bar and click More Info.

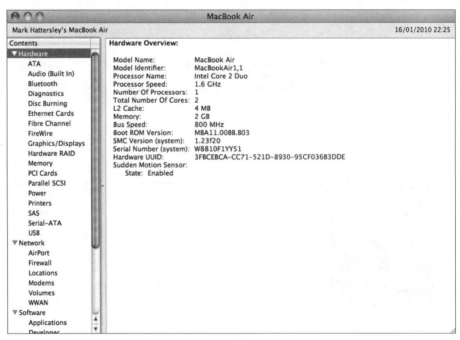

FIGURE 1-9: The System Profiler utility displays a wide range of information about a Mac, from the type of hardware it contains to the installed software.

> **TIP** When buying a secondhand Mac, make sure to get the installation discs for any software included in the sale. If you don't possess the physical discs, you may have legal problems regarding the license, and you may find it difficult to obtain updates. Also, if you don't have the installation discs, you won't be able to re-install the software if there are any problems.

CHECKING FOR HARDWARE ERRORS

One of the key concerns most people have when buying a secondhand Mac is whether it has an unknown fault with the hardware. Problems with the software can usually be rectified. Here is a list of items to check prior to handing over your money.

CHECKING THE HARD DRIVE

Open the Disk Utility application by choosing Go ➜ Utilities from the Finder menu (or pressing SHIFT+⌘+U) and double-clicking Disk Utility.

The first thing to check is the S.M.A.R.T (Self-Monitoring, Analysis, and Reporting Technology) status of the hard drive. You can check this at the bottom of the Disk Utility window, which should say "Verified," as shown in Figure 1-10.

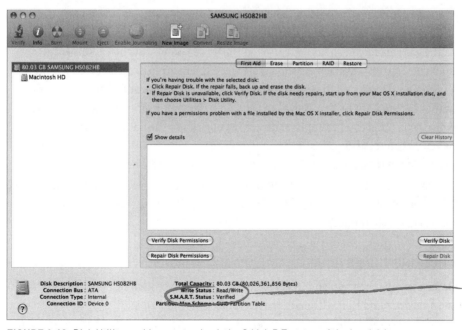

S.M.A.R.T.
status verified

FIGURE 1-10: Disk Utility enables you to check the S.M.A.R.T status of the hard drive.

One final method of checking for a problem is to physically listen to the noises the hard drive makes when idle and during use. A good way to listen to the hard drive in action is to copy a large file from one area to another—or highlight a large file, such as a movie clip, and select File ➜ Duplicate from the menu bar (or press ⌘+D). Normally the hard drive should remain relatively silent when not copying a file, and you may hear a faint clicking noise during copying. If the hard drive makes a scraping or whining noise, something may be amiss. A persistent audible high-pitched whine should be of particular concern.

▶ In addition to being annoying, this noise often occurs shortly before a hard drive goes kaput.

> **TIP** If you have never owned a Mac prior to buying one secondhand, try to get some time with one—either in a store or with a friend—prior to making a purchase. Familiarize yourself with the sounds that the device makes. Quite often, a computer component makes an odd noise before it fails.

CHECKING THE OPTICAL DRIVE

The optical drive is another area you should check prior to purchasing a secondhand Mac. Unlike with the hard drive, Disk Utility can't check the physical status of an optical drive (because the disks are, by nature, replicable). However, like the hard drive, an optical drive unit is prone to error and should be tested before use.

▶ Hard drives and optical drives both have moving parts, which makes them more error-prone.

The best way to do this is to insist on observing a Mac's optical drive in action. At the very least, you should ensure that the drive accepts and ejects CDs without problem. That is, the machine should eject a disc smoothly, with an electric whir. You should also ensure that you can copy files from the optical disc to the hard drive without error. As with hard drive, you should listen for any unusual noises. A slight whirring is normal, as the optical disc spins up prior to the data being read. However, be wary of any scuffing noises that suggest the disc isn't spinning cleanly in the drive. And as with hard drives, any high-pitched whines are not normal.

▶ You can't use mini-CDs in slot loading drives.

Most Macs (apart from the Mac Pro and MacBook Air) come with slot-loading optical drives. Replacing these is both expensive and difficult so make sure to test the optical drive thoroughly.

CHECKING THE KEYBOARD, TRACKPAD, AND MOUSE

Be sure to give the keyboard, trackpad, and mouse a thorough test prior to purchasing a secondhand Mac. Although these components are well built and sturdier than most, they are also the parts that receive the most physical use. To test the keyboard, open the TextEdit application by choosing Go ➜ Applications (or pressing ⌘+A) and double-clicking TextEdit. Type out some sample text.

CHECKING A MAC NOTEBOOK

When purchasing a Mac notebook secondhand, there are a few things you should check in addition to what you check when considering a desktop model:

▶ **Check for dents:** Aluminum MacBooks are sturdy creatures, but one sign of mistreatment (specifically that the device has been dropped) is to check for dents in the case.

▶ **Look for signs of scruffiness:** The white MacBook models are prone to collecting dirt. Although this isn't necessarily a problem, it may be a sign that the owner has taken less care of your new pride and joy than you will.

▶ **Check the lid:** Make sure the lid opens and closes smoothly, without difficulty. The modern MacBook range has a magnetic clasp that connects the lid to the base. Older MacBook Pro models have a silver tab on the front of the MacBook that you push in to release the lid. These tabs are particularly error-prone, so make sure the lid opens and closes smoothly.

▶ **Make sure the backlit keyboard works:** If the unit has a backlit keyboard, look at whether it works correctly. The only real way to test it is to darken the room.

▶ **Make sure the device sleeps:** When you close the lid, the notebook should go to sleep. The best way to test this is to look at the white Apple logo on the reverse of the display. This logo should light up when the notebook is in use and should quickly turn off when the lid is closed.

▶ **Ensure that the battery charges:** Make sure the device is plugged in during testing and that the battery charges correctly. The chargers on recent Apple notebooks should connect and be held in place magnetically (a system called *MagSafe*). A light on the side of the connection keeps you informed of charging status; orange signifies charging, and green indicates fully charged.

▶ **Ensure that the battery holds charge:** One thing you need to be careful of when buying a secondhand machine is the amount of charge the battery still holds. A MacBook battery, when new, provides between 5 and 8 hours of use (depending on the size and type of battery), but this capacity can drop over use. A full charge on an old battery lasting 30 minutes isn't unheard of, and eventually the battery will fail to hold any charge at all. You should check the battery life indicator in the menu bar and make sure it displays the time instead of the percentage by ⌘+clicking on the battery icon and choosing Show ➜ Time from the drop-down menu. Then you need to wait a few minutes for the notebook to operate without a charge and see how much remaining time is displayed.

Apple builds high quality machines, but Macs (like all computers) are complicated pieces of machinery, and there are lots of things that can go wrong.

GETTING A GUARANTEE

It may sound obvious, but the best thing you can do prior to buying a secondhand Mac is to ask the person selling it if he or she knows of any problems whatsoever. Of course, there's no guarantee of the person's honesty, but getting a guarantee prior to purchase in case you discover any errors is a good way to go about any sale. One advantage to purchasing via an auction site such as eBay (www.ebay.com) is that you can check whether the seller offers a guarantee and uses the PayPal Buyer Protection program and eBay Resolution Center (http://resolutioncenter.ebay.com) if there are any problems.

CHECKING THE APPLE WARRANTY AND APPLECARE

Apple offers 12 months of support and care with all new Macs. You can also purchase a longer support package called AppleCare that offers 3 years of coverage from the original date of purchase. AppleCare provides telephone support plus global repair of both hardware and software.

HOW MUCH IS THAT MAC WORTH?

There are two good ways to measure the worth of a Mac. The first is to head to a website called Mac2sell (www.mac2sell.com), to get an accurate valuation. Another way to determine the value of a secondhand Mac is to check a popular auction site, such as eBay (www.ebay.com), for auctions of the type of Mac you want that are just closing or have already completed.

Getting a Refurbished Mac

In addition to buying a new Mac or a secondhand model, you have a third option: You can buy a Mac from the refurbished section of the Apple Store (http://store.apple.com/us/browse/home/specialdeals). "Wait," you say. "Isn't *refurb* just another term for *secondhand* or, even worse, a term that means *previously broken*?"

Not only do you get the full 12-month warranty that comes with a new Mac, you also get the option to purchase an additional AppleCare plan to extend the period of service and repair to 3 years. That should be enough to calm your nerves about the quality of the product.

Typically you will save at least 10 percent on a machine, and this amount rises to around one-third off the retail price. So where do the refurbished products in the Apple Store come from? Some of them are Macs that were returned as faulty and have been repaired. But others may have been returned for other reasons, such as non-payment on a credit plan. Apple also loans equipment to media sources to test out, and for events and trade shows such as Macworld Expo. When the equipment has been used to show off Apple products, it is placed into the refurbishment scheme.

You shouldn't count on a refurbished model not showing any signs of previous use, but if you're happy to have a Mac that may have been used before but has been checked out, works properly, and comes with guarantee, then the refurb section of the Apple Store, as shown in Figure 1-11, is worth checking out.

> ► You can also get refurbished iPhones, iPods, AirPort Base Stations, and just about every other Mac product on sale.

> ► The last three Macs I've bought have been from the refurb section of the Apple Store. In each instance, I couldn't tell if they had been used before.

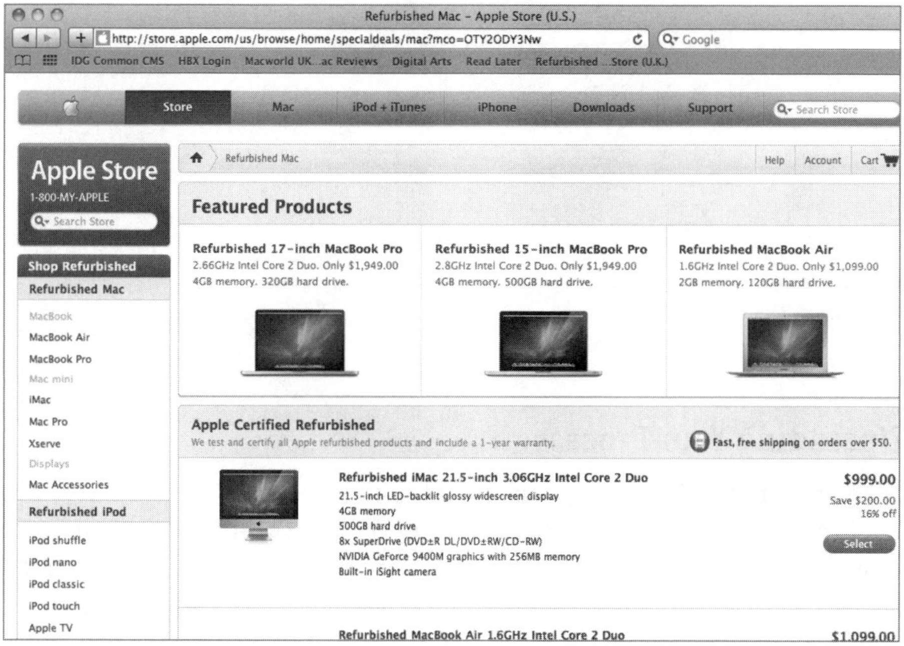

FIGURE 1-11: The refurb section of the Apple Store enables you to pick up a Mac that was returned to Apple and refurbished. Refurbs come with a 12-month warranty.

GETTING OPTIONAL EXTRAS WITH A MAC

When you purchase a Mac from the Apple Online Store, you need to select a number of options before you finalize your purchase. The range of options may seem a little daunting at first, as Figure 1-12 shows, but it's important to choose the right options.

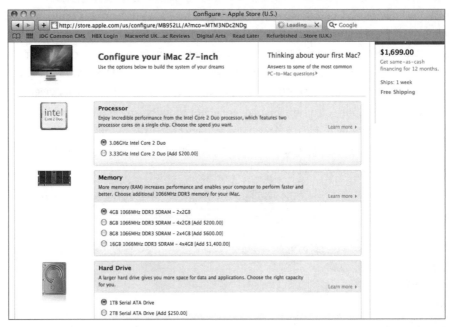

FIGURE 1-12: Apple offers a range of optional extras with a new Mac. Choosing the right options enables you to build the machine that is right for you.

Upgrading Your Processor

▶ It is sometimes possible to replace and upgrade a processor in a Mac, but it's extremely difficult and invalidates the warranty.

The processor option is normally available only with a brand-new Mac. Not every Mac has an upgrade option, and often the price of upgrading can be high. However, upgrading the processor is an option worth exploring. Processors are hardwired into all Macs, and upgrading a processor after you've purchased a Mac isn't an option.

A faster processor enables a Mac to perform complex tasks more quickly. Most Macs come standard with powerful processor units. A faster processor is unlikely to make a huge difference unless you do a lot of high-end work. Picking a base unit with the standard processor will give you many years of performance. Having said that, opting for a faster processor will extend the usable lifetime of your Mac.

Purchasing Extra Memory

Another option to consider when buying a new Mac is whether to purchase **extra memory**. More memory enables Macs to run programs faster and more efficiently and to run multiple programs at the same time. Prior to Mac OS X Snow Leopard, most applications ran in a 32-bit environment, where the greatest amount of memory available was 4GB. Since the introduction of Mac OS X 10.6 Snow Leopard, a Mac program can use up to **32TB of theoretical memory.**

> ▶ Even though Snow Leopard can support 32TB, the most memory a Mac currently supports is 32GB on the 8-Core Mac Pro.

> **TIP** If you want to get a bargain on memory, don't purchase it from Apple at the same time you purchase your Mac. Apple charges a premium for RAM, and you can typically purchase a RAM upgrade for less than the amount Apple charges. You can get RAM from a lot of different companies, such as Kingston (`www.kingston.com`) and Crucial (`www.crucial.com`).

Adding a Larger Hard Drive

Your hard drive is the central storage area for your Mac, and it's important to get one that fits your needs. If you're coming from an old computer, you might find the storage space on the latest Macs bountiful. But hard drives fill up quickly when you start installing applications, downloading movies, importing photos, and so on.

Whether you purchase a larger hard drive with your Mac depends largely on what you feel your needs are. Although most Macs come with a reasonably large hard drive (the MacBook Air is a notable exception), it is reasonably easy to upgrade the internal hard drive on most Macs. However, it's generally easier and more practical to add extra storage to a Mac in the form of an external hard drive.

> **CROSSREF** Chapter 6 has information on keeping your hard drive free from clutter, and Chapter 10 has more information on upgrading your hard drive space.

Getting a Display with Your Mac

Most desktop Macs come with a display attached, with the exception of the Mac mini or Mac Pro. So if you're purchasing one of these, unless you already have a display, you need to consider getting one. It is also possible to attach a second display to Mac notebooks and the iMac. Some people find that working with two screens makes life easier and more efficient. Attaching a larger screen to a Mac notebook (along with a keyboard and mouse) enables you to use it like a desktop computer.

Choosing Apple Keyboard and Mouse Options

If you purchase an iMac or Mac Pro from Apple, your purchase will include a mouse and keyboard by default. You can opt for different wired or wireless mouse options and choose international language keyboards before purchasing.

Adding an Apple Remote

An Apple Remote used to be standard with all Macs, but now it is an optional extra. The Apple Remote enables you to access the Front Row interface on a Mac and play music, watch videos, and display photographs from a distance. It is also used to control an Apple TV.

Getting a Mini DisplayPort Adapter

Apple recently included a new kind of display connection called a Mini DisplayPort. At this writing, the Mini DisplayPort is a relatively rare monitor connection. Apple includes three options to connect MiniDisplay ports to other common monitor connections:

- ▶ Mini DisplayPort to DVI
- ▶ Mini DisplayPort to Dual-Link DVI
- ▶ Mini DisplayPort to VGA

The adapter required depends on the connection used on your monitor. Typically, modern monitors (with the exception of those made by Apple) use DVI, with Dual-Link DVI required for monitors with 30-inch or larger displays. VGA is used on older monitors and is often found on projectors.

Selecting Software with Your Purchase

Apple offers a range of software that you can purchase along with your new Mac. Every new Mac comes with Mac OS X and the iLife suite of applications. Mac OS X has a wide range of programs included, for tasks such as using the Internet, sending e-mail, managing contacts, and other basic functions. It even has a built-in dictionary and text editing programs that function as a good—if somewhat basic—word processor.

Purchasing MobileMe with Your Mac

MobileMe is an online membership service that you pay for annually. MobileMe enables you to use your Mac from another location via the Internet. It includes e-mail, online iCal, and Address Book syncing; syncing of certain Mac OS X items such as preferences and Keychain; online storage; and remote access called Back To My Mac. It syncs information on Mac and Windows systems, so it's a good choice for users of multiple operating systems. Chapter 22 has more information on MobileMe.

▶ *You can usually save money by buying a boxed copy of MobileMe from an online retailer such as Amazon.*

Selecting One to One Membership

One to One is a scheme Apple offers that enables you to get personal training with a new Mac. Training typically takes place in Apple Retail Stores, in the form of an individual meeting with an Apple Genius. For more information on One to One, see www.apple.com/retail/onetoone.

▶ *Apple calls its in-store experts Apple Geniuses.*

Getting a Printer to Go with Your Mac

A printer to physically output information to paper used to be considered an essential accessory for any computer. These days, it's considered more of an extra. The type of printer you choose depends on your needs. Typically, people interested in printing graphics go for inkjet printers, and users with business needs go for laser printers or all-in-one units. Be aware that the biggest cost of a printer isn't the unit itself but the cost of replacement ink cartridges; this is especially true with inkjet models.

You may not really need a printer. Mac OS X can turn virtually any document into a PDF (Portable Document Format) file, which you can view on Macs, Windows PCs, and UNIX/Linux computers; e-mail to other people; and display on iPhones or iPods. More and more people are forgoing printers completely and using digital files instead.

▶ *To create a PDF file from just about any application, choose File → Print, click on PDF, and choose Save as PDF.*

CONSIDERING OTHER ACCESSORIES TO GO WITH YOUR MAC

Although Apple offers a comprehensive set of hardware and software options with a Mac, there are some other common items you might consider purchasing along with your Mac:

- ▶ **Apple Airport Extreme Base Station and Airport Express Base Station:** These are both extremely good Wi-Fi routers. While they require a modem to provide an Internet connection, they are both likely to provide much better service than a Wi-Fi router provided by your Internet service provider. The AirPort Express is smaller and designed to be taken on the road; the AirPort Extreme has multiple antennas for faster performance. Chapter 8 has more information on networking.

▶ **Time Capsule:** This unique device is similar to the AirPort Extreme Base Station but also includes a hard drive for remote backups. Chapter 7 has more information on backing up your Mac with a Time Capsule.

▶ **TV tuner:** The ability to watch and record digital television and radio on a Mac is a great inclusion, and a number of USB devices enable you to record programs.

▶ **External hard drive:** Getting an external hard drive is a relatively inexpensive way of increasing the amount of storage available. Also, you can use an external drive to back up a Mac, using Apple's Time Machine software.

▶ **Laptop bag:** If you're getting a Mac notebook, you probably want to also pick up a laptop bag to store it and carry it around safely.

▶ **Speakers and earphones:** Every Mac (even the Mac mini) has a built-in speaker, but the sound quality is better on some models than on others. If you have a Mac Pro or Mac mini, you might want to consider investing in a pair of external speakers. Alternatively, you can attach a pair of earphones to any Mac to listen to audio.

While there is any number of cool accessories to go with a Mac, you shouldn't feel the need to get carried away. A Mac fresh from the box packs plenty of power, and usually has all you need to get up and running. You can always add on extra features at a later date.

SUMMARY

The first step toward Mac nirvana is getting a machine, and just looking at all of the possibilities can be lots of fun in and of itself. When you purchase a new Mac, a secondhand Mac, or a refurbished Mac, you can be secure in knowing that your new machine will be of the highest quality. Whether you use your new Mac for business or pleasure, it comes equipped with plenty of software to get you up and running, and there is an abundance of additional software and hardware so that you can get your Mac to do whatever you need it to.

CHAPTER 2

Setting Up a Mac

Few things in life are more satisfying than unpacking and setting up a new Mac. The moment you open the box, it becomes apparent that something special lies inside. Apple takes design very seriously, and from the inside of the Mac to the outside of the box, everything is designed to work amazingly well.

In this chapter, we'll get just as serious about setting up a computer as Apple was about building it. This chapter provides tips for setting up your computer workstation that will make life much easier and help you prevent injuries. But the real magic begins when you turn on the power: booting up, setting up your user account, registering your Mac, and logging in. So let's get your Mac ready to roll.

UNPACKING AND SETTING UP A MAC

▶ Don't throw the box away. Mac packaging is small enough to store and it's easy to fit the Mac back into the original box, which adds to the resale value.

The first thing you'll want to do upon delivery is take your Mac out of the box and set it up.

If you purchased a new Mac, it will likely be sealed inside a paper sleeve. In addition, a MacBook will have a paper sleeve between the screen and the keyboard. Some people keep the paper in case they decide to re-box the Mac, but there's no real need for it. You will also find a white box labeled "Everything Mac" that contains an instruction manual, the Mac OS X installation discs, and some Apple stickers.

If you purchased a Mac with a display, you should also get a display-polishing cloth to wipe dust from the display.

▶ Keep the installation discs safe in case you ever need to reinstall Mac OS X.

You will also receive a power cord, and if you opted for a Mac notebook you'll get an external power supply unit. In the case of a Mac notebook, you'll receive a MagSafe power adapter with two cable options: an AC wall plug that connects the power adapter straight to the wall or a power cord. The wall plug is a more tidy option, whereas the power cord provides more length.

A Mac mini comes with a MiniDVI-to-DVI adapter that's used to connect the device to a DVI display.

Both the Mac Pro and iMac also come with a keyboard and mouse. Because the Mac Pro is designed to sit further away from you than the iMac, it also comes with a USB extension cable.

If you purchased a MacBook Air, you'll also receive a USB-to-Ethernet adapter. You use this adapter when you want a tethered network connection instead of a wireless AirPort connection.

Getting to Know the MagSafe Adapter

The power adapter that comes with a MacBook, as shown in Figure 2-1, is known as the *MagSafe Adapter* because it uses a magnetic connection, which is incredibly useful. It is designed to quickly disconnect from your notebook in the case of an accident (somebody tripping over the cable, for example).

Take a close look at the power supply unit provided with a Mac notebook, and you'll see that it has two extendable flaps. You can pull out the flaps to provide two hooks that you can wrap the cable around. At the end of the cable is a clip you can use to attach the wrapped cable together. If you use the plastic plug instead of the extension cable, you can wrap up the entire power supply into a package that fits neatly together and makes the whole thing easier to carry around.

FIGURE 2-1: The MagSafe Adapter is a power cord that attaches magnetically to the Mac.

The MagSafe Adapter also comes with a plastic housing that fits over the end of the connection. Because the adapter is magnetic, it may attract small metal particles, which can be difficult to remove. These particles can cause electrical shortages. You should therefore use the clear plastic housing over the MagSafe tip when you're carrying around the MagSafe Adapter.

> **NOTE** When you connect the power cord, you see an LED (light-emitting diode) appear on the socket connection. This LED has two states: orange to signify that the MacBook is charging and green to signify that the device is fully charged. There are lights on both sides of the housing, so you can connect the MagSafe adapter to the power cord socket in either orientation.

Setting Up The Keyboard and Mouse

If you purchased a Mac Pro or iMac, you received a wireless Magic Mouse and a keyboard (wired with the Mac Pro and wireless with the iMac). Mac mini computers and Mac notebooks do not come supplied with a keyboard and mouse.

The wireless keyboard and mouse need to be in proximity to the Mac, and you should turn them on before powering up the computer. (The Mac will deliver a reminder if they're not turned on.) The power button for the keyboard is located on the right-hand side of the keyboard. The keyboard requires two (or three, for older models) AA batteries, which you insert into the left-hand side of the device.

As with the keyboard, the mouse requires two AA batteries. To turn on an Apple Magic Mouse, you use the switch on the underside of the device.

You don't need to worry about turning off the mouse and keyboard when you're not using your Mac. They both turn off automatically and turn back on when you press a keyboard key or click the mouse.

If you purchased a wired keyboard, you need to connect it to one of the USB ports on the computer. If you opted for a wired mouse, instead of the wireless Magic Mouse, you need to plug the short cable into the USB port on the side of the wired keyboard.

▶ To open the battery compartment to check or replace the batteries on a keyboard, use a coin.

CREATING A GOOD WORKING ENVIRONMENT

The setup of your working environment can have a big impact on your health. Many people suffer injuries from working with computers. Repetitive strain injury (RSI), conjunctivitis, eyestrain, migraines, fatigue, neck and back strain, and carpal tunnel syndrome are common computer-related injuries. If you're careful, you'll encounter such injuries only in other people and be able to advise them about how to alleviate their troubles. Either way, this section of the book will be important to you.

Setting Up Your Desk

When you sit at your desk, your hands should be in a relaxed position, with your elbows at a 90-degree angle to the desk. Your wrists should feel relaxed when your hands are over the keyboard.

Keep your mouse as close to the keyboard as possible. You shouldn't have to reach or stretch to access your mouse. Sorry if this sounds a bit like Mom talking, but good posture is important. Your back should be straight, your feet should be flat on the

▶ If you have a raised keyboard, it's wise to invest in a gel wrist support. You can get these supports integrated with mousepads as well.

ground (or you should use a footrest), and you shouldn't slouch or hunch your shoulders. Invest in a good chair that supports the arch in your back. Your monitor should be at eye level, around 18 to 28 inches away from your face.

At the Ergotron website (www.ergotron.com), you can provide your height, and the site gives you exact measurements for your desk setup. Figure 2-2 shows an example of a good workspace layout.

> If you don't do anything else to create an ergonomic workspace, at the very least make sure your monitor is at the correct height. Most people have their monitors too low, and this can lead to neck, shoulder, back, and eyestrain.

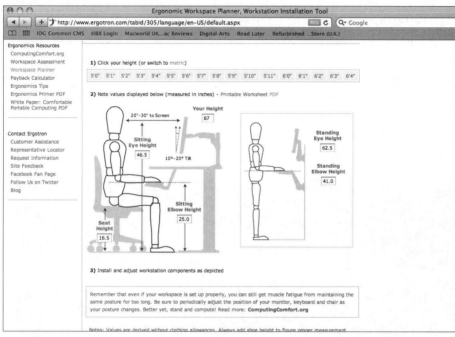

FIGURE 2-2: Especially if you'll be working on your Mac for a substantial part of the day, you should set up an ergonomic workspace.

Taking Regular Breaks from the Screen

Be sure to take regular breaks and look away from the screen periodically. Modern computer screens with LED displays are not as bad for eyes as older displays with cathode ray tubes (CRTs). (Looking at a CRT is essentially the same as looking at a light bulb.) Even so, if you spend eight hours a day staring at a computer screen, you will soon start to strain your eyes.

Computer work has a tendency to distort time, especially if you become engrossed. Most people don't take anywhere near the recommended length or frequency of breaks. If this sounds like you, then consider setting alarms, via iCal, or by using a physical alarm clock to remind you to break from your computer.

Medical experts suggest that it's better to take shorter breaks more often than longer breaks less often. For example, taking a 5- to 10-minute break after 50 to 60 minutes of work is better than a 15-minute break every 2 hours. But either schedule is better than working for hours on end without a break at all.

If you want help with taking breaks, you can install a program such as the free AntiRSI (http://tech.inhelsinki.nl/antirsi), as shown in Figure 2-3. This program monitors your usage and periodically suggests taking micro pauses (about 13 seconds) and longer breaks (about 8 minutes). A commercial application called MacBreakz (www.publicspace.net/MacBreakZ) provides similar functionality, and also monitors keyboard and mouse usage and provides advice on how to more ergonomically use your computer.

▶ I use AntiRSI all the time. You can postpone breaks, but be careful not to get too engrossed and turn off your reminder system. You need breaks!

FIGURE 2-3: Programs such as AntiRSI provide helpful reminders to regularly take breaks.

If you spend a lot of time typing in Microsoft Word (or another word processor), you might want to consider changing the default color scheme. Most word processing programs display black text against a white background, to simulate the look of paper. This combination isn't the easiest on the eyes, however, and many writers use a more ergonomic solution, such as a blue background and white text. In Microsoft Word, choose Word ➜ Preferences and select the General preference icon. Select the Blue Background, White Text check box and click OK. It takes some getting used to, but this color scheme is much easier on your eyes. This setting is local to your computer and used for display only. Documents print out as normal and display with the normal white background and black text on other computers.

Dealing with Problems (Before They Happen)

If you suffer from problems such as RSI, backaches, carpal tunnel syndrome, or other computer-related troubles, you should consider investing in special equipment. Here are some examples:

▶ **Ergonomic keyboard:** You can invest in ergonomic keyboards that are designed to fully minimize hand movement, such as those made by Maltron (www.maltron.com). These are a bit odd looking but can be wrist-savers.

▶ **Get a backpack:** If you carry a notebook around, you might consider investing in a backpack rather than a shoulder bag because it spreads the weight across your back.

▶ **Vertical mouse:** Like a Maltron keyboard, a vertical mouse is a bit weird looking and takes some getting used to. Evoluent (www.evoluent.com) is known for its vertical mouse range, which has been approved by the health services clinic at University of California at Berkeley.

▶ **Trackball:** The mouse is so ingrained as part of the computer interface setup that most people don't realize the benefit of using a trackball instead. Trackballs are far better for the wrist than the mouse, and they're great space-savers, too. Kensington (www.kensington.com) and Logitech (www.logitech.com) are two of the better-known trackball manufacturers.

▶ **Speech recognition:** Many RSI sufferers invest in custom software, such as MacSpeech Dictate (www.macspeech.com). This software enables you to dictate text documents, although it takes some practice to get it working effectively.

▶ **Monitor arm:** Another great tool in the ergonomic armory is a monitor arm. These handy devices attach to a monitor and hold paper documents and other items at eye level. If you have a MacBook or iMac, you can consider purchasing a stand to adjust the position of the built-in display.

This is by no means a comprehensive list. If you suffer from any computer-related problem, you should get a doctor to check you out.

LEARN DOUBLE-HANDED SHORTCUTS

A neat habit to get into (and it's one that very few people are aware of) is to use both hands for keyboard shortcuts. This method minimizes the scrunching up of fingers. For example, you can hold down the ⌘ key on the right-hand side of the keyboard with your right thumb and press the S key with the ring finger of your left hand. Got it? One hand holds the modifier, and the other presses the button.

SETTING UP MAC OS X

After you power up your Mac for the first time, the boot process begins. Owners of new Mac systems and those who have just done a clean installation of Mac OS X get to watch a stylish welcome video and go through the setup process.

The Setup Process

After the short setup video plays, you're taken to the Setup Assistant, which guides you through the setup process. The following sections describe the various windows in the Setup Assistant.

THE WELCOME WINDOW

▶ If you wait at the Welcome window for approximately 30 seconds, Apple's VoiceOver technology opens and a large dialog appears. VoiceOver is part of Apple's Universal Access technology for users with disabilities.

The first screen of the Setup Assistant is the Welcome window, which prompts you to select a country or region. If you live outside the areas displayed, you select the Show All check box to bring up a wider range of countries. When you've selected the appropriate country, click Continue.

THE KEYBOARD WINDOW

The Keyboard window enables you to choose a keyboard layout that matches your region. The default option is usually selected for you, based on the option you chose in the Welcome window. If this is the wrong area for your keyboard layout, or if you want to choose a layout different from the default, click the Show All button and select the appropriate keyboard.

DO YOU ALREADY OWN A MAC?

The Do You Already Own a Mac window is helpful to users who are upgrading from an earlier Mac system and who have it on hand, or to those users who have used Time Machine to back up their data. From this window you can launch a program called Migration Assistant, which enables you to transfer system information from one Mac (or Time Machine backup of a Mac) to another. The data on the original source remains unaffected.

To run Migration Assistant and transfer your information, you choose any of the first three options:

▶ From another Mac

▶ From another volume on this Mac

▶ From Time Machine backup

You can use Migration Assistant to transfer information from one Mac volume to the Mac you are setting up. Migration Assistant can transfer the following information:

▶ Users

▶ Networks and other settings

▶ The Applications folder

▶ Files and folders on the startup drive

> ▶ You can run the Migration Assistant application at any time, not only during the setup process. You can find Migration Assistant in the Utilities folder inside the Applications folder.

TRANSFERRING INFORMATION FROM ANOTHER MAC

To transfer information from another Mac, you need either to connect both computers via a FireWire connection or connect them both to the same network (by using a physical Ethernet connection or the same wireless network).

If both computers have FireWire ports, you can use a FireWire cable to connect the two machines. Restart the source Mac (the one from which you are transferring information) while pressing and holding the T key. This places the source Mac in Target Disk mode, which enables direct access to the hard drive. (In effect, it turns the whole computer into an external hard drive.) You can then select the type of information you want to migrate and click the Transfer button.

To migrate your information from one Mac to another via a network, you need to turn on the source computer and open the Migration Assistant application. Then you choose To Another Mac from the options and click Continue.

> **WARNING** It can take a long time to migrate information from one Mac to another. Typically you should set aside a morning or afternoon for the transfer, or leave your computer running overnight.

TRANSFERRING INFORMATION FROM ANOTHER VOLUME

The Transferring Information from Another Volume option is for Mac users who have more than one installation of Mac OS X on their Mac. This volume can be either another hard drive or another partition on the Mac's main hard drive.

> **CROSSREF** Chapter 9 has more information on partitioning disks.

TRANSFERRING INFORMATION FROM A TIME MACHINE BACKUP

Time Machine is an incredibly useful utility that was first introduced in Mac OS X 10.5 Leopard. It primarily acts as a simple backup and restore system feature that enables you to retrieve lost information. Time Machine also has a fantastic second use: You can use it to transfer system information from one Mac to another via Migration Assistant.

> **CROSSREF** Chapter 7 has more information on setting up and using Time Machine to back up your Mac.

▶ It's best to start making a full backup of your old Mac before unpacking the new one. The backup process can take a while.

Before you begin the process of using Time Machine to transfer information from the source Mac, you should first ensure that a full backup has recently taken place.

DO NOT TRANSFER INFORMATION RIGHT NOW

Choose this option if you are setting up a new Mac and don't have a previous model; or you can use this option if you want to perform a clean installation and start fresh. You can always run Migration Assistant later.

After you have finished migrating information from another Mac, or if you are setting up a new Mac, you'll be taken to a window that helps you to set up wireless network preferences.

SELECT A WIRELESS SERVICE

The Select a Wireless Service window enables you to quickly and easily join a Wi-Fi network if your Mac possesses an AirPort connection.

If your computer won't be connected to a wireless network, click Different Network Setup, which takes you to a window with a wider range of network options, including Cable Modem, DSL Modem, and Local Network (Ethernet). You can also click the My Computer Doesn't Connect to the Internet option; if you select this option, you bypass the Apple ID and Registration Information windows, as explained in the next section, and go straight to the Personalize Your Settings window.

> **CROSSREF** Chapter 8 has more information on setting up a wireless network.

ENTER YOUR APPLE ID

An Apple ID is your identification account with Apple. You primarily use your Apple ID to make purchases and download content from iTunes, log in to services provided on the Apple website, and use iChat. If you have a MobileMe account, you simply enter your name and password here. If you don't have an Apple ID, you can leave this box blank and click Continue. (You can create an Apple ID later if you like.)

REGISTRATION INFORMATION

The information you provide on the Registration Information page is automatically delivered to Apple via the Internet. You can't leave any fields on this page blank, and there is no button that enables you to bypass registration. If you want more information on why Apple is collecting this information about you, and what it is used for, click the Privacy Policy button.

> ▶ It is possible to skip registration. To do so, press ⌘+Q and select the Skip option.

CREATE YOUR ACCOUNT

You need to create a User account before you can use your Mac. You use the User account to log on, and as a security check (known as *authentication*) when you want to install a program or want to change something vital (such as deleting files in the Mac OS X System folder).

To create the User account, you need to enter a name and a short name. The name should be your full name and the short name an abbreviation that you will enter when authentication is required. You also need to type a password (and verify it by typing it again). It is vital that you choose a password that is both memorable and secure, because this main account you are setting up is an Administrator Account and has a high level of control over the operating system.

> **NOTE** There is no way to retrieve a password that you have forgotten, although you can reset the password on your computer by using the Reset Password utility on the installation disc.

Finally, you need to enter a password hint that will be used to jog your memory if you forget your password. If you enter an incorrect password three times in a row, the screen shakes and displays your password hint. When you're done with this screen, click Continue.

CREATING SECURE PASSWORDS

To create a secure password that is easy to remember, try the following:

▶ Combine multiple words with punctuation marks.

▶ Use a mixture of uppercase and lowercase letters, and replace some letters with numbers.

▶ Make sure the password is more than eight letters long.

▶ Avoid using single words, names of friends, local street names, or other personal information.

A good tip for a memorable password is to use random words connected with special characters such as ampersands (&) and plus (+) signs. For example, the password "red" is incredibly weak, but the password "red&yellow+pink&green" would be incredibly strong, and so is "r3d&ye11ow." Apple has some good thoughts on creating secure tips on its support website (`http://support.apple.com/kb/HT1506`).

You can also click on the Key icon next to the password text field to open the Password Assistant. This program offers suggestions for passwords. A pop-up menu enables you to change the type of password, and a length slider changes the number of characters used.

SELECT A PICTURE FOR THIS ACCOUNT

One of the great customization features of Mac OS X is the ability to use a picture on your account. This picture isn't just used when you log in; it also becomes part of your Address Book contact and e-mail account, and it's used in your iChat conversations. So make sure you're happy with the one you pick.

You can select an image from the picture library or the images Apple provides, but you can also take a quick snapshot of yourself using a Mac's built-in iSight web camera.

SELECT TIME ZONE

The Select Time Zone window enables you to select a time zone for your Mac. Mac OS X 10.6 uses Location Services to automatically detect your time zone based on the location of your network connection. If the operating system chooses the wrong location, or if you want to select another time zone, you can uncheck the Set Time Zone Automatically Using Current Location box and click on your location on the map. Alternatively, you can enter the name of a nearby city in the Closest City box.

SET THE DATE AND TIME

The Select Data and Time window enables you to set up the Mac's clock and calendar. You simply enter the correct date and time.

DON'T FORGET TO REGISTER

If you skipped the registration process earlier, you are prompted again at this point to register. Click Done to continue.

AUTOMATICALLY RENEW MOBILEME

If you are a MobileMe member and you entered your Apple ID, you are presented with an option to automatically renew your membership. After you select your option, press Continue.

THANK YOU

Finally, a Thank You window appears, telling you your Mac is set up and ready to use. You can click the Go button to start using your Mac.

Running Software Update

Apple periodically pushes updates to the Mac OS X operating system and the various applications that are included with Mac OS X. These are called *software updates*. It's common to find that the software included on a brand-new Mac has been updated in the time it's taken for the machine to leave Apple and arrive at your location. So the first thing you should do upon starting up a new Mac is run the Software Update application to check for the latest software.

From the Apple menu, choose Software Update to launch the Software Update utility. The application accesses the Internet and begins looking for new software. If your software is up to date, the application says so, and you can click Quit to continue. If the application finds new software, the Software Update window lists the updates available, and you can select which updates to install by using the check boxes. Typically you should select all items and click Install. You may be required to enter the password you used earlier to set up your account.

SUMMARY

Although unpacking and setting up your Mac might sound like teaching a duck how to swim, there is a lot more to setting up a good working environment than throwing a Mac on a desk and turning it on. You need to get your Internet connection up and set up a User account, which you will surely use for years to come. In addition, you should take the time to set up an ergonomic work environment—your body will thank you later. It's also well worth installing software such as AntiRSI to ensure that you take regular short breaks. As part of setting up Mac OS X, be sure to run the Software Update utility to ensure you're using the latest and greatest version of the Mac OS and other software.

CHAPTER 3

Running Windows and Other Operating Systems on a Mac

IN THIS CHAPTER

▶ Using Boot Camp to install Windows on your Mac

▶ Using Virtualization to install Windows on your Mac

▶ Keeping Windows and Mac safe with security

▶ Running Windows software on a Mac using CrossOver Mac

▶ Installing the UNIX operating system Ubuntu on a Mac

When you're part of the Mac community, it's all too easy to look down on other operating systems. But Microsoft Windows is a big part of the computer world, and other UNIX systems like Ubuntu are powerful, and interesting, even if they lack the finesse of Mac OS X. Mac owners have an ace up their sleeve, however. It is possible to run Windows and other operating systems on a Mac. You can do this in one of two ways: either as a standalone operating system that can be launched as an alternative to Mac OS X on startup or inside Mac OS X using a process known as virtualization. The latter option enables you to run Mac OS X and Windows programs side-by-side, with little discernable difference. Ready to click the Start button? Read on to get your Mac ready for Microsoft.

INSTALLING WINDOWS ON A MAC WITH BOOT CAMP

Boot Camp is an Apple program that enables you to install Windows XP, Windows Vista, or Windows 7 on your Mac. With Boot Camp, Windows is installed on a separate partition on your hard drive or on a second hard drive attached to your computer (frequently a second hard drive inside a Mac Pro). Mac OS X features a program called Boot Camp Assistant that takes you through the process of partitioning your hard drive to create a second volume and installing Windows, as shown in Figure 3-1. The other part of Boot Camp is a set of drivers included on the Mac OS X installation disc. These are installed into Windows to enable it to fully utilize all the Mac hardware.

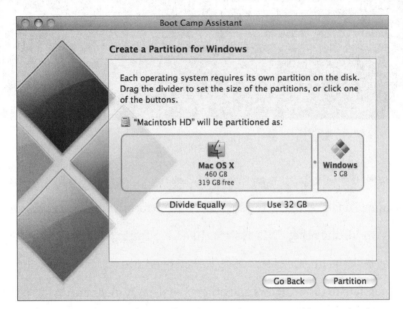

FIGURE 3-1: You can use Apple's Boot Camp software to partition your hard drive and create a second volume for a Microsoft Windows installation.

To install Windows on a Mac via Boot Camp, you need the following items:

▶ A licensed copy of Windows XP, Windows Vista, or Windows 7.

▶ Your Mac OS X installation disc or a CD with the latest Boot Camp driver downloaded from Apple (www.apple.com/support/bootcamp)

You'll learn how to obtain the latest drivers in the next section.

WORKING WITH WINDOWS GENUINE ADVANTAGE

Windows contacts Microsoft via the Internet for authorization, a process known as *Windows Genuine Advantage*. You're supposed to install a copy of Windows on only a single machine. You can install it on a limited number of machines before it fails authorization. If this happens, you can call Microsoft using a telephone number supplied with the Windows disc. Keep this in mind if you plan to install Windows on multiple Macs; you may need copies for each machine. If your copy of Windows fails authorization, it will run in a basic mode, without any visual effects and with limited access to the Windows functionality.

Updating Boot Camp Drivers

For Windows to run effectively on a Mac, you need a number of drivers for the Mac hardware (graphics card, keyboard, mouse and trackpad, and so on). These drivers are available on your Mac OS X installation disc.

When you first install Windows, the installation disc will be inside the computer, and the eject button doesn't work because the drivers aren't present. To get around this problem, you click the triangle next the Start button and choose Restart. Hold down the mouse button (or trackpad button on a Mac notebook) to automatically eject the Windows installation disc as your Mac starts up.

▶ Remember to hold down the Option key and select the Windows partition by clicking the arrow icon.

Updating Boot Camp

In the Update Boot Camp window, you choose Start ➜ All Programs ➜ Apple Software Update. If any new software is available, it appears in the Updates list.

Below the Updates list is a second list of optional new software. If you like, you can check these options to install additional Apple software such as Safari, iTunes, and QuickTime. Click Install when you're ready. You need to click Next on the following License Agreement window for each item you selected. When the User Account Control dialog appears, you click Yes to enable Apple Software Update to install the programs.

▶ Unlike Mac OS X, Windows typically needs to be restarted after new software has been installed.

RESIZING A BOOT CAMP PARTITION

It is possible to resize your Boot Camp installation after you have installed Windows XP or Vista (but not Windows 7, unfortunately). This can be really useful if you install Windows using a small partition and then decide you need more space later.

You can do this by cloning the Windows installation using a program called Winclone (www.macupdate.com/info.php/id/25932/winclone). You clone the Windows installation to an external hard drive, wipe the Boot Camp partition, and create a new—larger—one. Then use Winclone again to clone the Windows installation to the new Boot Camp partition.

Winclone is a free program, and the company has promised that Winclone 3.0 will have support for Windows 7, although support is somewhat sporadic.

Using the Boot Camp Control Panel

After you've installed Windows on a Mac, you can adjust the settings for Boot Camp by using the Boot Camp Control Panel.

When you first open the Boot Camp Control Panel, Windows presents a dialog that asks whether you want the program to make changes to the computer. Click Yes to enable Boot Camp to make the necessary changes to this Windows installation.

▶ Get used to seeing this security dialog, as Windows has a tendency to request confirmation when you are changing system settings.

CHOOSING A STARTUP DRIVE

By default, a Mac starts up from the main partition—the one that contains Mac OS X—when you start the Mac. It is possible to choose a different boot drive by holding down the Option key during startup by using the Startup preference pane.

Now that you know how to install Windows using Boot Camp, let's take a look at how to run Windows within Mac OS X.

USING VIRTUALIZATION TO INSTALL WINDOWS INSIDE MAC OS X

Virtualization is a rather grand and imposing term. But virtualization is easy; in fact, it's by far the easiest way to get Windows up and running on a Mac. *Virtualization* means running one operating system inside another. *Virtual* often means convincing but make-believe (as in virtual reality), but in this instance, there's nothing pretend about running Windows on a Mac in a virtual environment: You run a complete copy of Windows.

The key difference between using virtualization software and Boot Camp is that with virtualization, you run a copy of Microsoft Windows within and at the same time as the Mac OS X operating system. With virtualization, you launch Windows inside Mac OS X as you would any other application. It then appears inside a Mac OS X window, and you can interact with it as if it were any other program.

Cool, huh? Well it gets way cooler. Modern virtualization software on the Mac has the ability to strip away the Windows interface and integrate key Windows buttons (such as the Start button) on the Dock or menu bar. You can open Microsoft Windows applications inside regular Mac windows, some of them even re-styling the Windows applications to look as much like Mac applications as possible. In short, with virtualization, you get to run Mac programs and Windows programs side-by-side, right from inside Mac OS X.

Are there any caveats with virtualization? Well, running two operating systems at once puts a bit of strain on your Mac, and you're advised to install plenty of RAM.

▶ You should to go up to 4GB or even 8GB if you're looking to run Windows Vista or Windows 7 alongside Mac OS X.

CROSSREF Chapter 10 has more information on upgrading your Mac.

Even with plenty of memory installed, you'll only be able to allocate some of your system hardware to the virtual installation of Windows. Typically you'll find that processor usage is high and graphical prowess is limited compared to an installation running in Boot Camp.

TIP If you're planning to run Windows games with high-end 3-D graphics, you should use Boot Camp rather than virtualization for maximum performance. You can access a Boot Camp installation via Parallels or VMWare, albeit in a more limited way, through Mac OS X for occasional use, and you can start up directly from the Boot Camp drive to run programs that place high demand on the system.

But don't let the thought of a slower system put you off. Most Macs can run day-to-day programs, such as word processors, e-mail and calendar applications, and web browsers across both systems with ease. Only if you plan on using processor-intensive applications such as games or graphic design programs should you consider using Boot Camp rather than virtualization.

Choosing a Virtualization System

When it comes to Mac OS X virtualization programs, the number of options available is reasonably limited, so making a decision is relatively straightforward. If you're looking to run Windows on a Mac, you have these three options:

▶ **Parallels Desktop for Mac:** This was the first Mac solution and is generally regarded as the most user-friendly option. Parallels continuously adds new features and is particularly adept at integrating Windows into the Mac environment, using a feature called Coherence. Parallels Desktop for Mac also features comprehensive drivers that utilize multi-touch gestures from Mac OS X inside Windows. Installation is relatively straightforward, and Parallels Desktop even integrates with a prior Boot Camp installation. Parallels Desktop for Mac is currently on version 6 and costs $80. For more information, see the Parallels website (www.parallels.com).

▶ **VMware Fusion:** VMware has a long history in the virtualization market, as it's been making products for the enterprise market since 1998. VMware Fusion for Mac is generally seen as a more capable option than Parallels Desktop, particularly in graphical prowess. (However, recent updates to both VMware Fusion and Parallels Desktop have eliminated much of the difference.) More information can be found at VMware's website (www.vmware.com).

▶ **VirtualBox:** This is an open source, and therefore free, solution made by Sun Microsystems. Feature-wise, it's somewhat lacking compared to both Parallels Desktop and VMware Fusion, but recent updates have implemented 64-bit support and Open-GL graphics, and work on it is steadily coming along. VirtualBox isn't as user-friendly as either Parallels Desktop or VMware Fusion. Still, it's free and functional, so it may appeal to dabblers who have a spare copy of Windows lying around. More information can be found at www.virtualbox.org.

▶ *I go for Parallels Desktop myself. I find its feature set a little better than VMware Fusion's, and it performs slightly faster for me.*

Which system you choose largely depends on personal preference. Both VMware Fusion and Parallels Desktop for Mac are paid-for programs that offer similar feature sets, and both are easy to set up (far easier than installing Boot Camp). VirtualBox is more of an experimental system, which is fun to play around with (especially because it's a free download) but is not so good if you're looking for a stable installation of Windows on your Mac.

INSTALLING MAC OS X INSIDE MAC OS X

You can use virtualization software such as Parallels Desktop, VMware Fusion, or VirtualBox to install a variety of operating systems, such as Windows, Linux, OS/2, and Solaris. However, one thing you can't do is install a virtual copy of Mac OS X inside a virtual environment. This breaks Apple's Mac OS X licensing agreement. Because of this, no virtual environment provides support for this kind of installation. If this is the sort of thing that interests you, you can use Apple's s Mac OS X Server software (**www.apple.com/server/macosx**), which Apple does allow you to virtualize. This is also a cool way to set up and run Mac OS X Server without having to replace your day-to-day operating system.

Let's take a look at using Parallels Desktop for Mac to install a copy of Windows inside Mac OS X.

Deciding Which Files Open with Mac or Windows

If you're really going to town with integrating Windows and Mac, then you might want to take a closer look at which programs are natively associated with file types. Most files on your system will open with Mac OS X programs by default, especially files that are cross-format by nature (such as image, music, and movie files). However, you can change the file association and cause some files to open in Windows rather than Mac. There are two ways to look at file associations: from inside Finder or through Parallels Desktop.

To look at a file association in Finder, you highlight a file in Finder and choose File ➜ Get Info (or press ⌘+I). You use the Open With pop-up menu to choose a different application to associate with the file. Windows applications are highlighted with the Parallels icon (the same as files in Finder).

If you want to associate a lot of file types with a Windows program (such as all the different image types), it's usually quickest to use a Parallels feature called Smart-Select. To do this, you open the Windows program that you want to associate files with, right-click the program icon in the Dock, and choose SmartSelect. The Smart-Select window opens, displaying a list of file types that the program can open, as shown in Figure 3-2.

Choose to open applications with Windows or Mac

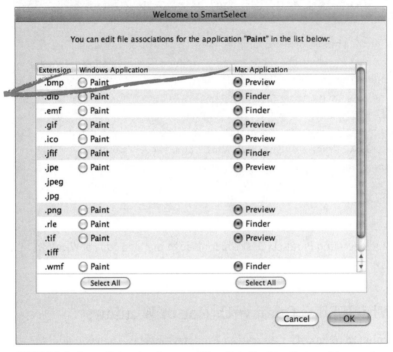

FIGURE 3-2: SmartSelect is a feature of Parallels Desktop that enables you to associate file types with either Windows or Mac applications.

A series of radio buttons enables you to set each file type to either the Windows program you selected or the default Mac OS X application. You can use the Select All buttons to change all file associations to the Windows program you used to open SmartSelect or their default Mac OS X associations.

Using Parallels Desktop for Mac with an iPhone

▶ The directions in this section use the term iPhone, but iPad and iPod touch can be substituted.

Before moving away from using Windows in a virtual environment, let's take a quick look at a neat trick you can do with a virtual environment. Armed with an iPhone, iPad, or iPod Touch, you can start up or turn off your virtual copy of Windows remotely.

To do this, you'll need to get a copy of the Parallels Mobile application from the iTunes App Store (http://itunes.apple.com/gb/app/parallels-mobile/id295531450?mt=8). Both Parallels Desktop for Mac and the Parallels Mobile app need to be set up before this will work.

You open Parallels Desktop for Mac and choose Parallels Desktop ➔ Preferences from the menu. Then you click on the iPhone icon to open the iPhone pane. Next, you click the Allow Connections from iPhone check box and make sure that the Send A List Of Your Mac's Accounts to Parallels Mobile check box is selected. You shouldn't click OK just yet, as you need this window open for now.

Next, you open the Parallels Mobile application on your iPhone and click the plus icon in the top right of the interface. You enter the hostname as it appears in the description in the iPhone pane in Parallels Desktop for Mac. Typically this is the name of your Windows PC, followed by a .lan extension (for example, john-pc.lan). Be careful of the capitalization because the iPhone tends to put capital letters in, and you need it to match exactly.

▶ The iPhone, iPad, or iPod touch and your Mac must be connected to the same network.

Now enter the Windows username, which is displayed in the iPhone pane in Parallels Desktop for Mac. You then need to enter the password that you enter when starting up the Windows virtual environment. Finally, you can click Save.

Now the Windows PC should appear in the Parallels Hosts list in the Parallels Mobile app. You click it to display the virtual machines available on your Mac. You can click one of the virtual machines to get a visual display of the screen. At the bottom of the screen, you see a selection of icons that enables you to control the status of your virtual machine:

▶ **On/Off:** Start up or shut down your virtual machine remotely.

▶ **Restart:** Restart the virtual machine.

▶ **Suspend/Resume:** Put the virtual machine to sleep. Click the triangular icon to resume.

▶ **Pause/Play:** Pause the virtual machine.

▶ **Refresh:** Update the display in the Parallels Mobile app.

Why would you want to do any of this from your iPhone? Well, many people find that working directly in Parallels Desktop for Mac is fine. But if you spend a lot of time setting up and testing virtual environments, the ability to remotely monitor and restart the machine is invaluable.

CROSSREF Chapter 19 has more information on accessing and controlling Mac OS X remotely with an iPhone, iPod touch, or iPad.

Shutting Down Parallels Desktop

If you have enough spare RAM in your Mac and you use Windows a lot, you might want to leave Windows running in the background all the time. (By default, Parallels Desktop for Mac adjusts the amount of necessary RAM to match your usage.) However, if you're an occasional Windows user and want to reclaim some of your system resources, you might want to quit the Parallels Desktop application when you're not using any Windows applications.

Be aware that quitting the Parallels Desktop application isn't quite as straightforward as quitting most Mac OS X applications because Parallels Desktop is running a whole operating system. If you use either of the Parallels options, you might notice that you have quite a few options to choose from. Choosing the right one can be difficult, so here's a handy guide:

▶ **Suspend:** This option freezes your virtual machine in its current state until you choose the Resume option. You typically use this option when you want to restart your Mac without interrupting the flow of work in the Windows machine. Although you can, you're not advised to use it when switching off the virtual machine for any length of time.

▶ **Shut Down:** Selecting this option safely saves all information in the Windows environment and switches off the virtual machine.

▶ **Restart:** This option turns off the virtual machine and boots it back up again. Sometimes Windows requests that you restart a machine in order for changes (such as new program installations) to be integrated with the operating system.

▶ **Pause:** This option temporarily pauses the virtual machine and frees up system resources for the Mac OS X operating system. Note that you should not quit Parallels Desktop while it is paused. Instead, you should resume the system and either continue using it or shut it down before quitting the application.

▶ **Stop:** This option forces the virtual machine to immediately quit. Using it is essentially the same as pulling the power supply on a computer. You should avoid using this option whenever possible to prevent damage to your virtual operating system. The Stop command is useful, however, when the virtual operating system freezes.

When you have shut down or suspended the virtual operating system, you can quit Parallels Desktop for Mac as you would any other program, as shown in Figure 3-3.

FIGURE 3-3: Remember to shut down or suspend the virtual machine before closing down Parallels Desktop.

INSTALLING SECURITY ESSENTIALS

Regardless of which installation route you take to put Windows on your Mac or which version of Windows you install, you need to install a security system. Mac OS X is remarkably resistant to Internet nasties, but your Windows partition may not be so hearty. It's running Windows, after all.

Fortunately, any Internet nasties you might encounter are likely to affect only your Windows partition. Even so, you really don't want malicious software messing around on your Mac. Thankfully, installing virus protection in Windows is a really straightforward process, and one that you can go about for free using Action Center. To begin, you click Start → Control Panel → System and Security → Action Center.

The Action Center window informs you that you have no virus protection available, so you can click Find a Program Online to launch Internet Explorer. If this is the first time you've launched Internet Explorer, it begins to go through a setup process (you can click Ask Me Later to skip it for now).

The web page that appears lists a wide array of security options. I recommend heading straight for Microsoft Security Essentials. It's a free option, is well supported, and offers seamless integration. And unlike some of the other free options, it

► Arguments rage about whether Mac OS X users should use security software. Most Mac users get by just fine without it.

► Action Center is known as Windows Security Center in Windows XP and Vista.

doesn't continuously attempt to get you to go for a paid-for option. You can click the Microsoft Security Essentials link here or get it directly from Microsoft's website, at `microsoft.com/security_essentials`. You click Download Now and Run to install it directly on Windows. You need to click Yes in another dialog to approve the installation. And as with other Windows programs, you need to go through a setup process and read a license agreement document.

With Microsoft Security Essentials installed, you should perform a quick scan of your computer (even if you haven't done anything yet). You need to ensure that the check box Scan My Computer for Potential Threats After Getting the Latest Update is selected and click Finish. Microsoft Security Essentials launches and immediately performs a download of the latest virus and spyware definitions from Microsoft. It then performs a scan of your system.

Microsoft Security Essentials sits in the background and protects the Windows partition of your Mac from malicious software. You can open it to run a full scan at any time by clicking Start ➜ All Programs ➜ Microsoft Security Essentials, as shown in Figure 3-4.

▶ Microsoft Security Essentials doesn't scan the Mac OS X operating system. However, it can scan the files on the Mac partition, or other volumes, for problems.

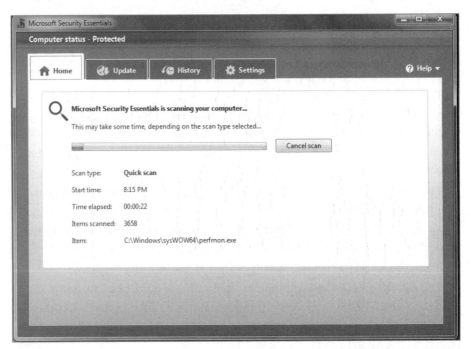

FIGURE 3-4: Microsoft Security Essentials is a free program from Microsoft that protects Windows from malicious software.

CHANGING A WINDOWS SECURITY SYSTEM

If you plan to ever move from one virus program to another—such as from Microsoft Security Essentials to an AVG program—it's imperative that you completely remove the first antivirus program before attempting to install another one. Antivirus software has a level of access to the machine that other programs lack. Many viruses try to disable antivirus software, so most antivirus software will prevent any program from disabling it (including other antivirus programs being installed). Having two antivirus programs running simultaneously can be extremely bad for Windows, and one may prevent successful installation, or function, of the other, leaving your system unprotected.

You click Save Changes to commit any adjustments from the Settings menu or press the red close icon on the top-right of the Microsoft Security Essentials Window to close the window.

BYPASSING WINDOWS COMPLETELY WITH CROSSOVER MAC

CrossOver Mac (www.codeweavers.com/products/cxmac) is an interesting Mac program that enables you to run Windows applications in Mac OS X without having to own or install a copy of Microsoft Windows.

There are some downsides to using CrossOver Mac. The biggest is that it doesn't work with every Windows program. Instead, compatibility is limited to certain programs, and some programs function better than others. CodeWeavers has an online service at www.codeweavers.com/compatibility that enables you to browse and search for compatible programs. Compatible programs are ranked as Gold, Silver, or Bronze. Gold programs typically work as they would in Windows, Silver programs work well enough to be stable (although some bugs prevent them from running flawlessly), and Bronze applications install and run but generally have enough bugs to be unstable.

▶ Save early and often is CodeWeavers's advice when running Bronze programs.

Installing Windows Programs with CrossOver Mac

CrossOver Mac makes it easy to install Windows programs without having to go through the effort of installing Microsoft Windows. The program automatically detects when a Windows installation disc has been inserted and runs accordingly, as shown in Figure 3-5.

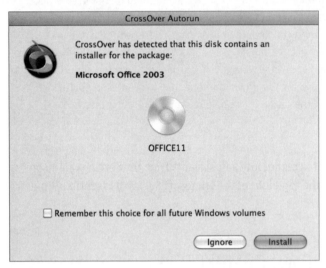

FIGURE 3-5: CrossOver Mac should automatically detect when a Windows installation disc has been inserted and offer to install the program for you.

NOTE CrossOver Mac may need to install fonts in order for the program to run correctly. If this is the case, you must accept the license agreement by clicking Yes.

By default, CrossOver Mac places applications in a folder called CrossOver inside the Applications folder, inside your Home folder. CrossOver Mac will create this folder if it doesn't already exist.

▶ This isn't the same Applications folder as the one located on the root of your hard drive (the one you access by pressing Shift+⌘+A).

Running Programs from CrossOver Mac

To run a program from CrossOver Mac, double-click a Microsoft Windows application file (within the CrossOver Mac/Applications folder) to open CrossOver Mac and start running the program.

TIP You can change the location of the CrossOver window through the application's preferences. You choose CrossOver ➜ Preferences and click Browse. Choose the folder you want and click Choose. I don't recommend using the regular Mac OS X Applications folder unless you create a CrossOver folder within it first.

CrossOver Mac programs run inside their own window, as shown in Figure 3-6, and—like Microsoft Windows programs—display the menu inside the window itself rather than using the menu bar like regular Mac OS X applications. The menu bar displays options related to CrossOver Mac. It's possible to install and run programs from the menu bar, as well as access recent files.

▶ Applications within CrossOver Mac can open and save documents to the Finder, like any Mac OS X program.

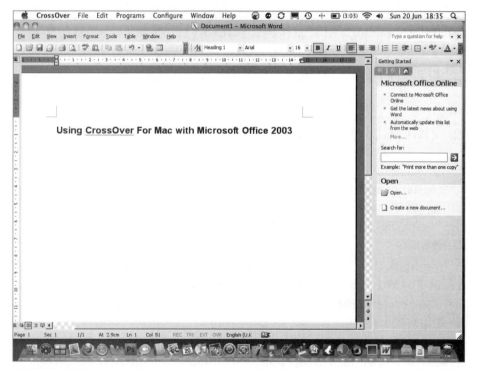

FIGURE 3-6: Windows applications running in CrossOver Mac appear inside a regular Mac OS X window.

Removing Windows Programs from CrossOver Mac

Windows applications installed using CrossOver Mac are known as *bottles*. Each bottle is a complete Windows environment within a single file (containing a unique drive, application code, and the application itself).

Every time you install an application, you create a bottle for it. It's possible to install the same application multiple times and have each application run in its own environment, without interfering with another application.

The distinction is important because you don't remove programs installed via CrossOver Mac by dragging them from the Finder to Trash or by using an application such as AppZapper. Instead, you have to remove applications by using the Bottle Manager program supplied with CrossOver Mac. To do so, you open CrossOver Mac and choose Configure ➜ Manage Bottles. The Bottle Manager window displays all the installed applications in a list on the left. To remove a program, you highlight it in the list and click the minus icon located in the bottom left of the window. Then you click Delete to remove the bottle.

▶ This is useful for developers. Web developers, for example, can run multiple instances of different web browsers at once.

▶ You can also use the Bottle Manager to install and repair bottles. Find out more at www.codeweavers.com/support/docs/crossover-mac/officesetup.

MOVING BEYOND WINDOWS INTO LINUX

Most people are familiar with Mac OS X and Microsoft Windows, but any number of other operating systems can be run on a Mac, including the UNIX family of operating systems. UNIX isn't actually just one operating system, but a whole host of different distributions. Mac OS X itself is a UNIX operating system, based on the open source Mach kernel.

▶ UNIX distributions are also known as distros and flavors.

In addition, there are also operating systems that are called *UNIX-like*, the most famous of which is Linux. Many people, in fact, confuse Linux with UNIX itself. Beyond that, many popular distributions (Ubuntu, Debian, Slackware, and so on) are all based upon Linux.

Confusing, huh? The world of UNIX is based on a vast army of individuals, corporations, and scientific and educational establishments driving forward an open source project. It's not surprising that you might be a bit confused.

It's also interesting and exciting, though, and UNIX sits at the heart of much of our computing experience, so it'd be a shame for any computer geek not to get to know this exciting world.

▶ I'm going to make things easy for you by suggesting that the UNIX system you start off with is Ubuntu.

ISN'T MAC OS X A UNIX SYSTEM?

You might already know that Mac OS X is a UNIX-based system. So if Mac OS X is based on UNIX, what's the point of installing a UNIX operating system on your Mac? Can't you just use UNIX programs on a Mac and vice versa? These are good questions, and they're easy to answer.

Mac OS X is officially a UNIX-certified operating system (many flavors of UNIX lack certification), so in many senses Mac OS X is more UNIX than many UNIX operating systems. On the other hand, it places Apple's unique Aqua interface over an open source kernel called Mach. Although the Mach kernel is open source and is capable of running UNIX processes, the Aqua part is all Apple. This is why programs created for Mac OS X—such as iTunes, iPhoto, and iMovie—can't run on non-Apple computers, even UNIX ones. It's possible to access and use powerful UNIX commands by using Terminal, and run UNIX programs with the X11 interface.

Why would you want to run a UNIX flavor (such as Linux) instead of Mac OS X on a Mac? Different UNIX flavors offer different insights into what an operating system can be, and they provide refreshingly different (if not exactly easy) ways to go about using your computer.

Installing Ubuntu on a Mac

In this section, you'll install Linux on a Mac. To make things simple, you should use a flavor called Ubuntu Desktop Edition 32-bit (www.ubuntu.com). Ubuntu is really great because it focuses on features and accessibility, making it the most straightforward and easy Linux operating system to install and use. It also comes pre-installed with a wide range of free software, such as OpenOffice, Firefox, and GIMP. A nice touch is that it comes with a built-in software manager that enables you to search and download open source software of just about every type.

> ▶ These are a Microsoft Office–like suite of programs, a web browser, and an image editing package, respectively.

Typically, there are two options available for installing UNIX on a Mac:

▶ **Run it live from the CD:** You can run Ubuntu as a live operating system straight from the installation CD, without putting any files on your computer. This is a great option if you want to check out the system before installing it.

▶ **Use virtualization software:** As with Windows, you can use Parallels Desktop, VMware, or VirtualBox to install Ubuntu.

Some options that aren't listed here are installing to a second partition (by using Boot Camp) and installing to an external hard drive, a USB Flash drive, or an SD card. It's possible to install Ubuntu to these places, but because Mac uses a different boot system than Ubuntu, getting a Mac to start up into Ubuntu from a partitioned drive or an external drive is a difficult process that isn't recommended.

GETTING TO KNOW EFI AND REFIT

EFI (Extensible Firmware Interface) is a modern update to the older BIOS (Basic Input/Output System) that is used primarily to boot a computer and start up the operating system. Macs use a custom EFI variation that is extremely robust for Mac OS X but not so good if you want to use a different operating system. Apple has provided a workaround for Windows users who want to install another OS in the form of Boot Camp. But if you want to install other operating systems and have them boot natively, you need to modify the EFI. You can do this by using the open source application rEFIt (`http://refit.sourceforge.net`). While this isn't a simple operation, you can create a bootable CD from rEFIt so you don't need to permanently change the EFI of your Mac. You can find more information on this on the Ubuntu forums, at `https://help.ubuntu.com/community/SwitchingToUbuntu/FromMacOSX`.

In fact, installing Ubuntu via Boot Camp or installing it on an external drive is such a major operation that I'd go so far as to suggest that you don't do it. Instead, it's generally considered the best approach to use virtualization software such as VMware, Parallels Desktop, or VirtualBox to install Ubuntu.

The first step is to download the latest version of Ubuntu (`www.ubuntu.com/desktop/get-ubuntu/download`).

▶ Get the 32-bit version, not the 64-bit one. It's better for desktop computers, and you probably don't need all the power of the 64-bit version.

For the installation, you need to boot from the installation file. This means you need to copy it to a CD and boot from the CD. One of the really neat features about Ubuntu is that you can boot into it and start using the operating system before deciding whether you want to keep it.

NOTE   It's possible to install Ubuntu from a USB Flash drive, but you have to use Terminal to convert the file type, and the process is not reliable. Ubuntu advises Mac users to create a bootable CD.

When you have the Ubuntu.iso file, you need to use this file to create a bootable CD or DVD:

1. Open Disk Utility.

2. Insert the blank CD/DVD. It should appear in the left pane in Disk Utility.

3. Drag and drop the Ubuntu.iso file to the left pane in Disk Utility.

4. Select the .iso file in the left pane, as shown in Figure 3-7, and click Burn in the toolbar to create this installation disc.

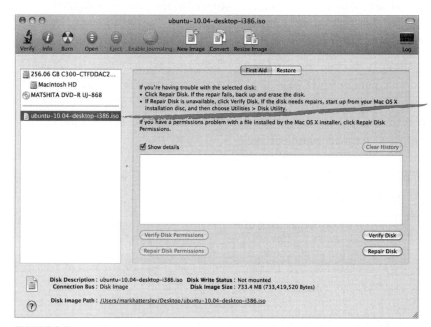

Creating an installation disk

FIGURE 3-7: Use Disk Utility to burn the Ubuntu.iso file to a recordable CD or DVD to create an installation disc.

With your Ubuntu installation disc in hand, you can begin the process of installing it on your computer by using a virtualization program.

Using VirtualBox and Ubuntu

One of the easiest and most reliable ways to install Ubuntu on a Mac is to use a virtualization platform. Both Parallels Desktop and VMware Fusion provide good support for Ubuntu. But in this section, you'll combine the open source operating system with VirtualBox (www.virtualbox.org), a free open source virtualization program. To get started, you download, install, and then open VirtualBox.

VM NAME AND OS TYPE

▶ If you type Ubuntu in the Name text box, VirtualBox chooses the correct menu items automatically.

To begin, you click the New icon in the toolbar, click Continue, and then enter a title for your operating system in the Name text box. Next, you choose Linux from the Operating System pop-up menu and choose Ubuntu from the Version pop-up menu.

MEMORY

In the Memory window, you choose the amount of RAM you want to dedicate to the virtual operating system. The recommended base memory size is 512MB.

VIRTUAL HARD DISK

In the Virtual Hard Drive window, you choose either Create New Hard Disk or Use Existing Hard Disk. If this is the first time you've used VirtualBox, you should select Create New Hard Disk. VirtualBox displays a new window called Create New Virtual Disk Wizard. When you click Continue, Virtual Box will take you through the windows described in the following sections.

HARD DISK STORAGE TYPE

The Hard Disk Storage Type window provides the following options:

- ▶ **Dynamically Expanding Storage:** This creates a smaller file size but dynamically adjusts it as you create files and install programs.

- ▶ **Fixed Size Storage:** This sets aside a specified amount of hard drive space (8GB by default) for the Ubuntu installation.

VIRTUAL DISK LOCATION AND SIZE

▶ Click the down-pointing disclosure triangle in the Finder window to reveal more information about the location of the file.

By default, Ubuntu saves virtual disk files in a folder called Hard Disks inside the VirtualBox folder, which is inside the Library. You click the yellow folder icon in the Virtual Disk Location and Size window to choose a new location.

Even if you've selected Dynamically Expanding Storage, you can still adjust the size of the virtual hard disk. This is the size that is reported to Mac OS X as the maximum size the hard drive should be. When you're ready, you click Continue. You should check all the settings and click Done. At this point, you've finished setting up your virtual machine.

Installing Ubuntu in VirtualBox

Now that you've set up your virtual machine, it's time to install Ubuntu in it. You need to make sure the Ubuntu installation CD is inserted in your Mac and click the Start button. VirtualBox displays a warning that every time the VM window is activated, it captures all keystrokes.

VirtualBox now displays the First Run Wizard. You click Continue to get started, and it asks you to display the host drive; by default, this should display the pop-up menu with your CD drive and no other options available. Click Continue and then Done.

VirtualBox is now ready to start installing the Ubuntu operating system. You need to go through the following windows in the Ubuntu installation:

1. **Welcome:** This window offers a number of language options and two buttons, as shown in Figure 3-8:

   ▷ **Try Ubuntu:** This runs Ubuntu from the CD, without making any changes to your virtual machine. Click this if you just want to see what Ubuntu looks like. If you select this option, you can ignore the rest of the steps in this list.

   ▷ **Install Ubuntu:** This places Ubuntu in the virtual machine. Click this option if you want install Ubuntu. If you select this option, you should follow the rest of the steps in this list.

2. **Where Are You?:** This window displays a graphical map of the world. Click on the location closest to you or use the Region and Time Zone pop-up menus to select your area.

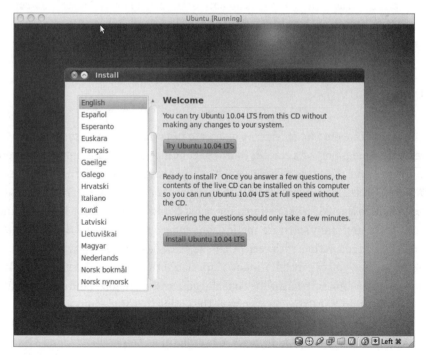

FIGURE 3-8: Ubuntu lets you run the operating system directly from the installation disc without even having to install it on your Mac.

3. **Keyboard Layout:** Based on your information in the previous window, this window guesses about the keyboard layout of your Mac. If you want, you can choose a different keyboard layout or click Forward.

4. **Prepare Disk Space:** The top of this window it should say This Computer Has No Operating System. You can choose either Erase and Use the Entire Disk or Specify Manual Partitions. In this case, you should stick with the default option, Use the Entire Disk, and click Forward.

5. **Who Are You?:** You need to enter a name, a username, a password, and the name of the computer. Suggested options for your username and the name of the computer are based on your initial name entry, but you can opt to change them. Click Forward.

6. **Install:** Check that you are happy with all the information and click the Install button.

7. **Restart:** Finally, you need to restart Ubuntu (not Mac OS X) to start using the operating system. You need to press Return to complete the restart when Ubuntu displays a black screen containing white text messages.

You now have Ubuntu installed on your machine. To log in, you double-click your account name and enter the password you selected during installation.

As you can see, there really is no barrier to setting up and running a second operating system with Mac OS X. And using Ubuntu with VirtualBox is a free, and relatively simple, way to get a second OS up and running.

SUMMARY

This chapter covers a lot of territory on how to run other operating systems, and their respective programs, on a Mac. As well as expanding your options, integrating your Mac with the world of Microsoft Windows will help you work alongside other people using Windows-based PCs. In most cases, you can share and edit files with Windows users by using native Mac OS X applications. Too, most hardware works with both Mac and PC computers, and many software applications come in Windows and Mac versions that produce files compatible with each other. For those cases where you want to take things a step further, you can install Windows on a Mac both via Apple's Boot Camp application and virtualization software, which enables you to run Windows (and other operating systems) within Mac OS X. You even have the option to install Linux and other flavors of the UNIX operating system on a Mac. Although I typically advise you to stick with Mac OS X for most of your day-to-day work, one of the great things about being a Mac owner is that you can run all of these operating systems from just one machine.

CHAPTER 4

Getting the Most out of Mac OS X Software

IN THIS CHAPTER

▶ Finding out about the applications that come with Mac OS X

▶ Installing new Mac OS X applications

▶ Removing all traces of applications when they're no longer needed

▶ Activating and deactivating programs

▶ Using preference panes to extend the functionality of Mac OS X

▶ Working with Dashboard and widgets

Mac OS X 10.6 Snow Leopard is Apple's most comprehensive operating system ever. It comes packed with applications, utilities, and functions that enable you to get far more out of the operating system than you probably thought possible. Mac OS X includes the superb contact and management software Address Book and iCal. It also offers superb Internet tools, such as Safari, Mail, and iChat. And it has applications that are prevalent and offer many fine features, such as the superlative Preview app. This chapter takes a look at the applications that come with Mac OS X, including how to install and cleanly remove them. There's a lot more to running applications than meets the eye.

WORKING WITH MAC OS X APPLICATIONS

Mac OS X comes with a large number of applications that help you get the most out of your Mac. Most of these applications reside in the Applications folder, as shown in Figure 4-1, or within another folder inside Applications called Utilities. These applications enable you to perform just about every task you can think of, from surfing the Web to managing your contacts and watching movies.

> ▶ It's possible to have a comprehensive computing experience without ever installing a single additional program.

FIGURE 4-1: Most applications are stored within the Applications folder, located at the root of your hard drive.

In addition to the applications included with Mac OS X, Apple also includes a collection of software called *iLife* with every new Mac. The iLife collection of applications consists of iTunes, iPhoto, iMovie, GarageBand, iWeb, and iDVD. The Mac OS X installation discs supplied with new Macs contain the latest version of iLife, but if you purchased a future upgrade to the Mac OS X operating system, it doesn't contain an update to the iLife suite, so it's not considered a part of Mac OS X itself. Apple typically updates iLife every 18–24 months, and the cost of a new version is usually reasonably priced. (At this writing, iLife '09 costs $79 for a single-user license.)

All the applications included with Mac OS X are installed in the Applications folder, located at the root of your hard drive.

You can access this folder by opening a new Finder window and choosing Applications under Places. Alternatively, you can navigate to the root of the hard drive and open Applications. You can also use the Shift+⌘+A shortcut to open a new Finder window displaying the Applications folder.

SOFTWARE TERMINOLOGY

People who create and use computer programs use a number of terms interchangeably, including *software*, *program*, *utility*, *application*, and *app*. In practice, these terms are interchangeable, but each has a specific meaning, as described here:

▶ *Software* is the general term for code that runs on a computer to perform a task; the Mac OS X operating system itself is software.

▶ *Systems software* comprises the operating system itself, and technical applications that comprise its component parts and are used to maintain the system. Aside from Mac OS X, the most common systems software you'll encounter are utilities. For example, Disk Utility enables you to manage disks in Mac OS X. You may also hear the term *tool*, which usually means utility.

▶ *Applications software* is code that runs specific tasks; these are made up of processes, which are in themselves pieces of code. Put together these processes make up what people typically call *programs*, or *applications*, which usually refers to the visible tools people use in an operating system (such as Microsoft Word or Adobe Photoshop). In this sense, the terms *program* and *application* (and increasingly *app*) all mean the same thing.

Installing Applications

Mac OS X comes with a wide array of applications that cover virtually every aspect of computing. Sooner or later, though, you're going to go through the process of adding new applications.

Mac OS X has a few different means by which to install new applications, and they're all fairly straightforward. Most installations are delivered on a volume and transferred to your hard drive. The volume that the application is delivered on is often an optical disc, such as a CD or DVD. However, a volume may be delivered as a disk file known as a *disk image*; these files have the extension .dmg. Double-clicking a disk image file opens up a volume containing the application installation files.

Another option is to download an application directly as a file, typically inside a compressed folder that has a .zip or .rar file extension. You must uncompress these files in order to access their contents. Mac OS X can uncompress .zip files natively, but you may need a program such as UnRarX (www.unrarx.com) to uncompress files with the .rar extension.

There are two main methods of installing applications. The most commonly used method is drag-and-drop: You simply drag an application icon from an open volume directly to the Applications icon. The second method is via a custom installer included with the installation volume. You don't get to choose which installation method you use; a program usually offers only one option. How can you tell which method to use? Typically the window containing the installation file contains some visual clue about which method to use, as shown in Figure 4-2. If it doesn't, you can take a look at any included documentation.

▶ A volume is a single partition of a hard drive or optical disc. Mac OS X can create virtual volumes from files that look and act just like you've inserted an optical disc.

▶ Usually a text file called readme.txt, or documentation, will be included with any new program installation that details the installation process.

> **NOTE** Don't worry if you choose the wrong installation method. Dragging an installation program into the Finder doesn't cause any problems, and the program will usually run just as well from the Finder as it does from the installation volume. Just don't forget to delete the installation file after you finish the installation. Likewise, opening an application icon in the installation folder runs the application as normal, without causing any ill effects. Still, you shouldn't really run applications from installation volumes; you should install them into the Applications folder.

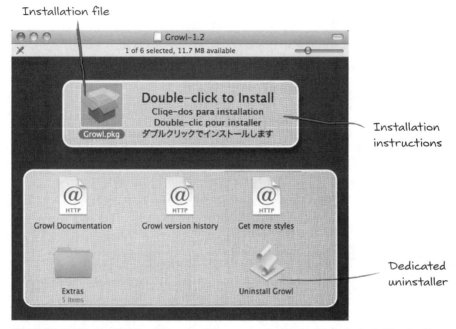

Installation file

Installation instructions

Dedicated uninstaller

FIGURE 4-2: Most installation folders contain some sort of instructions for installing the file.

Removing Applications

The reverse of installing applications is, of course, removing them. Removing applications from Mac OS X can be as simple or as complex a process as you want it to be. It just depends on how fastidious you are regarding the overall cleanliness of the file structure on Mac OS X. At the most basic level, removing an application from Mac OS X is a case of locating the application in the Applications folder and dragging it to the Trash in the Dock, as shown in Figure 4-3. Although you can't run applications that have been moved to the Trash, as shown in Figure 4-3, you can Ctrl+click (or right-click) a file and choose Put Back to move it back to its original location.

> **NOTE** You may be required to enter your Administrator password.

You can leave the application in the Trash as you would any other file. It will be deleted for good when you empty the trash (by choosing ➔ Empty Trash). As with any other item, you should be sure you don't want to use it again before emptying the Trash.

Ctrl+click and
choose Put Back
to move to original
location

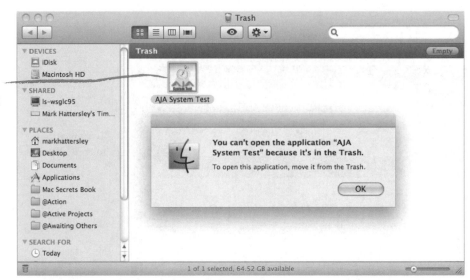

FIGURE 4-3: Delete applications by dragging them to Trash. Applications can't run when they're in the Trash, but you can recover them.

But is deleting a program really so simple? Well, no, it isn't. Here's the thing: Most of an application is contained within the file you drag to the Applications folder, but when you run the application for the first time, it creates other files and folders on your computer. These files and folders remain on your computer when you drag the application to the Trash.

Apple's reasoning seems to be that these supporting files are generally quite small and don't slow down the Mac, so it's better to keep them on your hard drive than to remove them. One benefit of this is that if you ever re-install an application, all your system files and preferences are kept intact.

However, the downside of this deletion method is fairly obvious: You end up with lots of flotsam and jetsam in your Library folder. And if you regularly install and remove software over time, the amount of detritus in your system can become annoying. Whether it actually slows down a system is up for debate, but it certainly wastes space on your hard drive and makes searching for files more difficult.

▶ Personally I
think it does. Plus,
it's just untidy.

You can deal with the detritus problem in two ways. The first approach is to search for these orphaned files and folders in your system and get rid of them, either at the same time that you remove the program itself or sometime later, when you do a regular cleanup. The second approach is to install a program, such as the AppZapper application described later in this chapter, to help you uninstall applications and clean up unwanted files. The following sections discuss both of these techniques.

MANUALLY REMOVING ORPHANED FILES FROM FINDER

To manually remove orphaned files from Finder, you drag an unwanted application to the Trash as normal but make a note of its name. This will help you to hunt down its associated files. Next, you need to manually check through the Library folders on your Mac. The Library folders contain items that are used to provide support to applications. To complicate matters, Mac OS X contains not one but two Library folders: One is contained in the user folder, and the other is contained in the root area of your main volume.

Inside the Library folders, you find an array of other folders related to Mac OS X. You should scan through the folders because sometimes (albeit rarely) an application creates a folder within the Library to contain files and folders. Most of the time, however, applications disperse various system files throughout the standard set of folders inside the Library. The following are some common folders to examine:

▶ **Application Support:** As the name suggests, this folder contains other folders that directly relate to applications. It's fairly likely—although by no means guaranteed—that there will be a folder here related to your application.

▶ **Caches:** Files and folders placed here are used to store information on a temporary basis. Mac OS X cleans out caches over time, but you can speed up the process by deleting any files or folders in here.

▶ **Logs:** An application may create text logs that are used to troubleshoot problems with the application. You are unlikely to need any logs that refer to your deleted program, so drag any corresponding files here to the Trash.

▶ **Preferences:** Just about every application places files or folders inside this folder. These files are typically used to store settings or adjustments that have been made to the program so that they will be remembered the next time the application is launched.

Just to confuse matters more, there is also a third Library folder, which resides inside the System folder in the root of your main volume. This folder contains mostly files and folders that are essential to the running of Mac OS X.

Just about everything inside the System folder is used and required by Mac OS X. Files are typically added to and removed from this folder inside Mac OS X itself; for example, screen savers are added using the Desktop & Screen Saver system preference pane and removed using the same pane. Adding and removing screen savers from this part of Mac OS X adds to and removes files from the Screen Saver folder inside the Library folders inside the System folder. I generally advise that you don't play around with this folder. If you want to remove functions from Mac OS X, it is better to do so through the regular Mac OS X interface so you don't damage the Mac OS X installation.

▶ The user folder is inside the Users folder and typically shares the same name as your account.

> **NOTE** If an application has problems, try deleting items from the Library or the Preferences folder. Cleaning the cache can help, too. Just don't clear out items from Application Support, as these files can be vital to running an application.

REMOVING THE IWORK TRIAL FROM A MAC

As an example of how to completely remove an application from a Mac, let's take a look at how to completely remove the iWork trial applications. Deleting this app suite represents a type of problem you could encounter: The trial installation could prevent you from installing the full version of the program.

The iWork trial from Apple (`www.apple.com/iwork/download-trial`) gives you 30 days to try out the suite of office applications. If you like iWork, you can purchase a serial number online from Apple to continue running it. However, if you purchase a physical copy of iWork instead of getting the online serial number, you'll find that the serial number provided with the physical copy doesn't activate the trial version. If you drag the iWork trial to the Trash and reinstall it using the installation disc, it still won't work. That's because the iWork trial has placed other system files and preferences related to the trial version all over your computer. You have to remove those files and preferences before you can correctly install the new version you have bought.

Let's look at an example of the clutter left behind by uninstalling via the drag-and-drop method.

1. Locate and then drag the iWork 09 folder to the Trash.

2. Open your user folder and choose Library, Caches and delete the following files: com.apple.iwork.Fonts, com.apple.iWork.Numbers, and com.apple .iWork.Pages.

3. While still inside the Library folder in your user folder, choose the Preferences folder and delete the following files: com.apple.iwork.Keynote.plist, com.apple.iWork.Numbers.plist, and com.apple.Pages.plist.

4. Go to the root folder on your hard drive and choose Library , Application Support, locate the iWork 09 folder, and drag it to the Trash.

5. Locate the Preferences folder within the Library and delete com.apple. iwork09.installer.plist and com.apple.iwork09.plist.

6. Locate the Receipts folder and move the iWork09Trial.pkg file to the Trash.

Finally, you've managed to completely remove iWork (unless there's something else hidden that even I don't know about). The .pkg file in the Receipts folder is the culprit preventing you from moving from the downloaded trial to the paid-for version. Once it's gone, you should be able to install the full version of iWork 09 from the installation disc, and then the serial number should work correctly.

UNINSTALLING PROGRAMS WITH APPZAPPER

From some of the methods outlined in this chapter, you can see that completely getting rid of programs can be something of a chore. Manually going through all the different folders and searching for all the files related to an application is a time-consuming and fiddly business. Of course, you shouldn't feel that this is something you have to do.

Many users find leaving stray files on the Mac unacceptable, though, and Apple's refusal to include a comprehensive uninstaller in Mac OS X is a puzzling situation. If you find yourself in need of a clean and tidy Mac OS X system, take a look at AppZapper (www.appzapper.com) or Mac Uninstaller, part of Smith Micro's Spring Clean Deluxe suite of Mac OS X applications (www.smithmicro.com).

These applications keep an eye on programs you install and the files that are associated with them. When you decide you no longer want a program, you can remove it using AppZapper, as shown in Figure 4-4, which automatically moves all files associated with the program to the Trash.

▶ Apple makes it clear that to get rid of applications you should simply trash them and leave the support files on the system in case they're needed again.

FIGURE 4-4: AppZapper keeps track of files associated with applications and moves a program and all its related files to the Trash for a clean uninstall.

REMOVING A PROGRAM WITH APPZAPPER

To remove a program with AppZapper, simply complete the following easy steps:

1. Double-click the AppZapper icon in the Applications folder to open the program. A window appears with a downward-pointing arrow icon and the message "Drag Apps Here."

2. Click an application icon or folder in the Applications folder and drag it to the AppZapper window, which turns blue as you drag the application icon or folder over it.

3. Let go of the mouse to attach the unwanted icon to AppZapper. The AppZapper window expands to display both the application icon and any files it believes are associated with the program you're trying to remove. To the left of each item is a check box (selected by default).

4. Click Zap! to move the selected items to the Trash. The screen flashes, and a zapping sound effect confirms that the deletion has taken place.

By default, AppZapper keeps the Apple applications on your Mac safe. It doesn't show them or delete them. But Apple applications can go unused, too, and you might want to consider deleting unused files when clearing out space on your hard drive. To get AppZapper to include Apple applications choose AppZapper ➜ Preferences and deselect the Keep Apple Applications Safe check box.

REMOVING MULTIPLE ITEMS AT ONCE WITH APPZAPPER

You can use AppZapper to delete several applications and all their associated files in one fell swoop. This is a great technique for recovering lots of space on a Mac's hard drive. It's especially useful if you've installed lots of programs that you no longer use. In addition to removing applications, AppZapper can also remove widgets, preference panes, and plug-ins—and all their related files.

1. Double-click the AppZapper icon in the Applications folder to open the program.

2. Click the switch icon, which is marked with a downward-pointing icon, in the top right of the window. When you click the icon, it displays a magnifying glass and the AppZapper window enlarges to display multiple items contained on your Mac.

3. Underneath these icons is a size slider, which is set to 0 MB by default. Drag the size slider as needed to search for items over a certain size. This example uses 58MB, as shown in Figure 4-5.

▶ If you want to keep any files, you simply deselect their check boxes.

▶ It's possible to recover an item that you've deleted with AppZapper. You simply drag the program out of the Trash, and the associated files are re-created when you run that program.

▶ This is a great way to see what installations are taking up the most space on your hard drive.

4. **A second slider,** which is set to Last Day by default, enables you to filter out apps that have been used in a certain period of time. Drag the slider to the right to filter applications that haven't been used in days, weeks, months, or even in the past year. This example uses Last Year, as shown in Figure 4-5.

▶ This option enables you to find applications on the Mac that you are least likely to use.

FIGURE 4-5: You can use AppZapper to search for applications over a certain size or to search for applications that you haven't used for a set period of time.

5. Choose the pull-down menu to choose a sort order for the applications. By default, the name sort order is used, but you can also sort by file size or the files you last used.

▶ This is a great way to see what installations are taking up the most space on your hard drive.

6. Click an icon in the main window to display all its related files. By clicking the items in the lower section, you can select or deselect them.

7. Click Zap! to move the selected items to the Trash.

TIP Applications inside the Applications folder usually appear as a single file instead of inside a folder. Double-clicking an application opens it. But appearances can be deceiving; these files are actually folders in disguise. If you want to see what's inside an application, Ctrl+click (or right-click) and choose Show Package Contents from the context menu. This opens a new Finder window that displays the contents of the application.

DEACTIVATING PROGRAMS BEFORE YOU UNINSTALL THEM

Some programs must go through a process called *activation* before you can use them. In this process, the application contacts a server online and verifies that it is a legitimate copy, and that it has only been installed on the permitted number of machines. In some extreme cases, an application limits the number of machines on which it can be installed, and it refuses to run if it's been installed on too many machines.

▶ Adobe and Quark software are both notorious for limiting the number of activations that software can have. Both typically limit activations to two machines.

If a program was activated online, you should ensure that you deactivate it before removing it from your Mac. This process, known as *deactivation*, is important because it tells the online server that you will no longer be using that program on the registered machine. This frees up the program to be installed on a new machine. If you fail to deactivate the program before removing it from your computer, you may not be able to re-install it on a different computer.

The deactivation process depends on the program in question. Typically it can be performed from within a program itself. (Check any documentation or the program manufacturer's website for more information.) For example, you deactivate Adobe software by opening an Adobe program and choosing Help → Deactivate. You select the Erase My Serial Number from This Computer After Deactivation Completes check box to remove the serial number you entered during installation. (You should select this option if you are passing on the computer, or the software, to another person and won't be re-installing it on the computer at a later point.) You click Deactivate to contact Adobe's server and inform it that you are no longer using the software.

Installing and Removing Preference Panes

Some pieces of software are installed as *preferences* and added to the System Preferences window rather than to the Applications folder or Utilities folder.

▶ System Preferences can be found by choosing → System Preferences from the menu bar. It's the Mac OS X equivalent of the Windows Control Panel.

Typically, preferences are extensions to Mac OS X. They are applications that run permanently and extend the functionality of the operating system. A typical example is Perian (http://perian.org), which enables Mac OS X's built-in video player, QuickTime, to play just about any video format.

Installing preference panes is typically a straightforward process, largely the same as installing most applications. Typically preference panes are delivered as digital downloads inside a .dmg volume. Inside the .dmg volume is usually an install file that you can double-click to go through the process of installing the preference pane.

When a preference has been installed, it appears in the Other section of System Preferences (choose → System Preferences). Clicking a preference's icon opens the System Preference pane and displays the options available.

To remove a preference, you Ctrl+click (or right-click) its icon in System Preferences and select Remove "Application" Preference Pane from the context menu.

Installing and Removing Widgets

Mac OS X 10.4 Tiger introduced a new environment to Mac OS X called Dashboard. This environment overlays small applications, called *widgets*, over the Desktop, as shown in Figure 4-6. Widgets can be practically anything, although they tend to be lightweight programs, such as calculators, weather apps, and world clocks. Another main use for widgets is to provide quick access to data stored in Mac OS X, such as contacts, calendars, and sections of web pages.

You can access Dashboard by clicking the Dashboard icon in the Dock or by pressing the F12 key (or the F4 key on newer Mac keyboards with specific icons for Mac OS X functions).

▶ Windows has a similar feature called Gadgets that appear on the Windows Sidebar.

▶ Press this same key again—or click in any empty area of the Dashboard—to close the Dashboard.

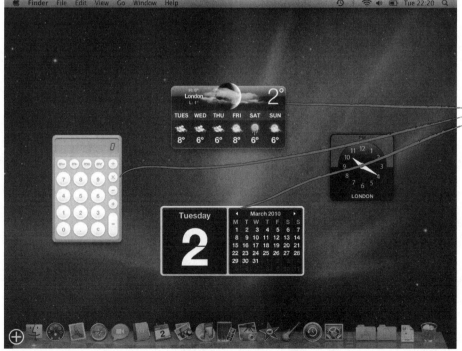

Widgets

FIGURE 4-6: Widgets are lightweight applications that can be added to and removed from the Dashboard.

When you access Dashboard, the desktop fades out, and the applications zoom in from the outside of the screen. With Dashboard enabled, you can use the widgets as you would any other application. By clicking and dragging widgets, you can move them to another part of the screen.

Unlike standard Mac OS X applications, widgets don't use the menu bar to offer pull-down options. In fact, none of the regular Mac OS X interface options are available in Dashboard, and clicking on any part of the screen that doesn't contain a widget closes Dashboard and takes you back to Mac OS X.

By default, Dashboard displays the following applications: Calculator, Weather, iCal, and World Clock. Dashboard in Mac OS X also contains 20 widgets installed in the Mac OS X operating system that cover a wide range of functions. Table 4-1 lists the widgets included with Mac OS X.

TABLE 4-1: Widgets Included with Mac OS X

WIDGET NAME	DESCRIPTION
Address Book	Provides a text search box that returns results from the Address Book application.
Business	Provides information on local businesses from the Yellow Pages online service.
Calculator	Provides basic calculation functionality.
CI Filter Browser	Provides information for developers on Core Image filters used by Mac OS X.
Dictionary	Serves as a reference tool for accessing the library of word descriptions in Mac OS X. Three options are available from the pop-up menu: Dictionary, Thesaurus, and Apple (a reference of Apple and Mac OS X–related terms).
ESPN	Provides the latest sports news and scores.
Flight Tracker	Provides information on airline flights.
Google	Provides a search box that opens your default web browser with the entered term in Google's search engine.
iCal	Provides information from the iCal application.
iTunes	Functions as a quick-access remote control for the iTunes application.
Movies	Provides information on upcoming movies.

WIDGET NAME	DESCRIPTION
People	Provides directory information on people.
Ski Report	Provides weather information for skiers.
Stickies	Allows you to type and store short text notes.
Stocks	Provides information on the latest stock charts.
Tile Game	Functions as a simple game based on moving tiles around to create a picture.
Translation	Takes a text input and translates between numerous languages.
Unit Converter	Converts units (such as length, weight, or currency) from one format to another.
Weather	Provides local weather information.
World Clock	Displays the time in a specific time zone as a visual clock.

It's worth taking time to set up Dashboard correctly, as some of the widgets can be real time-savers. You can locate more Widgets online from Apple's Web site by visiting this address: www.apple.com/downloads/dashboard/?r=dbw.

ADDING WIDGETS TO DASHBOARD

To add a widget from the installed list to Dashboard, follow these steps:

1. Open Dashboard and click the Add (+) icon at the bottom left of the screen. The screen moves up, and the Dashboard Shelf, shown in Figure 4-7, appears.

   The Dashboard Shelf displays a row of widgets available to Mac OS X at the bottom of the screen. Arrows on the side of the Dashboard Shelf can be used to display more widgets.

2. To add a widget to Dashboard, click and drag the icon in the Dashboard Shelf to the main screen. Let go of the mouse (or trackpad) to add the widget. It is added with a rather stylish water-drop effect.

> **NOTE** It's possible to add a widget to Dashboard more than once and to have multiple versions of the same widget running on Dashboard.

Manage widgets

FIGURE 4-7: The Widgets widget enables you to add and remove Dashboard items.

REMOVING WIDGETS FROM THE DASHBOARD

To remove a widget from Dashboard, follow these steps:

▶ You can also delete widgets from the Dashboard Shelf by holding down the Option key to display the x icon.

1. Open Dashboard and click the Add (+) icon in the bottom right of the window to display the Dashboard Shelf. (This is the same process as for adding widgets.)

2. Notice that each widget on Dashboard now displays a small x icon in the top left of the widget. You click this x icon to remove the widget from Dashboard.

Note that this doesn't uninstall the widget from Mac OS X. It simply removes that instance of the widget from Mac OS X.

WIDGET PREFERENCES

Although widgets don't have menu options, many of them have a set of preferences you can use to determine and change the information they display. Look out for a small circled *i* icon on the widget. Clicking this *i* icon flips around the widget and displays its preferences information.

MANAGING WIDGETS IN THE DASHBOARD SHELF

Removing a widget from Dashboard doesn't uninstall it from Mac OS X. The widget remains in the Dashboard Shelf. Dragging it back to the main window places it back in Dashboard.

You can't delete the widgets that come with Mac OS X from Dashboard. However, it's possible to remove them from the Dashboard Shelf by using a widget called Widget Manager, which enables you to manage the various applications used and displayed in the Dashboard Shelf.

> **TIP** You can delete the widgets that come with Mac OS X by deleting them from the /Library/Widgets folder. You can also add widgets to the Dashboard by placing them in the ~/Library/Widgets folder (in your Home folder) but it's inadvisable because although they will appear on the Dashboard Shelf they won't appear in Widget Manager. I advise you to leave the stock Mac OS X widgets alone and use Widget Manager unless there's a problem.

To delete widgets from Dashboard, follow these steps:

1. Open the Dashboard Shelf by clicking the Add (+) icon in Dashboard and click Manage Widgets. Widgets in use by Mac OS X are displayed in a list.

2. Deselect the check box to the left of each widget to prevent it from appearing in the Dashboard Shelf.

3. Unchecking a widget disables it and prevents it from appearing in the Dashboard Shelf, and removes any corresponding widgets in use by Dashboard.

You can download additional widgets online, from Apple's website as well as other websites. To create Dashboard widgets, a developer uses technology similar to that used for websites, and Apple provides a program called Dashcode, which can be found in the Developer Tools on the Mac OS X installation discs.

> **NOTE** If you want to learn how to create widgets, investigate *Dashcode for Dummies* by Jesse Feiler.

You can download extra widgets from Apple's website, which is accessible from within Dashboard. Follow these steps:

1. Display the Dashboard Shelf and click Manage Widgets.

2. Click More Widgets from the Widget Manager or point your web browser to www.apple.com/downloads/dashboard.

3. Select a widget and click Download to save it to your Downloads folder.

4. By default, the file opens, and a dialog asks if you want to install the widget and open it in Dashboard. You can click Install to open Dashboard and get a preview of the widget. You can click Keep to add the widget to Dashboard and the Dashboard Shelf.

To remove an installed widget, you open the Widgets widget and click the red Remove (-) icon to the right of the widget. A dialog asks if you want to move the widget to the Trash. You can click OK to remove the widget from Dashboard and uninstall it.

PLACING WIDGETS ON THE DESKTOP

Here's a cool tip that enables you to place the widgets from Dashboard onto the Mac OS X desktop: Open Terminal and type `defaults write com.apple .dashboard devmode YES`. This turns on developer mode in Dashboard. Now hold down F12 (or F4 on recent Mac keyboards) to display Dashboard; while holding down F12, start to move a widget around. Keep the mouse held down on the widget and let go of F12 (or F4). Now the widget is permanently displayed on the desktop. This is handy if you like using a certain widget all the time. To move the widget away from the Mac OS X desktop and back to Dashboard, you simply repeat these steps.

SUMMARY

Mac OS X is an intuitive operating system, and adding applications and utilities is an easy process. Because there are several methods for doing so, you're bound to find one that works best for you. Uninstalling applications from Mac OS X is no less difficult; however, the process may be slightly more involved if you want to track and remove the extra files that applications tend to leave behind on your system. Although you might encounter some problems with regard to activating or deactivating software when removing applications, this process, too, is generally easy. On the fun side, you can also work with preference panes and widgets. These not only extend the functionality of your Mac, but they make your Mac more productive, and more fun to work with.

CHAPTER 5

Getting the Most from Mac OS X Utilities

IN THIS CHAPTER

- ► Finding out what makes the Utilities folder so valuable
- ► Understanding what the various Mac OS X utilities do
- ► Running utilities from Mac OS X server
- ► Running utilities from the Mac OS X installation disc

What separates a Mac user from a Mac genius? Good question!

Typically, a Mac genius is the sort of person who doesn't just use a computer but also controls it; a genius is a person others turn to when things go wrong. A Mac genius is the sort of person who knows not just how to use a computer but also how a computer works. And when it comes to Mac OS X, a lot of the times a person is considered a genius because he or she knows how to use the programs sitting inside the Utilities folder. You're almost certainly familiar with the Applications folder, but the Utilities folder holds a rarer breed of programs. A lot of the cooler things you'll learn from this book involve tinkering with the programs in the Utilities folder, so this chapter describes all the utilities included and provides references to other chapters where you'll learn how to use them. This chapter also includes a section on how to run utilities from the Mac OS X installation CD.

LOOKING AT THE UTILITIES FOLDER

You might be wondering what the difference is between an application and a utility. Technically, they're the same sort of thing: Both are programs that run in Mac OS X. Most of them (with the exception of Exposé and Spaces) open in the Dock, provide menu bar options, and perform various functions.

The difference is that utilities are programs that are by-and-large used to control the operating system. You don't tend to create anything here—as you might with a word processing or image editing program—but you do get to discover how things work and how to fix things when they don't. Disk Utility, for example, can help you format and fix a hard drive; Activity Monitor is used to monitor what's going on inside your Mac. All the utilities are located inside the Utilities folder, which sits inside the Applications folder, as shown in Figure 5-1. To access the Utilities folder, open a new Finder window, navigate to Applications, and scroll down to the tail end of the alphabet.

▶ Exposé and Spaces run all the time, like Dashboard. Running them from the Utilities folder is the same as clicking the appropriate icon in the Dock.

The Utilities folder is found in the Applications folder.

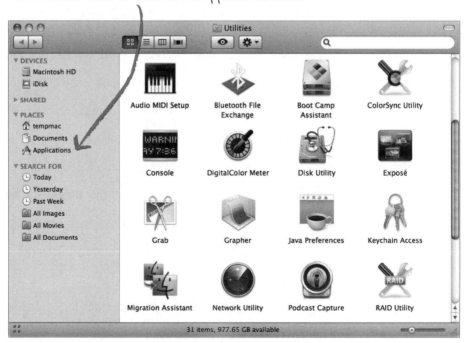

FIGURE 5-1: The Utilities folder contains a range of programs used to maintain, repair, and investigate Mac OS X.

There are also three shortcuts to the Utilities folder that are worth getting to know:

▶ Choose Go ➜ Utilities from the Finder menu bar.

▶ Press Shift+⌘+U.

▶ Type Utilities into Spotlight and choose the Utilities folder from either Folders or Top Hit.

With the Utilities folder open, you'll find a range of programs to use. Table 5-1 lists all the utilities included with Mac OS X.

EXTENDING THE UTILITIES

You can install other utilities. Some utilities are installed with applications such as Adobe Utilities—which contains Adobe Updater, Pixel Bender, ExtendScript Toolkit, and others—which is included with Adobe Creative Suite applications.

TABLE 5-1: Utilities Included with Mac OS X

UTILITY	FUNCTION
Activity Monitor	Displays information about a Mac's hardware and software activity, such as CPU usage, memory, disk activity, disk usage, and network usage.
AirPort Utility	Adjusts settings for wireless devices, including the AirPort Base Station and Time Capsule. (Chapter 8 has more information on AirPort Utility.)
AppleScript Editor	Edits scripts that can automate Mac OS X tasks.
Audio MIDI Setup	Configures MIDI audio input and output devices.
Bluetooth File Exchange	Transfers files to and from devices wirelessly via Bluetooth technology.
Boot Camp Assistant	Partitions a hard drive and installs Windows as a second operating system. (Chapter 3 has more information on running Windows on a Mac.)
ColorSync Utility	Enables color management, including synchronizing color across displays, scanners, and printers.

continues

TABLE 5-1: Utilities Included with Mac OS X *(continued)*

UTILITY	FUNCTION
Console	Displays information on the Mac OS X log, which records underlying UNIX activity on the Mac. (Chapter 22 has more information on UNIX.)
DigitalColor Meter	Displays the color of the pixel underneath the cursor; used by graphic designers, especially web designers.
Disk Utility	Assists in managing, partitioning, and formatting hard drive volumes. (Chapter 9 has more information on Disk Utility.)
Exposé	Displays all active windows on the screen simultaneously for quick navigation.
Grab	Takes screenshots of the display and individual windows, and saves them as image files. (Chapter 17 has more information on working with images.)
Grapher	Enables you to create complicated 2-D and 3-D graphs.
iDisk Utility	Displays information on your iDisk (part of Apple's MobileMe service) and enables you to open other users' iDisk folders. (Chapter 20 has more information on iDisk.)
Keychain Access	Stores passwords for websites, servers, wireless networks, and other password-protected areas. (Chapter 15 has more information on Mac security.)
Migration Assistant	Transfers documents, applications, and user accounts from one Mac OS X installation to another. (Chapter 2 has more information on Migration Assistant.)
Network Utility	Provides detailed information on network activity. (Chapter 8 has more information on networking.)
Spaces	Enables you to access up to 16 virtual desktops that can each display different application windows.
System Profiler	Provides detailed information about the hardware and software available on a Mac.
Terminal	Serves as a line-based editor for inputting UNIX commands directly into the system. (Chapter 22 has more information on UNIX.)
VoiceOver Utility	Reads aloud text displayed by programs (including web browsers), enabling visually impaired users to use Mac OS X more effectively.
X11	Interfaces with the X Window system, which enables UNIX applications to run under Mac OS X. (Chapter 22 has more information on UNIX.)

Running a utility, such as DigitalColor Meter shown in Figure 5-2, is straight-forward: Simply double-click the appropriate utility icon in Finder to launch it and select Quit from the application's menu to close it.

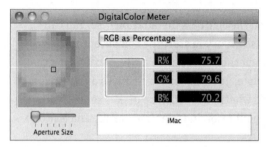

FIGURE 5-2: The DigitalColor Meter utility enables you to get color values from the pixel underneath the cursor.

> **TIP** Due to the sheer volume of utilities, it's usually easiest to use Spotlight to launch them. If you know the name of the utility you want to use, open Spotlight and type the utility name, and the utility will appear under Applications.

RUNNING UTILITIES FROM MAC OS X SERVER

Some utilities aren't included with Mac OS X, but are added to Mac OS X by a Mac running Mac OS X Server. This is because the utilities on the client computer work in conjunction with programs running on the server.

▶ A Mac running Mac OS X is known as a client, and a Mac running Mac OS X Server is known as a server.

The most notable of these utilities is a program called Podcast Producer 2. This program enables users to record video and audio to create a podcast, which is then run by the server.

> **TIP** If you don't have two computers, it is possible to run Mac OS X Server inside Mac OS X using virtualization software—such as Parallels Desktop or VMWare—which enables the one computer to act as both the client and server. Chapter 3 has more information on using virtualization software.

However, hooking up a Mac to Mac OS X Server enables a whole host of extra features, such as Address Book Server, iCal Server, and Wiki Server 2, as well as a host of sharing and networking features. You can find out more about Mac OS X Server from Apple at www.apple.com/server/macosx/features.

RUNNING UTILITIES FROM THE MAC OS X INSTALLATION DISC

Some Mac OS X utilities are included on the Mac OS X installation disc. You can run these utilities directly from the disc when you start the computer, without having to launch Mac OS X itself. This method is useful in a wide variety of situations. If a Mac fails to start, for example, you can use the utilities on the installation disc to check disk integrity and whether the startup disk is set correctly. You may be able to fix the problem without resorting to a time-consuming Mac OS X re-installation.

> **CROSSREF** Chapter 21 has more information on using the utilities on the installation disc to troubleshoot Mac OS X problems.

Some programs provide additional functionality when you run them via the installation disc. For example, Disk Utility cannot repair the main hard drive (containing Mac OS X) if it is running from that hard drive. But opening Disk Utility from the installation disc enables you to repair problems on the main hard disk.

> **NOTE** It's often better to run utilities from Mac OS X than from the installation disc, if possible. Not only do utilities run much faster from within Mac OS X, but also these utilities are more up-to-date. Software Update regularly updates all programs, including utilities, in Mac OS X with new features and data, including updates to permissions from various installers. The copy of Disk Utility on the installation disc has data only from the time the installation disc was created.

The Mac OS X installation disc also contains some utilities that aren't installed as part of Mac OS X; these utilities must be run from the installation disc. Two notable utilities relate to security: Reset Password and Firmware Password Utility. If you want to use these utilities, you have to run them from the installation disc.

> **CROSSREF** Chapter 15 has more information on Mac security and passwords.

Starting Utilities from the Installation Disc

To run the utilities from the Mac OS X installation disc, you need to start your Mac from the installation disc:

1. Insert the Mac OS X installation disc into the Mac's optical drive.

2. Restart the computer by pressing → Restart and clicking Restart.

3. Hold down the C key. This shortcut ensures that the Mac starts from the installation CD instead of from the Mac OS X installation on the hard drive.

Be aware that it takes quite a long time for a Mac to boot from the installation disc. When the installation begins, you are prompted to select the language. (Don't worry: You won't go through the installation process and replace Mac OS X!) Choose Use English for the Main Language (or another language) and click the right-arrow icon to continue. You are taken to the first window in the Mac OS X installation process, but of course you don't want to continue with that. Instead, ignore the main window and use the options from the menu bar to access utilities.

Locating Utilities on the Startup Disc

The utilities on the installation disc are located under Utilities in the menu bar. You can run them on the Desktop as if you were running them in the Mac OS X installation on your hard drive. You can run only one utility at a time from the Mac OS X installation disc. Remember that a utility will run considerably more slowly from the disc than from the hard drive.

Table 5-2 describes the utilities you can access from the Mac OS X installation disc.

▶ There are some differences between running a utility from a hard drive and running the same utility from the startup disc. For example, you can't change preferences or access services when running utilities from the installation disc.

TABLE 5-2: Utilities Included with the Mac OS X Installation Disc

UTILITY	FUNCTION
Startup Disk	Enables you to choose a different default startup disk for the Mac.
Reset Password	Enables you to reset the Mac OS X password. This is useful if you purchase a Mac and don't know the password or if you forget a password. (Chapter 15 has more information on Mac security.)
Firmware Password Utility	Enables you to set a firmware password that will prevent a person from starting up the Mac from another hard disk or from a CD or DVD such as the startup disc. It essentially prevents people from using the Reset Password function to access Mac OS X.

continues

TABLE 5-2: Utilities Included with the Mac OS X Installation Disc *(continued)*

UTILITY	FUNCTION
Disk Utility	Enables you to format, partition, and repair drives. You can use Disk Utility from the Mac OS X installation disc to work on the main hard drive.
Terminal	Enables you to enter UNIX commands into Mac OS X. You can run this utility from the Mac OS X installation disc to move, edit, and copy files to and from a hard drive.
System Profiler	Displays information about the Mac hardware and software. (Chapter 1 has more information regarding System Profiler.)
Network Utility	Enables you to diagnose and correct problems with networks to which a Mac is connected. (Chapter 8 has more information on Network Utility.)
Restore System From Backup	Enables you to replace the Mac OS X installation using a Time Machine backup volume. (Chapter 7 has more information on using Time Machine to back up and restore Mac OS X.)

As with quitting a utility that you run from within Mac OS X, when you finish using a utility that you launched from the installation disc, choose Quit from the application's menu bar and restart your Mac.

> **TIP** Because you can't run the Finder from the installation disc, the only way to edit and move files from the startup disc is to enter UNIX commands into the Terminal application. Chapter 22 has more information on using UNIX to manage files.

▶ You can force a Mac to eject the disc during startup by holding down the mouse button or trackpad button.

Mac OS X boots from the designated startup disk even with the Mac OS X installation disc inserted into the drive. The Mac should not start up from the installation disc unless you are holding down the C key during startup.

SUMMARY

This chapter includes a preview of the important utilities that come with Mac OS X. The Utilities folder houses a wide range of tools for all kinds of tasks. Typically, utilities are used to manage functionality of the Mac OS X operating system. They're great for getting to know what's going on under the hood and can be used to fix a wide range of problems. Getting to know the programs in the Utilities folder will separate you from the common computing herd, turning you into a Mac genius to whom others turn for help. Play around with the Utilities folder, and if you're hungry for more info, skip around to the referenced chapters. Remember that you can get more information by choosing Help from each utility's menu bar.

Keeping Your Mac in Great Condition

By now, you've probably noticed that Macs are great machines. Apple's computers are stunning to look at, easy to use, and capable of amazingly powerful processing. It'd be a shame if, over time, that amazingly powerful and gorgeous piece of machinery deteriorated. But that's what happens, over time, to a machine that isn't kept locked away and unused. The hard drive fills up with junk, the external casing gets tarnished, and the insides attract dust and dirt that slow down the machine and, in extreme cases, stop the machine from working. In this chapter, we're going to take a look at keeping your Mac in healthy condition, inside and out. This isn't just vanity: Keeping your machine in good condition extends its life span, maintains its value, and ensures that it remains in peak condition.

TIDYING UP YOUR HARD DRIVE

Using a Mac makes changes to the structure of the hard drive. Installing programs and creating files adds data to the hard drive; moving files to the Trash and then emptying it does the opposite: It opens up space on the hard drive. You might think of the hard drive like a bucket that fills up with water (or data, in this case) until it's full. Although this is a handy metaphor, it's slightly disingenuous because when you remove data, the rest of it doesn't slosh down the hard drive but remains in its place.

When new data is added to a hard drive (from adding programs or creating files), it's placed in the spare sectors on the hard drive. The more you add and remove files from your hard drive, the more the data ends up sitting all over the place, a process referred to as *fragmentation*.

▶ Fragmentation doesn't mean the Finder (the visible representation of your files and folder) becomes untidy. It's the actual data sitting on the hard drive that is strewn around.

Defragmenting the Hard Drive

▶ Called defrag, for short.

The antidote to fragmentation is called, appropriately, defragmentation. The good news is that Mac OS X largely takes care of defragmentation for you, and most of the time you shouldn't really need to worry about it. Mac OS X runs disk optimization (including defragmentation) after installing system updates or large applications.

Mac OS X is extremely clever about file management. If you're using the HFS+ file system (the Mac OS X default), Mac OS X intelligently removes larger files that you have recently deleted first. If a file is reasonably small (under 20MB) and fragmented into more than eight sections, Mac OS X automatically defragments the file when it is opened. It does this by moving the file to a spare area of the hard drive.

> **TIP** Some optimization features in Mac OS X work only on drives that are formatted to HFS+ Journaled mode. Try to have all additional drives (such as second hard drives and external drives) in HFS+ Journaled mode, too. They often come formatted for Windows, and if you leave them that way, you'll miss out on Mac OS X's special features.

Mac OS X 10.3 and later includes a process called *Hot File Adaptive Clustering*. In this system, Mac OS X keeps track of files under 10MB that are opened frequently, and it periodically moves these "hot" files to an area on the disk called the *Hotband* (which is the part of the disk that Mac OS X has determined is the fastest). The size of the Hotband is determined by the size of the hard drive; the Hotband is 5MB per 1GB of hard drive. As the files are moved into the Hotband, Mac OS X automatically defragments them.

According to Apple, there are two scenarios in which you should consider defragmenting the data on your drive:

▶ If you have lots of large files (such as large video clips)

▶ If you are low on disk space (typically if you have a hard drive that is 90 percent full)

If this sounds like your hard drive—and sooner or later it probably will—what can you do to defrag your hard drive?

> **TIP** If you think fragmentation is the reason your Mac is running slowly, you can use an extreme but largely effective method: You can make a complete backup of your files, reinstall Mac OS X, and then copy the files back to the Mac.

Unlike Windows 7, Mac OS X doesn't come with a built-in defragmentation tool—mostly because the system itself takes care of the vast bulk of fragmented files. However, you can purchase a tool called iDefrag (www.coriolis-systems.com/iDefrag.php). iDefrag provides detailed information about the state of your hard drive, as shown in Figure 6-1, which in itself is quite illuminating.

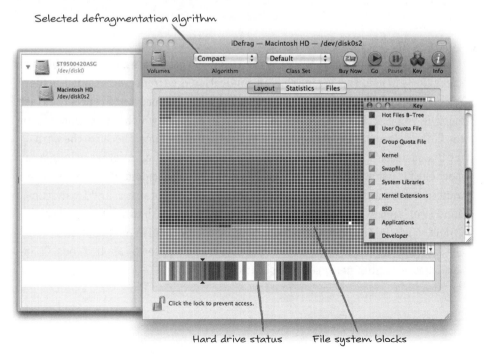

FIGURE 6-1: An application called *iDefrag* provides comprehensive information on the state of the data structure of a hard drive.

> **TIP** As a safety measure, I recommend backing up your hard drive completely before performing any defragmentation. Chapter 7 has more information on backing up a Mac.

CRON JOBS

You may hear from many Mac users that the Mac runs optimization scripts overnight, so you should leave your Mac on 24 hours a day. These scripts are sometimes called *cron jobs* because they used to run via a UNIX facility called cron; however, they now run using a UNIX facility called *launchd*.

The leave-on-overnight advice is still partly good advice: If left on overnight, a Mac will run optimization on the hard drive between 3:00 and 5:30 a.m. (depending on your time zone settings). However, it used to be the case that not leaving your Mac on overnight meant that these scripts didn't run at all. Today, however, they'll run when you next run Mac OS X. You may notice sluggish performance, though, as your Mac tries to perform both your daily computing tasks and its maintenance routines.

Sometimes when you try to empty the Trash, you get a warning dialog telling you that a file is in use. This means that an application is currently accessing the file. You can click Continue to carry on deleting the other files or Stop to cancel the Trash emptying process. The best course of action is to examine which application is using the file and close it. (Sometimes this is easier than other times, because the warning dialog doesn't tell you which application is using the file.) Alternatively, you can move the file out of the Trash if it has been moved there accidentally and you don't want to remove it. If you're sure that you want to get rid of the file, and Trash stubbornly won't remove it, then you can use Secure Empty Trash to delete it. You can Ctrl+⌘+click the Trash icon and choose Secure Empty Trash to remove all files from the Trash, as shown in Figure 6-2, even if they are being used by applications. Chapter 15 has more information on Mac security.

Secure
empty trash

FIGURE 6-2: Ctrl+click (right-click) the Trash icon in the Dock and choose Secure Empty Trash to force deletion of all files.

Compressing Files

One way to conserve space on your Mac is to compress unwanted files and folders by using compression technology. The downside of compression is that compressed files are typically unusable in a compressed state; to use the files, you need to uncompress them.

▶ Compression is a process that involves removing all the gaps in a file to reduce its file size.

Compression of files is a technique that has been around for a while, and there are a number of programs you can use to compress files, as well as several different file types. The most common file type is .zip (which is integrated with Mac OS X); other common types include .rar, .sitx, .lzh, .arj, and .gz.

Typically, compressing a file enables you to save approximately one-third of the space the files take up, depending on the type of files being compressed. It's possible to rename compressed files. However, when you uncompress them, the folders and files retain their original names. You can also move compressed files to different areas of the hard drive or to removable media.

You highlight the files and folders you want to compress in the Finder and then do one of the following:

▶ **Ctrl+click and choose Compress from the contextual menu.** If you have selected just one item, the screen says "Compress" and the name of the item. If you've highlighted multiple items, it says "Compress Items" with the number (for example, "Compress 3 Items").

▶ **Choose File → Compress from the Finder menu.**

> **NOTE** Compressing a file in Mac OS X doesn't remove the original file. Remember to move it to the Trash to save space.

Although the .zip file format is the most popular, you're likely to encounter different file types. Probably the most comprehensive file compression and uncompression application is Smith Micro's StuffIt (www.stuffit.com). A free version called StuffIt Expander is handy if you ever need to uncompress a compressed file that's not a .zip file. If compressing and uncompressing files is a regular part of your disk management, you should consider purchasing the full version of StuffIt, which gives you much more control over compressing and uncompressing files.

A relatively new option for compressing files is to use the program Squeeze by LateNiteSoft (www.latenitesoft.com/squeeze), as shown in Figure 6-3. This program makes use of support included in Mac OS X 10.6 Snow Leopard for HFS+ file compression.

▶ Squeeze works only on HFS+ formatted drives (the default for Mac OS X).

Squeeze works by removing some of the space taken up by files and folders without rendering them unreadable. It installs as a System Preference pane, and you have to add files and folders from the Finder to Squeeze. You can do this by dragging files or folders from Finder to the main window in Squeeze or by clicking the Add (+) icon and choosing items from the dialog.

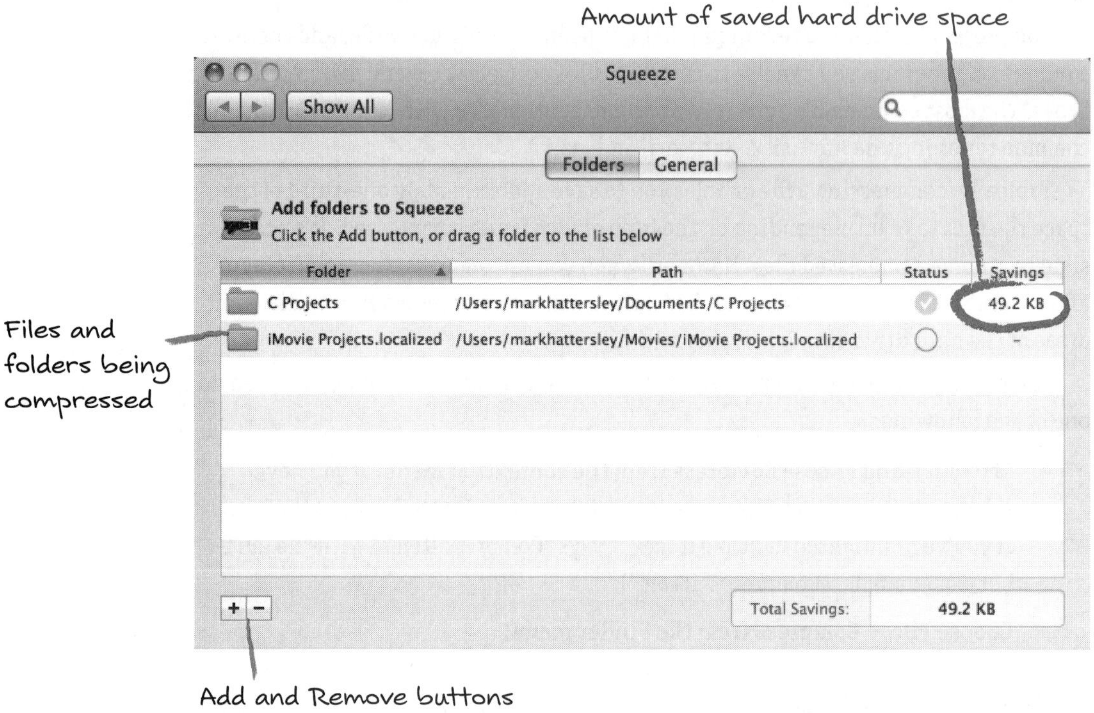

Amount of saved hard drive space

Files and folders being compressed

Add and Remove buttons

FIGURE 6-3: Squeeze is an innovative program that compresses and expands files as you work.

Squeezing files using HFS+ compression isn't as efficient as compressing them, but the files and folders remain completely usable.

Clearing Out System Logs and Caches

As applications run, they often create files to help them in their functions. Of these, two types are most common: system logs and caches. *System logs* are used by Mac OS X and applications to report information; programmers use them to check for errors. Applications use *caches* to temporarily hold information on the disk instead of trying to fit it all into RAM. System logs don't tend to take up much space, but caches can be quite large and are worth periodically checking.

There are three main caches in Mac OS X, and all three are located inside a Library folder. One is located at the root of the hard drive, the second in the System folder at the root of the hard drive, and the third inside your user folder. Here are the roots for all three:

- ▶ /Library/Caches
- ▶ /System/Library/Caches
- ▶ ~/Library/Caches

You can delete files from the caches folders with impunity. They are considered temporary by nature, and any application that needs a cache will re-create it when you next use it. One file in the /System/Library/Caches folder is locked: com.apple.Spotlight cache. This file is required by Mac OS X's Spotlight search tool, and you shouldn't delete it unless you are having a problem with Spotlight.

Note that Mac OS X applications use caches to speed up performance on repetitive tasks. However, overly large caches can result in applications performing slowly. Clearing out a cache for an application is a great way to solve performance problems, but you shouldn't do it needlessly and repetitively; applications do use caches for good reason.

▶ Deleting /Library/Caches causes Spotlight to re-index all the files in Mac OS X. This is a time-consuming process that results in the creation of the same file. It's a handy trick if you're having problems with Spotlight, though.

> **NOTE** Safari, in particular, is notorious for creating a large cache that has a negative impact on performance.

REMOVING UNUSED APPLICATIONS OR PREVIOUS OPERATING SYSTEMS

Applications take up a large amount of space on a hard drive. If you need more space, clearing out unwanted applications is a good way to start.

> **CROSSREF** Chapter 4 has more information on removing unused applications from Mac OS X.

When you install Mac OS X on a Mac that already has a version of Mac OS X on it (such as when doing an upgrade or a re-installation), you are given an option called *Archive and Install*. This option retains the previous system on your hard drive. Mac OS X holds this system in a folder called *Previous Systems* at the root of the hard drive. You can drag this folder to the Trash to delete it.

▶ You will need to enter an administrator password.

Getting Rid of Support Files

An application is likely to have files—mostly templates—that support the application. Although these files are useful, they can take up a lot of space, and if you rarely use the themes (either because you rarely use the application or because you're proficient enough to work without templates), getting rid of the support files can be a good way to conserve hard drive space.

A good place to start is iDVD. You can find the iDVD themes in ~/Library/Application Support/iDVD/Installed Themes. You can drag the Themes folder to the Trash to remove these themes. While you're in the Application Support folder, you might want to take a look at other files you might not need.

Cleaning Out iTunes and iPhoto

Some applications in Mac OS X manage files directly rather than accessing them purely via the Finder. Two notable culprits are iTunes and iPhoto. Both of these applications act as managers for files in the Finder, and removing files from within these applications is a great way to free up space on your Mac.

▶ A great way to spot large iTunes tracks is to sort them by Size. Choose View → View Options, select the Size check box, and click OK. Then click the Size sort triangle so it points downward.

Removing files from iTunes is simple enough. You highlight the files you no longer require and press Delete (or choose Edit → Delete). iTunes brings up a dialog asking if you want to keep the file in the iTunes Media folder or move it to Trash. You should select Move To Trash.

You delete pictures from iPhoto using largely the same process as in iTunes. You can either delete individual images or entire events. Depending on the size of the image files, you can save considerable space. However, a key difference is that iPhoto has its own Trash, independent of the Trash in Finder, as shown in Figure 6-4. You will need to empty Trash from within the application to recover space on your hard drive.

You can view the contents of the iPhoto Trash by selecting Trash in the Recent list in the iPhoto sidebar. When you're ready to get rid of files from iPhoto, you click on iPhoto → Empty iPhoto Trash.

Empty Trash to delete photos

FIGURE 6-4: iPhoto has its own Trash, and pictures deleted from iPhoto continue to take up space until you empty it.

Check the Movies Folder

If you're into watching, creating, or sharing digital videos, you might find that they fill up your hard drive pretty quickly. Digital video is probably the most data-hungry of all file types, and video files tend to be much larger than other type of file. Obviously, with such large files hanging around, you should ensure that you really need the files on your system and delete any that you don't.

You should especially be aware of movie files that you've imported into iTunes. If you have the Copy Files to iTunes Media Folder When Adding to Library option checked in iTunes Preferences (the default option), when you add a movie to iTunes, you also add a second copy inside the iTunes library. With HD movies taking up such huge amounts of storage space, having two copies on your hard drive will soon cause trouble.

▶ This is especially true if you watch high-definition movies. A typical two-hour movie in HD takes between 10GB and 16GB of hard drive space—more than you can probably afford to spare.

Buying a Second Hard Drive

Of course, if you find yourself running out of space, one option to consider is to attach more storage space to a Mac. This can take the form of an external hard drive, which you attach to the Mac typically by using USB or FireWire. An external hard drive enables you to easily add a second hard drive with plenty of free space for minimal cost. Mac Pro owners might want to consider adding an internal drive, as it's a neater, faster, and usually cheaper option.

CROSSREF Chapter 10 has more information on upgrading hard drive space.

Owners of Mac notebooks might want to consider a network-attached storage (NAS) hard drive. Instead of connecting directly to your Mac, a NAS typically has an Ethernet connection and attaches directly to a network. (In your home, this is typically a spare Ethernet port on your Wi-Fi router). A NAS drive enables you to copy files to and from the hard drive when you are connected to the network, doing away with the need for a direct connection. This can be a great boon to MacBook owners who use their Mac notebook in different parts of the house. It also means that multiple Macs can access and use the same hard drive. Because NAS drives can be permanently switched on, and connected to your router, they often have advanced features, such as remote access, file transfer protocol (FTP), and BitTorrent downloads. These are often set up through an interface in the web browser, and setup can be fairly complicated. This is something to bear in mind when you're being sold on extra features.

NOTE Increasingly people are using online storage solutions such as iDisk and Box.net to store files remotely. By storing files remotely, you save space on your hard drive, and you can access files wherever you are.

Using OmniDiskSweeper to Clear Out Files

Going through the Finder and looking for files you can delete is a great way to free up space, but it's time-consuming. A simpler option is to use a program that does the work for you. One of the best I've found is a free program called OmniDiskSweeper (www.omnigroup.com), which scans a volume looking for large files. It's also good at determining which files Mac OS X is using and which are just hanging around.

After you launch OmniDiskSweeper, you highlight the main volume (typically Macintosh HD) and click Sweep *"Macintosh HD"* Drive (where *"Macintosh HD"* is the name of the main volume). The OmniDiskSweeper window reveals the contents of the volume in a window reminiscent of the Finder window in Column View mode, as shown in Figure 6-5. It lists files and folders, along with the amount of space they take up on the hard drive. The files and folders are color coded, with red objects taking up the most space, purple ones taking up intermediate amounts of hard drive space, and green objects taking up very little space. You can drill down folders by clicking on them in the window; the contents appear in the column to the right.

You can also use OmniDiskSweeper to remove items from the Finder. To do so, you highlight the item in the window and click the Delete icon. A dialog appears, asking you to confirm the deletion. You click Destroy to remove the item.

▶ Be warned that the file or folder is immediately removed from the Mac instead of moved to Trash.

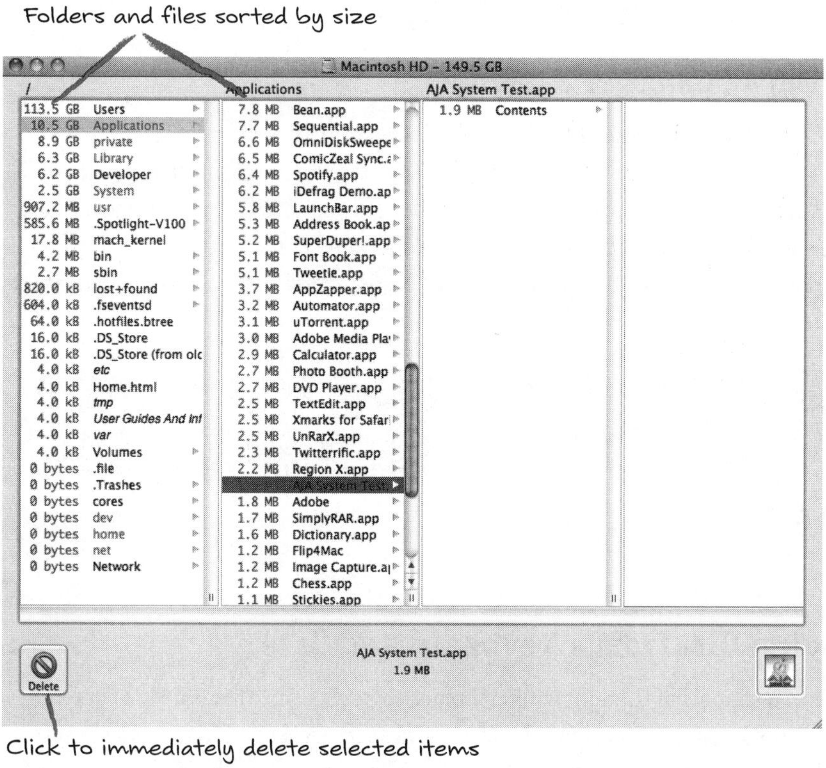

Folders and files sorted by size

Click to immediately delete selected items

FIGURE 6-5: The free OmniDiskSweeper application is great for scanning a hard drive for files, folders, and applications that take up a lot of space.

KEEPING YOUR MAC PHYSICALLY CLEAN

Cleaning up may not be the most thrilling part of being a computer guru, but it's important on a few levels. Dirt, dust, and grime can be computer killers, clogging up

► The screen, keyboard, and mouse of a Mac are particularly susceptible to gunk.

electronics and jamming moving parts. Aside from the practical reasons, there's also the issue of appearance. Obviously, a computer covered in grime isn't going to be nice to use (although each user's grime-resistance may vary), but Macs are particularly susceptible to looking scruffy. Those shiny white and aluminum computers you see in an Apple store can look a grubby gray after a few months use. Sooner or later—either through a general desire for cleanliness or because you can no longer use the mouse or see through the screen—you'll end up cleaning your Mac, which is covered in the following sections.

Cleaning a Computer Screen

The best way to clean a computer screen is to use a soft clean cloth and liquid. It's largely recommended that you don't spray the liquid directly on the screen, and obviously you shouldn't pour liquid cleaner directly onto your computer; instead, spray it onto the cloth and then use that to rub it on to the screen. When it comes to liquids, I typically recommend buying a specific screen-cleaning product, such as iKlear or 3M Screen Cleaner.

> **WARNING** You may hear that you should use rubbing alcohol to clean displays. Stop! This is a throwback to the glass CRT displays, and you should never use alcohol, ammonia, or any other solvents on modern LCD or LED displays. Stay away from alcohol when cleaning a Mac display!

Removing Dirt from a Keyboard and Case

► You can take a vacuum cleaner to a keyboard if you don't have compressed air, but be careful not to suck up any loose keys.

There are two schools of thought when it comes to keyboards. One is called "get a wet cloth, cotton swabs, and compressed air and then use a combination of scrubbing and blowing to clean the keys." The other is to use custom computer cleaning products. These products typically are gel-like substances that look like putty; you squeeze the substance between the keys, lifting up dirt as you go. Personally I prefer the scrub-and-blow method. A can of compressed air is a tech geek's best friend and worth far more than any cleaning gel. If you want to really clean up, use compressed air to blow out any dust and hairs and then get some cleaning fluid and some cotton swabs; dip the cotton swabs in the cleaning fluid and scrub between the keys. Then dab the fluid onto a lint-free cloth and scrub the surface of the keys.

Keeping the Inside of a Mac Pro Clean

Compressed air is your best friend when it comes to cleaning the inside of a Mac Pro, because by far the biggest problem is dust. The fans on a Mac Pro suck dust into the system, and this dust can clog up components and interfere with electrical connections.

Fortunately, it's pretty easy to deal with dust. You can pick up cans of compressed air from most computer stores. A quick blast inside the case deals with the dust easily. Whenever you open up your Mac, whether specifically for cleaning or to upgrade components, it's a good idea to give it a blast of compressed air to remove any dust from the system.

> **WARNING** Be careful not to use compressed air too close to the circuit board as the extreme cold can damage circuits. Although most cables are protected inside a Mac Pro, you should check for any loosened any cables attached to the PCI cards.

Removing Dirt from a Mouse

The mouse is another part of your Mac that will quickly lose its clean appearance. If you're an owner of an Apple Magic Mouse, you needn't worry unduly: You can clean the surface of the device by using the same approach as cleaning the case or keyboard, described earlier.

However, owners of older Mighty Mouse devices have an additional problem that can be quite frustrating. The small ball on the top of the device (called the Scroll Ball) frequently stops working when it becomes covered in dust and grease from fingers. Getting it working again can be a pain, but try the following steps:

1. Push down on the surface of the mouse and scrub your finger up and down on the Scroll Ball to dislodge any dirt.

2. Hold the mouse upside down and roll the ball around with your fingers. (Some users also claim that using a sheet of paper to move the Scroll Ball around while holding it upside down works.)

3. Dab a lint-free cloth in a little alcohol-free cleaning fluid (not too much) and use it to firmly clean the Scroll Ball and mouse. This is a more extreme approach than the method described in step 2, and you may have to wait for the cleaning fluid to dry before the Scroll Ball works properly.

▶ Despite sounding crazy, this upside-down method was Apple's official advice for cleaning the mouse.

▶ Don't forget that you can use any USB mouse, and many Mac users prefer mice made by other manufacturers, or even trackpads and graphic tablets.

Typically, most users try all of these methods during the course of the Mighty Mouse's lifetime. Apple's replacement for the Mighty Mouse, called the *Magic Mouse*, replaced the Scroll Ball with a touch-sensitive surface that's less prone to clogging up.

GETTING THE MOST OUT OF A MACBOOK'S BATTERY

Most Macs sold these days are notebooks, and they all come with internal batteries that enable you to use them out and about. This is great news for digital nomads; but sooner or later, any roving computer user will come up against the problem of battery life.

The great news is that most current Mac notebooks have really long-lasting batteries. Apple has developed some great technology, and current Mac notebooks can run for 7 to 10 hours on a single charge. Notebook battery charge diminishes over time, however, and you will likely need to replace your notebook battery at some point. However, Apple promises that the latest models are good for up to 1,000 charges before they need to be replaced, and that should provide around five years' worth of functionality before you need to consider replacing the battery.

> **CROSSREF** Chapter 10 has more information on replacing the physical battery in a MacBook or MacBook Pro.

Selecting the Best Energy-Saving Options

Apple notebooks offer a range of options designed to control the length of battery life. Typically, these options offer some form of trade-off between the amount of battery power that the machine uses and the performance it can offer. However, you shouldn't necessarily think that there's a direct correlation between battery life and performance; many changes to the settings you make will increase battery life without affecting performance.

The place to be if you want to maximize the battery life of your machine is the Energy Saver preferences pane. The following sections describe how to get the best performance from your notebook battery.

CHOOSING THE RIGHT GRAPHICS SETTING

Some Mac notebooks contain two different graphics cards: one that offers high performance and one that offers long-lasting battery power. On the latest range of

Mac notebooks, Mac OS X automatically moves from one graphics card to another, depending on the task. If you are using regular programs (such as Mail or Safari), it sticks with the energy-efficient graphics card; if you open an application with higher performance requirements (such as Aperture or Final Cut), your Mac switches to the high-performance card.

It's possible to override the automatic switching so that the high-performance graphics card (with heavy battery requirement) is permanently turned on. You need to ensure that the Automatic Graphic Switching check box is deselected.

Older Mac notebooks require you to manually switch between graphics cards. If you have one of these Macs, you'll see two options: Better Battery Life and Higher Performance. If you choose an option different from the highlighted one, a dialog appears, saying "Changing Graphics Settings Requires You to Log Out." You click the Log Out button to sign out of your account. You then need to close down all open programs to move to a different graphics card setting.

CHANGING THE ENERGY-SAVING OPTIONS

You use two sets of controls—Computer Sleep and Display Sleep—in the Energy Saving preferences pane to fine-tune the power requirements of the Mac. You can adjust the following options:

- **Computer Sleep:** A slider controls the amount of time a Mac waits without user input before entering sleep mode. When in sleep mode, the computer essentially turns itself off: The CPU powers down, the hard drive spins down, the fans stops, and the display turns off. In this mode, the Mac draws very little power.

- **Display Sleep:** As in sleep mode, the Mac draws less power when the display is blank. However, it is still capable of performing tasks such as checking for e-mail or downloading large files.

- **Put the Hard Disk(s) to Sleep When Possible:** This check box, which is selected by default, enables the hard drive to spin down after 10 minutes of inactivity. The advantage to putting a hard disk to sleep is that it saves energy, and it also saves wear and tear on the engine that spins the physical drive. Some users find the slight delay as the hard drive comes back into action annoying; it is usually marked by a spinning rainbow wheel.

▶ The graphics card designed to offer high performance is often called discrete. This is because it sits separately from the CPU and typically has its own RAM.

▶ If you don't have a Graphics option in the Energy Saver preferences pane, your Mac notebook doesn't have multiple graphics options.

▶ You can quickly put a Mac to sleep by holding down Option+⌘+Eject for about two seconds.

▶ If you have one of the newer solid state drive (SSD) hard disks, deselect the Put the Hard Disk(s) to Sleep When Possible option. Because the SSD doesn't use power when it's inactive and doesn't spin, there's no advantage to putting it to sleep.

> **TIP** If you transfer large files that take longer than 10 minutes to move from one drive to another (such as transferring a large file over a wireless network), you might find that the file transfer is interrupted by the hard disk going to sleep (especially if you leave the computer to transfer the file). If this happens, you should deselect the Put the Hard Disk(s) to Sleep When Possible check box before transferring the file.

▶ **Slightly Dim the Display When Using This Power Source:** This check box appears only underneath the Battery tab in the Energy Saver preferences pane on a Mac notebook. With this option selected, the screen slightly dims (by three bars, or approximately one-fifth of the power) when the Mac is running off the battery. You can manually increase the power by using the Brightness setting in the Display pane in System Preferences or by pressing the brightness up button on some Mac keyboards (typically the F2 key). This option is selected by default and draws slightly less power over prolonged periods of time.

▶ **Wake for Network Access:** This check box appears only underneath the Power Adapter settings. Mac OS X has a feature called *Bonjour Sleep Proxy* that enables supporting devices (such as a Time Capsule or an AirPort Base Station) to wake up a Mac to perform a task before putting it back to sleep. Typical tasks include an iTunes Sharing request, printer sharing, and Back to My Mac (a remote access feature provided as part of Apple's MobileMe service). These functions cannot access the Mac if it's completely switched off but can if it is in sleep mode.

▶ **Automatically Reduce Brightness Before Display Goes to Sleep:** With this option selected, the display automatically dims before the display turns off. The amount of time between the display dimming and the display turning off depends on the Display Sleep setting. If your Mac's display is set to turn off after 2 minutes, the display dims after 1 minute and 45 seconds.

> **TIP** If you watch movies or download large files, you might want to consider moving the Computer Sleep and Display Sleep sliders to the Never setting so the display doesn't go blank mid-movie or with a large file half downloaded. It's best to do this with the settings only in the Power Adapter window, as you will seriously hamper battery life if your computer stays on permanently. You should also deselect the Automatically Reduce the Brightness Before Display Goes to Sleep check box to prevent the screen from going dark soon after you start watching a movie.

▶ **Restore Defaults:** You click this button to return the settings to their original status. Only the Battery or Power Adapter settings are returned to their default, depending on whether the Battery or Power Adapter tab is selected.

▶ **Show Battery Status in the Menu Bar:** You select this option to display the battery icon in the menu bar. It gives a visual guide about how much energy the battery contains, as shown in Figure 6-6. When the battery is less than 10 percent full, the icon turns red.

▶ **Schedule:** Click this button to schedule times for the Mac to start up, sleep, restart, or shut down. A Mac notebook will start up only if a power adapter is connected. You might want to do this to turn on a Mac before you come to work and turn it off automatically at night.

▶ *Click the Battery icon in the menu bar and choose Show Time to get an indication of how much battery life is left. The time displayed is an estimate and becomes more accurate as energy is used.*

Delselect fpr permanently faster performance

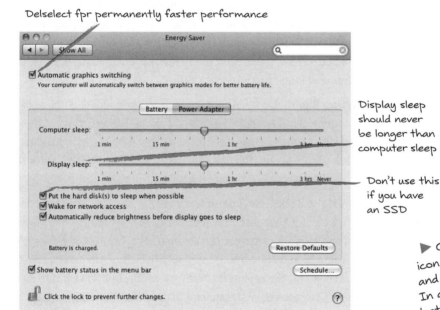

Display sleep should never be longer than computer sleep

Don't use this if you have an SSD

FIGURE 6-6: The Energy Saver system preference pane offers plenty of options to maximize a MacBook's battery life.

▶ *Click the Battery icon in the menu bar and choose Show Time. In addition to the battery icon, you now get an indication of how much battery life is left in the Mac.*

Turning Off Unwanted Features

Many parts of the Mac OS X operating system consume energy, and turning them off can extend the battery life. Note, however, that typically these features provide functionality to the Mac, and turning them off isn't always necessarily a good thing. There's little advantage in stripping down the operating system to the point where you no longer enjoy using it.

Check out these suggestions and decide whether you actually want each particular feature:

▶ **Turning Off AirPort: AirPort** requires a lot of power to work, and switching it off is a great way to boost the amount of power you can get from a Mac.

▶ *This is Apple's term for Wi-Fi.*

▶ **Switching Off Flash:** Adobe Flash is a popular plug-in for web browsers such as Safari. It's used for powering much of the interactive content on the Internet, including most video, audio, and animation. It is a well-known memory and power hog, though, and turning it off can boost your battery life when you're using the Internet. There's no straightforward way to switch off Flash in Safari, but you can remove the plug-in to temporarily prevent it from working. The Flash plug-in is called *Flash Player.plugin* and is located in Home/Library/Internet Plug-Ins. Inside this folder you also see a folder called *Disabled Plug-Ins*. You can move the Flash Player.plugin file to Disabled Plug-Ins to disable Flash. You need to quit the Safari application and reopen it for the change to take effect. If you want to use Flash again, you need to move file back to Internet Plug-Ins and restart Safari.

▶ **Deactivating Bluetooth:** Bluetooth is a technology used for wireless communication. Apple's wireless mouse and keyboard use it to connect to Mac OS X, and it can also be used to transfer files and other data. As with AirPort, Bluetooth takes a lot of power. You open System Preferences, click Bluetooth, and ensure that the On check box is deselected.

▶ *Obviously this isn't a good idea if you're using a Bluetooth mouse or keyboard.*

▶ **Turning Off the Backlit Keyboard:** MacBook Pro and MacBook Air models come with a backlit keyboard that automatically brightens up the keys in dim lighting conditions. You can use the Keyboard Brightness control keys (sitting alongside F5 and F6 on a Mac notebook) to change the strength of the lighting. If you find the keyboard lighting valuable but still want to manage battery use, you can reduce the amount of time that Mac OS X waits between input before dimming the lights.

▶ **Reducing the Screen Brightness:** You can turn down the screen brightness to preserve battery life. You can adjust the brightness of the screen by using the Screen Brightness control keys (sitting alongside F1 and F2 buttons on most Mac keyboards).

▶ **Ejecting Optical Discs:** Make sure you eject any discs from the optical drive. If the optical drive contains a disc, it spins around to read the disc, drawing power as it goes.

▶ **Quit Unused Programs:** Mac OS X is great at multitasking, but having more programs in memory draws slightly more power. Although this isn't as big a drain as other resources, you can slightly increase battery life by sticking to just the programs you need. Removing unused Dashboard widgets can also increase performance. (Chapter 4 has more information on adding and removing widgets in the Dashboard.)

If you get rid of one of these features, you'll have more energy; if you keep it, you'll get more functionality.

Inverting the Screen Color

Some users claim that inverting the screen color, as shown in Figure 6-7, gives an extra 30 minutes or so of battery life. The theory is that displaying large quantities of black pixels draws less power than displaying white ones. You can invert the screen by pressing Ctrl+Option+⌘+8. This mode is effective in low light conditions. You may want to combine this option with a low display brightness setting to extend battery life.

▶ This feature is designed to make the screen easier for disabled users to see.

FIGURE 6-7: Inverting the screen color is a feature offered for visually disabled users, but using it also extends battery life.

Calibrating the Battery

Calibrating a MacBook battery ensures that you get the longest runtime from it and is easier than you think; it essentially involves running the battery all the way until it is drained. This helps Mac OS X gauge how much performance is available from the battery, which enables it to accurately display how much runtime is left after you've recharged the battery.

You calibrate a Mac battery by performing these steps:

1. Plug in the battery adapter and charge the Mac notebook until it is fully charged.

2. Allow the battery to remain fully charged for two hours or longer.

3. Disconnect the power adapter and use your computer until the battery starts to run out.

4. When Mac OS X delivers a low-battery warning, close down all the applications and save your work. Keep using the Mac until Mac OS X goes into sleep mode. Allow the Mac to remain in sleep mode for at least five hours. Do not plug in the power adapter during this time.

5. Connect the power adapter and leave it connected until the Mac is fully charged. You can use the computer during this final process.

▶ I've found that you can wait a few months between calibrating the battery.

Apple recommends that you calibrate the battery in a Mac notebook when you initially purchase it (or if you have installed a new battery) and then once per month after that. Many owners never intentionally calibrate a Mac notebook's battery, but the process happens organically during regular use.

USING AN INVERTER TO CHARGE UP IN AN AUTOMOBILE

You can charge up a Mac notebook in a car by using the power adapter with an inverter. *Inverters* change the current from the 12-volt outlet into a form that your notebook can use. A good option is the Kensington Auto/Air Power Inverter (http://us.kensington.com/html/17163.html). It provides an electrical outlet and two USB ports to charge your MacBook and a couple other devices at the same time.

▶ Don't confuse the 20mm connection on a MagSafe Airline Adapter with an automobile's power port. Although they're physically similar, you shouldn't plug the MagSafe Airline Adapter into your car.

USING AN IN-FLIGHT ADAPTER TO CHARGE IN THE AIR

Many airlines now offer power supplies from the comfort of your seat. Apple provides a MagSafe Airline Adapter that plugs straight from the airplane's power adapter into the MacBook. Two types of connections are used: EmPower and 20mm. The MagSafe Airline Adapter powers your MacBook during the flight, although it doesn't provide enough power to charge the battery.

GET ACQUAINTED WITH EXTERNAL BATTERY OPTIONS

On older PowerBook and MacBook Pro models, it's possible to remove the battery from the notebook by using a battery release latch or locking lever. On early models, you turn this latch a quarter-turn clockwise, usually with a coin. On later models, you pull the locking lever outward.

If you own a Mac notebook that has a removable battery, you can purchase multiple batteries. Then when you're away from a power supply, you simply use up one battery, shut down the notebook, and insert the next battery.

More recent Mac notebooks have replaced the removable battery with a fixed internal unit. Although this might seem rather foolish, given that mobile owners typically use more than one battery to provide a steady stream of power, the fixed internal unit lasts much longer—almost doubling the amount of time a notebook can be used. However, it does mean that you're somewhat stuck if you're on a long journey without access to a power supply. Help is at hand, though, from two companies: HyperMac (www.hypermac.com) and Battery Geek Inc. (www.batterygeek.net). Batteries are available in different sizes; the largest one can power a MacBook for around 30 hours.

> **NOTE** HyperMac's batteries automatically detect which model of MacBook is connected and adjust the power accordingly. If you have more than one kind of Mac notebook, you need only one HyperMac battery. Battery Geek Inc.'s batteries only charge up the MacBook when it is turned off.

KEEPING YOUR MACBOOK SAFE

Because Mac notebooks are premium products, they're magnets for quick-fingered thieves. Although you're unlikely to let your Mac notebook out of your sight, you might want to consider some of the security options discussed in the following sections.

Using the Kensington Security Slot

Kensington lock slots are present on both the MacBook and MacBook Pro models (but not the MacBook Air). Situated next to the optical drive slot, the Kensington lock slot is a small reinforced metal hole that can be used to attach a locking cable. These cables typically feature a key or combination lock and a sturdy cable that can be looped around a permanent object (such as a table leg).

You typically use a Kensington cable to keep a Mac notebook safe while in a public place, such as a coffee shop or library. However, the cable can be circumvented if enough force is applied (although this often damages the case). Adept thieves who are armed with a few simple tools can also pick the lock. However, many shops, offices, and companies attending trade shows use these cables to prevent people from wandering off with notebooks.

> **WARNING** Keeping your notebook secure is especially important if you keep confidential information on it. Barely a day goes by without a news story about someone losing a notebook with thousands of customer details, confidential company reports, or even confidential medical information. It's one thing to lose a notebook; it's another to lose data and then lose your job.

Installing Tracking Software

Several companies offer anti-theft software solutions that help locate stolen MacBooks. Typically these involve installing a program on the Mac that sits in the background and sends information remotely. In the event that a Mac notebook is stolen, you can report the loss to the service provider, which then activates the software and tries to track down the machine.

Undercover 3 by Obicule (www.orbicule.com/undercover) and LoJack for Laptops (www.absolute.com/products/lojackforlaptops) are the most prominent of these software-based solutions. They also use software that imitates hardware faults in the hope that the MacBook will be taken to an authorized repair shop, at which point it displays a message reporting the MacBook as stolen.

▶ Undercover recommends creating a dummy account with no administrator abilities. This enables a thief to play around on the Mac and activate the tracking software. Although this might be successful, I still have my doubts.

I have doubts about software-based anti-theft solutions. They require Mac OS X to be running and logged in. You should always require login to get into your Mac for security reasons. There's a way for a knowledgeable thief to overcome the login, but the thief is more likely to attempt to wipe the operating system. You can prevent a system wipe by using a Firmware Password (see Chapter 15 for more information), which leaves a thief with an unusable computer, but then it's also a computer that Undercover or LoJack can't recover.

Tagging Your Notebook

Thieves typically want to steal something so they can sell it. One way to discourage theft in the first place is to physically tag the device with information. A company called STOP (Security Tracking of Office Property) can supply you with a metal tag that is attached to a Mac and is extremely difficult to remove. In fact, even if you do remove the tag, you'll damage the Mac case and expose the contact number etched below it. The tag has a toll-free number, a website URL, and a barcode number that is registered online with your personal details. When you register with STOP, your notebook is added to their database, and if the police or a concerned citizen recovers your machine, they can use the service to get your equipment back to you. You can find more information on STOP online at www.stoptheft.com/site/index.php.

Protecting your Mac is a great idea, but really the best practice is not to let it out of your sight. Macs are high profile, premium devices that thieves love to get their hands on.

▶ The real benefit of tagging isn't recovering stolen equipment but deterring thieves from taking it in the first place.

SUMMARY

This chapter covered a lot of software and hardware basics designed to keep your Mac in great condition. From cleaning up the files on your hard drive to keeping your Mac physically clean on the inside and out, you'll want to protect your investment and keep it operating at peak levels of performance. Far from being an act of vanity or organization, keeping a Mac clean ensures that it stays in good shape and helps prevent hardware errors.

Keeping your Mac notebook battery in good shape it also key, and there are a number of options for getting the most battery life out of your Mac, including several methods for charging up while on the go. If you work on the move, you should prepare yourself not only to use one of these mobile charging methods, but also to think about safety options, including physical locks or tagging options that might discourage a thief from taking your Mac in the first place. But in the event your computer is stolen, at you least you have some innovative software options that can enable you to track down your stolen notebook and remotely wipe the data contained on it.

CHAPTER 7

Backing Up Your Mac

IN THIS CHAPTER

► Setting up and customizing Time Machine to create backups of your data

► Setting up an Apple Time Capsule and backing up your files

► Using Time Machine to locate and restore deleted files

► Discovering backup options such as backing up your files manually or cloning your hard drive

► Backing up your data by using an online service

► Syncing your data online

Backing up data is a vitally important process, yet few computer users invest time or effort in setting up a backup system. You should laugh at them, look down on them, and giggle when they come to you for help. But don't get caught without a backup yourself, or you'll look and feel like a chump. Losing valuable files isn't funny, so let's take a look at your options.

USING TIME MACHINE TO CREATE A BACKUP

▶ Typically, a backup consists of files or folders you want to keep safe. It can also be the entire contents of your hard drive.

With Mac OS X 10.5 Leopard, Apple introduced a remarkable new backup solution called *Time Machine*. Time Machine is extremely clever in lots of different ways. Obviously, the fact that it backs up all your files makes it a pretty smart, but it's also intelligent enough to back up only changes to files. It's also clever because it doesn't just back up the current contents of your drive but also the way your hard drive has looked over time (hence the name). So you can roll back files and folders to how they looked an hour ago, last week, last month, and so on.

But Time Machine is especially smart because it's so easy to set up and get working that it barely needs an explanation. You simply attach a new hard drive and click Use As Backup Disk in the dialog that says "Do you want to use this as a Time Machine drive?" as shown in Figure 7-1. That's it. See you in the next chapter.

▶ Make sure the hard drive you use for Time Machine has no files on it that you want to keep. It'll be wiped in the process.

Do you want to use "UNTITLED" to back up with Time Machine?

Time Machine keeps an up-to-date copy of everything on your Mac. It not only keeps a spare copy of every file, it remembers how your system looked, so you can revisit your Mac as it appeared in the past.

(?)   (Decide Later)   (Don't Use) (Use as Backup Disk)

FIGURE 7-1: Setting up Time Machine is as simple as attaching a drive and clicking Use As Backup Disk.

Still here? Okay, so here's a bit more detail: The drive you use for Time Machine has to be formatted using the default Mac OS Extended format for Mac OS X hard drives. However, most hard drives you buy are preformatted using MS-DOS (FAT) because this format ensures that the drives are compatible with computers running Mac OS X or Windows. If your drive is in MS-DOS (FAT) format, a dialog warns you that the disk must be erased before you can use it for Time Machine.

> **NOTE** One caveat to using Time Machine is that you should dedicate the entire attached hard drive to the Time Machine backup. Although it's possible to copy files to and from Time Machine, doing so isn't really recommended.

The Use As Backup Disk dialog only appears if you haven't already set up Time Machine. If you've already set up Time Machine but want to change the drive, you need to set up Time Machine manually using the Backup preferences pane. You also need to go through the manual process if you want to change the backup drive.

HOW BIG IS YOUR BACKUP HARD DRIVE?

Although Time Machine uses compression to squeeze the data on your main volume into the Time Machine backup, it incrementally adds data to this volume as it continually backs up the data, and over time will fill up the drive. The larger the backup drive, the farther back in time you can retrieve files. I recommend that the backup drive be at least twice the size of the main drive.

Setting Up Time Machine Manually

You set up Time Machine manually through the Time Machine preferences pane, as shown in Figure 7-2.

Making the first backup can take quite a long time. It may be several hours before you can use Time Machine to restore files. It's a good idea to set your first Time Machine backup to take place overnight and to set the Computer Sleep setting to Never in the Energy Saver system preferences pane so that the Mac runs all night. Chapter 6 has more information on the Energy Saver system preferences pane.

NOTE When you set up a volume to use for Time Machine backup, the icon changes to a blue volume icon with the Time Machine logo (a circular arrow clock). The name of the volume also changes to Time Machine Volume.

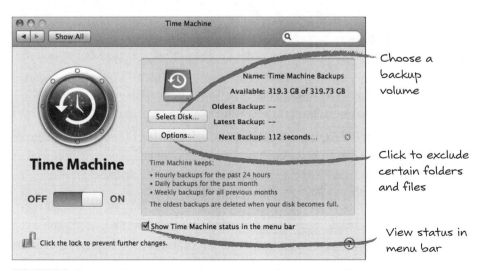

FIGURE 7-2: Time Machine makes creating backups as simple as attaching a drive and turning it on.

Following the initial backup, Time Machine performs hourly backups of your data. It keeps hourly backups for the past 24 hours, daily backups for the previous month, and weekly backups until the backup drive is full. In addition, you can manually perform backups in the interim periods. To do so, you click the Time Machine icon in the menu bar and choose Back Up Now.

Customizing Options for Time Machine

Time Machine doesn't let you granularly select which files, folders, or other items to back up. In many ways, this is its strength: You don't have to go through a complex process of deciding what files and folders you want to back up.

> You can choose which files and folders you don't want to back up.

However, you do have some options when setting up Time Machine. These options can speed up the Time Machine process and minimize the impact that Time Machine may have on your system. You find the options for Time Machine in the Time Machine pane within System Preferences: You click Time Machine and then click Options to display the following settings:

- **Exclude These Items from Backup:** Items added to this list are ignored during the backup process, as shown in Figure 7-3. By default, this includes any external hard drive volumes, but you can also add files or folders from Finder in one of two ways:

  - Drag and drop files or folders from Finder directly into the window.

  - Click the Add (+) icon and use the Finder window to choose a file or folder, and then click the Exclude button. Click the Show Invisible Items check box to see hidden items.

- **Back Up While on Battery Power:** This check box appears on Mac notebooks and is selected by default. If you deselect this check box, Time Machine performs a backup only when connected to a power adapter. This helps maximize battery performance and is a good way to ensure that backups take place when the machine is likely to be on for a while.

- **Notify After Old Backups Are Deleted:** When Time Machine starts to fill up, it deletes older files from the backup. This option, which is selected by default, ensures that Time Machine warns you after it removes old backups.

> So how big is large? Any file larger than 1GB that you regularly modify qualifies for consideration to the list of excluded files.

So what kind of files should you exclude from a Time Machine backup? Apple recommends that you exclude large files that you regularly modify. Remember, you don't have to exclude anything from a Time Machine backup; excluding files just speeds up the process.

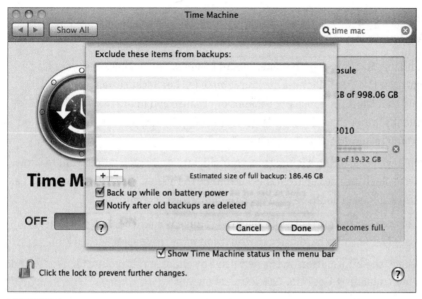

FIGURE 7-3: You can exclude large files from Time Machine to reduce the amount of time it takes to create a backup.

You might want to consider excluding the following files and folders from the Time Machine backup:

- Applications folder
- Virtualization files
- Movies folder
- iTunes Music folder
- iPhoto library

Adding some or all of these items to the list of excluded files speeds up the backup process, but keep in mind that you won't be able to access these files if you lose them. In some cases (especially the iPhoto Library) you might want to investigate a separate backup solution.

> ▶ Virtualization software such as Parallels Desktop and VMware Fusion uses virtualization files (also called virtual machines). A virtualization file is typically a single large file found within the Documents folder.

> ▶ You can use iPhoto's Export or Burn features to backup photos.

WARNING If you exclude items from the backup and intend to use Time Machine along with Migration Assistant to move from one Mac OS X installation to another, you should clear the list of excluded files and folders and do a complete backup before beginning the migration process.

Transferring Time Machine Backups from One Volume to Another

Although Time Machine is pretty smart about compressing old backups, your Mac might outgrow the Time Machine backup volume (either because you have used it for so long that there are too many backups or because you upgraded your Mac's hard drive, and it's larger than the Time Machine backup). As Roy Scheider famously said in *Jaws*: "You're gonna need a bigger boat."

If you need to keep the backup from your old hard drive, you might want to transfer the Time Machine backup from the old volume to the new one. This process isn't as straightforward as it should be. You need to follow these steps:

1. Ensure that the current Time Machine volume is connected. Also connect to your Mac the new hard drive to which you want to transfer the backup.

2. Check the information on the new drive by choosing the volume in Finder and choosing File ➔ Get Info. Check the following:

   ▷ Ensure that the format displays Mac OS X Extended (Journaled). If it's any other format, you need to use Erase feature in Disk Utility to format the drive. (Chapter 5 has more information on using Disk Utility to format drives.)

   ▷ Make sure the Ignore Ownership of This Volume check box is not selected. This check box doesn't appear on all hard drives; if you don't see it on your drive, don't worry.

3. Open Disk Utility and highlight the drive. Check that the Partition Map Scheme is set to GUID Partition Table (or Apple Partition Table if you're using an older G5 Mac). If it isn't, use the Erase feature to format the new hard drive.

4. Open System Preferences, click Time Machine, and move the Time Machine switch to Off.

5. Double-click the old Time Machine volume in Finder to reveal its contents.

6. Copy the Backups.backupd folder from the root of the old hard drive to the root of the new one.

7. Enter an administrator username and password to copy the file.

8. Return to Time Machine in System Preferences and click Select Disk. Now choose the new hard drive volume and click Use for Backup.

9. Eject the old hard drive volume from Finder (by highlighting the volume and choosing File ➔ Eject). Then disconnect the old drive from your Mac.

Mac OS X now carries on backing up to the new volume, and you can use Time Machine to recover files from the new drive.

SETTING UP A TIME CAPSULE

If you own a Mac notebook, you might have already spotted a flaw in Apple's Time Machine technology. It requires you to attach an external hard drive to a Mac, something you're unlikely to do on a permanent basis because it limits the portability of the device.

▶ There's nothing stopping you from using an external drive now and then to back up your data.

Apple has created a special device called *Time Capsule* that combines the wireless capabilities of its AirPort Extreme Base Station Wi-Fi router with a built-in hard drive. Setting up a Time Capsule device enables a Mac to wirelessly back up and retrieve data. And because the Time Capsule uses the 802.11n wireless standard, it can transfer data much faster than most wireless routers. The 802.11n standard transfers data at up to 300 Mbps, compared to a max of 54 Mbps for the more common 802.11g wireless routers; this compares pretty favorably to the 480 Mbps provided by a USB 2.0 connection. This speed makes transferring and backing up files with a wireless connection feasible.

> **NOTE** This is a theoretical maximum speed. The closer you position the Mac to the Time Capsule, the faster the connection will be. An Ethernet connection offers 1000 Mbps, though, which is the fastest connection of all.

Connecting a Time Capsule to Your Network

Like Apple's AirPort Base Station, Time Capsule creates a wireless network, but it doesn't have its own built-in ADSL (Asymmetrical Digital Connection Line) connection, so you typically have to connect it to your current network.

▶ This is the connection on a modem to which you connect the telephone line.

In a home setting, you do this by directly connecting Time Capsule to your cable or DSL broadband modem via an Ethernet cable. (You attach the cable to the port marked WAN on the Time Capsule and to any Ethernet port on your modem.) It's also possible to attach a Time Capsule to a regular network, such as the type found in office environments, by connecting it to the network with the Ethernet cable. You connect the power supply to Time Capsule after you've connected it to the network.

Determining the Time Capsule Settings

You now use a program supplied with Mac OS X called *AirPort Utility* to set up Time Capsule. Located within the Utilities folder (which you access by choosing Go ➜ Utilities from Finder), the AirPort Utility is used to set up Apple AirPort Base Stations and Time Capsules.

You have to connect your Mac to Time Capsule, either by using a second Ethernet cable and attaching it to your Mac and a spare port on Time Capsule or by locating the default wireless network Time Capsule provides. Typically this will be called *Apple Network* followed by a hexadecimal number (for example, Apple Network 8a7e2b), as shown in Figure 7-4.

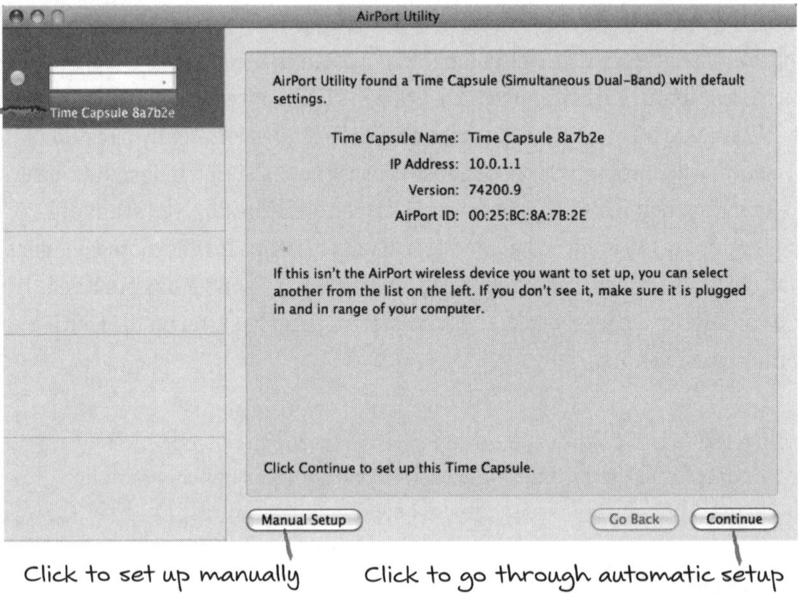

Base Station(s) located on the network

▶ Connecting your Mac directly with an Ethernet cable is a good idea because you can also use it for the first backup. The Ethernet cable is a lot faster than the wireless connection.

Click to set up manually   Click to go through automatic setup

FIGURE 7-4: You set up Time Capsule by using a Mac OS X program called Airport Utility.

▶ This password isn't the same as the wireless network password.

AirPort Utility displays an icon of Time Capsule and some information about the device. You click Continue. On the next dialog, you give Time Capsule a name (by default, it's your name followed by *Time Capsule*) and a password. The password is used to access and change Time Capsule settings.

Most of the setup process is straightforward, but the final window offers two puzzling options:

▶ DHCP (dynamic host configuration protocol) and NAT (network address translation) are technologies that automatically assign IP (Internet protocol) numbers to the devices that access a router, which assigns a unique IP address to each device.

▶ **Bridge Mode:** You should select this option if your current router is using DHCP and NAT to provide IP addresses to your network. Most routers supplied by ISPs provide DHCP and NAT, so you typically use this mode.

▶ **Share a Single Address Using DHCP and NAT:** This is the default option. You can use this mode if you're confident about turning off DHCP and NAT functionality in your current router, or if your router doesn't provide this functionality. You shouldn't choose this option if your router already uses DHCP and NAT.

Typically, the router you attach Time Capsule to assigns the IP addresses, so you should choose Bridge Mode; otherwise, both your current router and the Time Capsule will try to assign IP addresses to the devices on the network.

If you select Bridge Mode, you must enter the TCP/IP (transmission control protocol/Internet protocol) information from your Internet service provider. Fortunately, this step isn't as confusing as it looks. You simply need to choose Configure IPv4 → Using DHCP and click Continue. (Your router most likely uses DHCP to assign an IP address to Time Capsule.)

The final screen displays all the settings you applied, and you click Update to send the information to Time Capsule. When a warning dialog appears, informing you that Time Capsule will be temporarily unavailable, you click Continue and wait for Time Capsule to restart.

> CROSSREF Chapter 8 has more information on using DHCP and NAT as well as IP addresses and setting up networks.

When Time Capsule restarts, you should be automatically connected to it, and you can perform the initial backup via either a wireless connection or your Ethernet connection.

If you plan to regularly perform backups wirelessly, I recommend setting up a 5 GHz network alongside your regular one. More recent Apple AirPort Base Stations and Time Capsules offer dual-band functionality that enable regular 2.4 GHz networks and faster 5 GHz networks to work side-by-side.

USING TIME MACHINE TO RESTORE FILES

Making backups is only one part of a backup strategy. The other part—the part you're likely to appreciate the most—is restoring missing files and folders.

Time Machine replaces your desktop with a starry space field background that represents time travel, as shown in Figure 7-5. The middle of the screen displays the currently active window, stacked above copies of the window repeated into infinity. Each window represents how that folder or application looked at a specific point in time. If you don't have an open Finder window or a window from a compatible application, Time Machine opens a new Finder window that displays the contents of the desktop.

▶ If you select the wrong option here, AirPort Utility will issue a warning, and the Time Capsule will display a blinking amber light.

▶ Use the Energy Saver settings in System Preferences to make sure your Mac doesn't turn off during the night. If your Mac is turned off during a backup, the backup process picks up where it left off when you next turn it on.

▶ Time Machine integrates directly with some Mac OS X applications, including Finder, Mail, Address Book, iPhoto, and GarageBand.

▶ There are actually only 10 windows repeated, but they animate into infinity, so you get the idea.

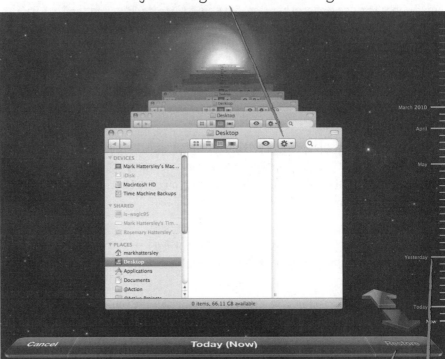

Adjust settings with the Action Cog

Choose files and click here to restore

Scrub timeline to move back in time

FIGURE 7-5: The interface for Time Machine is a highly visual star field. Think *Star Trek*, and restoring files will never be the same.

> TIP You can examine the contents of files from inside Time Machine by using the Quick Look feature. To do so, you highlight a file and click the Quick Look icon (which looks like an eye) in the window's toolbar.

Highlight files and click Restore to bring them back to the present. If there's already a file in Finder that has the same name as the one you're restoring, you are prompted to keep the original file, keep both files, or replace the original file. If you keep both files, the text *(original)* is appended to the name of the current file.

> TIP The Settings menu enables you to adjust settings from inside Time Machine. You can delete old backups from this menu to free up space on the Time Machine backup drive.

DISCOVERING ALTERNATIVE BACKUP OPTIONS

For most people, Time Machine and its companion hardware Time Capsule represent by far the best approach to backing up a Mac. But this isn't the only option, and it's also not the most comprehensive or smartest option. Indeed, for a serious user or a savvy technologist, a dazzling array of online and offline backup options are available. And many of them offer advantages over Time Machine (although typically ease of use isn't one of them). In the rest of this chapter, we'll look at some of your other options for backing up Mac OS X.

Manually Backing Up Your Files

When it comes to making backups, one option is to forgo all solutions, schedules, programs, and plans and just copy the files you want to keep safe onto a separate drive or disc. Then you just need to keep that drive or disc safe. Although this method might seem old-fashioned and a little bit clunky, manual backups are easy to make and permanent (or at least long-lasting) records of files you want to keep physically safe.

Manual backups are also less system dependent. Time Machine is great, but it works only with Mac OS X. Your long-term backup should work not just with your current computer but with any computers you might use in the future.

WHAT HAPPENS TO YOUR BACKUP IF YOU LEAVE MAC OS?

You may not think you'll ever move away from Mac OS X, but think about OS/2, NeXT, and BeOS; and with Google creating a Chrome OS and Apple moving into mobile OS with the iPad and iPhone, there's no guarantee that you'll be using Mac OS X in the future. What then? If your backup only works with the computer you currently run, you might regret it when you no longer use that computer. Fortunately, many files are cross-platform, and support for them is likely to stick around.

It's a good idea to use Time Machine for day-to-day backups but also to crank out a copy of important files on a semi-regular basis. What format should you use to perform a manual backup? As with all other backup solutions, it should certainly be something separate from your main hard drive volume. Here are some of the more popular options:

▶ **Optical media:** Recordable CDs and DVDs are a common storage medium for making backups. CDs can hold up to 700MB of data; DVDs can hold 4.7GB on a single-layered disc or 8.5GB on a double-layered disc. Most Macs have a CD- or DVD-recording SuperDrive, although support for optical media is thought to be waning on the whole.

▶ **Blu-ray Disc:** This is another form of optical media, albeit a less common variant. The advantage of Blu-ray Discs is that they can hold up to 50GB of data. Apple does not support Blu-ray Disc at the moment, and you will need to purchase an external Blu-ray Disc drive to both record and read the discs as well as a third-party recording software such as Roxio Toast Itanium (www.roxio.com).

▶ **Solid-state storage:** This format is becoming increasingly popular. Solid-state storage (often referred to as *SSD* or *flash*) records data onto a solid block of memory, with no moving parts. Solid-state storage can be purchased as small independent drives (often called *memory sticks*) that attach via USB 2.0 or as small cards that fit inside devices such as digital cameras and your Mac. A common type is the SD card, for which some Macs currently have a port built in. Larger solid-state drives are also sold as replacements for internal hard drives.

▶ **Hard disk:** If you've set up Time Machine to record to an external hard drive, you're already familiar with this option. But due to falling costs and increasing storage sizes, an external hard drive can make a suitable repository for long-term storage.

▶ **Network storage:** If your Mac is connected to a large network, it may be worth considering backing up data to the network. Alternatively, you can use an online backup solution, discussed later in the chapter.

I suggest that you stick with either optical discs (probably DVDs because of their size) or solid-state storage for manual backups to ensure their durability.

The following sections discuss these various options.

Backing Up with EMC Retrospect

As good as Time Machine is, it's not the only automated backup option. You can combine the flexibility of a manual backup with the consistency of Time Machine by using a custom backup solution. There are quite a few Mac backup programs on the market, but few offer the simplicity and ease of use of Time Machine.

If you're looking for something more powerful than Time Machine, I suggest that you look into a program called EMC Retrospect (www.retrospect.com). Retrospect enables you to control the backup of multiple computers, both Mac and PC, all from a single machine. Retrospect is therefore ideal for use in business and workgroup environments, as well as at home if you're running multiple computers.

If you use Retrospect on more than one computer, one of them acts as the main machine that controls all the backups and has the pool of storage (typically internal or external hard drives) attached to it; this is known as the *server*. The other machines on the network back up their content to the drives attached to the server; these are known as *clients*.

Setting up Retrospect is a bit more complex than using Time Machine. In addition to having servers and clients, Retrospect comes in three parts:

▶ **Retrospect Engine:** This is the backup and restore software that runs on the computer that is acting as the server (that is, the computer with the backup storage attached to it). After installation, the Retrospect Engine runs in the background and doesn't offer any options except for Stop or Start. You can verify that it's installed and running by opening System Preferences and clicking Retrospect Server.

▶ **Retrospect Console:** This program, installed on the server, displays the interface used to control backup functions. You use this to create scripts that determine what information to back up and how often backups will take place; you can also get reports and monitor the activity of client computers.

▶ **Retrospect Client:** This program, installed on every client machine, enables a client machine to back up to the Retrospect server. Like the Retrospect Engine, it offers little in the way of options, and backups are determined and controlled from the Retrospect Console running on the server.

Once you have the Retrospect Engine and Console installed on the server and the Retrospect Client software installed on any remote machines you want to back up, you use the Retrospect Console software to set up and control backup operations.

▶ Setting up Retrospect backup operations is a complex process. Inside the installation folder is a document called Retrospect 8 Getting Started.pdf that walks you through the process.

Cloning Your Hard Drive

Another option for backing up your Mac is to create an exact duplicate of your internal hard drive and store it on a second volume (typically an external hard drive). This process, known as *cloning*, has a number of advantages over other backup methods discussed so far:

▶ **It's a perfect replica.** A cloned hard drive is an exact copy of your data, all the way down to the 1s and 0s on the hard drive.

▶ **You can boot from the clone drive.** It's possible to boot from the clone and run your computer.

▶ **It enables complete restores.** This is a good alternative to using Time Machine when you're moving your Mac OS X installation from one hard drive to another.

▶ **You can physically swap the drives.** If you clone the volume to a hard drive that's physically identical to the internal drive you boot from, it's possible to physically swap the original drive with the cloned copy.

▶ Cloning a drive usually wipes all the data from it. Be careful to check the drive first for data you might want to keep.

However, there are downsides to cloning your hard drive. The most notable one is that it isn't an automated process. This means that you're unlikely to consistently back up your computer, and when you do a restore, your backup may be from some time ago. Also, because you're performing a complete backup, it isn't as easy to restore individual files. Finally, although it's possible to use cloning programs to incrementally back up changes, those programs don't remember earlier states, so you can revert only to the most recent backup.

There are many programs available to Mac users who want to clone their drives. (It's also possible to use Retrospect, mentioned earlier, to perform a complete clone.) However, I recommend two programs that are highly regarded in the Mac community: Carbon Copy Cloner (www.bombich.com) and SuperDuper! (www.shirt-pocket.com).

CHANGING THE STARTUP SYSTEM

When you have more than one Mac OS X boot volume attached to the computer (as is the case when you clone your internal Mac OS X to a second volume), you can boot the computer from either volume. To choose the boot volume, open System Preferences and click Startup Disk. The Select The Startup Disk You Want To Use to Start Up Your Computer dialog appears with a set of icons, one for each volume from which your Mac can boot. You highlight the volume you wish to start up from and click Restart. (Note that the Startup disk you choose here will be used every time you start your Mac until you change the System Preferences and choose another volume.)

It's also possible to choose the startup volume while the computer is starting up by holding down the Option key. Before Mac OS X starts up, a dialog prompts you to choose a startup volume.

Backing Up Your Data Online

Another increasingly popular option is to back up all your data by using an online network. The advantages here are manifold: You don't have to worry about purchasing, maintaining, or protecting an external volume; you can back up your files wirelessly from anywhere; and you can restore your files from anywhere.

You need to consider a couple caveats about using online services, however. Obviously, this involves backing up your data online, and even with a fast Internet connection, the initial backup (and any subsequent restores) can take quite a while. Plus, you're trusting an external service with your personal data, so you need to be sure it's a company you can trust not to lose or abuse all your private information.

There are a few different services available for backing up your data online. I recommend a service called CrashPlan (www.crashplan.com), as shown in Figure 7-6, for several reasons: The pricing is reasonable, it offers secure unlimited backup, and because CrashPlan is largely geared to support the enterprise market, it's widely regarded as one of the most professional backup services.

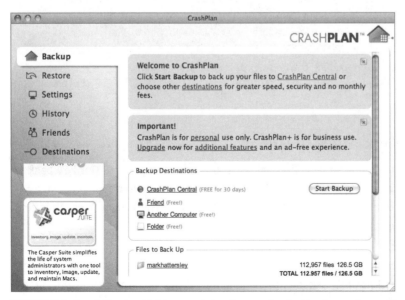

▶ Because CrashPlan is an online service, the first time you run it, you're asked to create an account with CrashPlan. This involves choosing a username and password and entering your e-mail address.

FIGURE 7-6: CrashPlan is a highly regarded online service that backs up all your files to a remote server.

By default, CrashPlan is set up to back up the contents of your main volume to the CrashPlan Central data center (located in an underground vault in Minneapolis, Minnesota), although backing up to other volumes is possible.

Open CrashPlan and click Start Backup, and you begin transferring data from your Mac to the online server. Because the initial backup can take such a long time, you might want to consider limiting the number of files you back up from the hard drive by specifying individual files.

▶ The first backup can take more than 100 hours. You should stop your Mac from turning off during this time by using Energy Saver preferences pane.

By default, CrashPlan saves all your files to the CrashPlan remote server. However, you can also use the program to save files locally to an attached drive or to other computers on a network. You can also set up networks with friends whereby you back up your data to each other's computers.

Restoring files with CrashPlan is a straightforward process. You click Restore in the list of options on the left-hand side of the CrashPlan window. Then you use the file list to select files and folders that you want to restore to the Mac and click Restore. By default, all restored files and folders are placed on the Desktop.

SAVING DATA TO A FRIEND'S COMPUTER

CrashPlan enables friends to save data to each other's computers, using a backup code system. To use this option, you click Destinations and Friends and then look for a six-digit alphanumeric code under Is Your Friend Already Running CrashPlan? CrashPlan sends this code to your friend, and your friend can then back up his or her computer to storage attached to your Mac. If you receive a backup code from a friend, you can back up to that person's computer. You just enter the code in the text box and click Start Backup.

Syncing Your Files Online

Another option for backing up files online is to use a syncing server. Unlike a backup option, which stores data online and passes it back to a computer upon request, a *syncing service* uses an online system to ensure that files and folders on multiple computers are constantly synchronized.

This kind of service is primarily used to enable people with multiple machines to work more effectively. It enables individuals to work on a file on one computer and then keep working on it, using another computer, without having to concentrate on copying the file from one machine to another. Syncing is particularly useful for mobile workers and anyone who typically uses both a notebook and a desktop Mac.

One neat side effect of syncing is that if your Mac's hard drive fails, another machine has the same data on it. And most syncing services enable you to access the shared files by using a remote Web-based interface. Some services also contain a history of backed-up files, combining the best of synchronization and backup.

Sounds neat, huh? Well, it is, and there are quite a few services to choose from, although I typically recommend two: Dropbox (www.dropbox.com) and SugarSync (www.sugarsync.com). As with Mac or PC, iPhone or Android, Pepsi or Coke, the arguments run, and different people have different favorite services. Me? I like SugarSync because it syncs up folders and files in Finder, whereas Dropbox provides you with a folder in Documents that you use to contain files you want to sync.

▶ Most services also offer iPhone and iPad apps that enable you to access stored files on the go, using your portable devices.

SUMMARY

In this chapter, we've taken a look at backing up your Mac. Fortunately, Mac OS X makes it incredibly easy to back up files with Time Machine, which is more powerful than you might think. It's a bit basic, though, and some people prefer to use a more advanced program like EMC Retrospect or clone their hard drive using Carbon Copy Cloner or SuperDuper!. You can combine multiple different solutions for extra secure backup.

It's a good idea to keep a separate backup of important personal files, such as photographs, stored on physical media somewhere safe. Recording these to optical media is a popular choice, although creating a backup to solid-state storage is becoming the way to go. Online backup is also a fashionable way to secure your files, although you need to be careful to choose the right service. I highly recommend Dropbox and SugarSync because they not only back up your data but also sync it across multiple machines. They're perfect if, like me, you have several Macs and PCs on the go at any one time.

CHAPTER 8

Working with Networks

Networking is pretty much at the heart of the modern computer experience. Basically, networks create connections between computers—and other devices—to share data. Whereas networks were at one time complicated and used mainly in office environments, they're now much simpler and common in homes. A modern Mac can stream audio to your home entertainment system, bounce photos to a photo display unit, and play video on your television. And then there's the Internet.

A computer not connected to a network offers little in the way of modern-day computing prowess, so it's little wonder that network troubles rank highest among computer users' problems. Macs are pretty good at networking, though. Locating devices on a network or connecting to the Internet is usually a breeze with a Mac. But there are many powerful networking features to discover in Mac OS X, so let's take a look.

SETTING UP AN AIRPORT BASE STATION

▶ The Time Capsule combines an AirPort Extreme router with a disk drive to create a wireless network capable of backing up data.

You can use an Apple AirPort Extreme or Time Capsule base station to create a wireless network that other Macs or other wireless devices (such as iPhones and iPads) can join. Unlike many other wireless routers, the AirPort Extreme and Time Capsule do not contain their own modems. Therefore, they cannot connect directly to the Internet. Instead, you'll most likely connect the AirPort base station to a router supplied by your ISP or attach it to a wired network to provide wireless functionality.

GETTING TO KNOW WI-FI STANDARDS

Wi-Fi is based in a standard called IEEE 802.11. The IEEE 802.11 standard is subdivided into the 802.11a, 802.11b, 802.11g, and 802.11n standards. (Sometimes you'll find companies advertise products as Wireless G, Wireless N, and so on.) Table 8-1 provides more information on Wi-Fi speeds and range, based on their IEEE standards.

By far the most popular two wireless standards are 802.11g and 802.11n. Most wireless routers today, including those supplied by Internet service providers (ISPs), use one of these two standards. Apple's latest generation of AirPort routers (AirPort Extreme and Time Capsule) use the 802.11n standard.

TABLE 8-1: Wi-Fi Standards

STANDARD	FREQUENCY	SPEED	RANGE
802.11a	5 GHz	54 Mbps	115 feet
802.11b	2.4 GHz	11 Mbps	125 feet
802.11g	2.4 GHz	54 Mbps	125 feet
802.11n	2.4 GHz/5 GHz	600 Mbps	230 feet

▶ Typically you'll just connect it directly to your existing router at home (or into an Ethernet network in an office environment).

To set up AirPort Extreme or Time Capsule, you connect the device to a network by using the supplied Ethernet cable, connecting it to a power outlet, and opening

AirPort Utility. Then you follow the Assist Me screens to perform the initial setup, which includes the following:

1. **Password settings.** The first thing you need to do is enter a name and password for the AirPort Extreme or Time Capsule.

▶ This is the password you use to log in and administer the device, not the one you use to join the network.

2. **Select what you want to do.** These options determine how you want the AirPort Extreme or Time Capsule to work with your current network (if there is one).

3. **Provide a name and security.** This is the SSID that the device will broadcast and the password that you enter to join it wirelessly. If you want help with selecting a suitable password, click the Actions cog to open the Password Assistant, as shown in Figure 8-1. More information on Password Assistant can be found in Chapter 15.

4. **Select whether AirPort Extreme/Time Capsule should operate in bridge mode or share an IP address using DHCP or NAT.** If you're already using a modem and router to serve devices in the home, you should select Bridge Mode. The current router is assigning IP addresses to the devices on the network. Selecting Bridge Mode ensures that the AirPort base station doesn't start providing conflicting IP addresses.

Choose different password types

Adjust password complexity

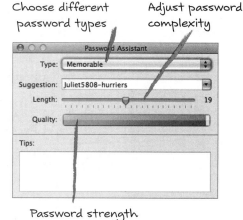

Password strength

FIGURE 8-1: The Password Assistant offers suggestions and advice on creating strong passwords.

5. **Enter the TCP/IP information.** Typically, the Configure IPv4 drop-down menu should be left at the default DHCP. Otherwise, you need to enter the TCP/IP information supplied by your ISP.

6. **Time Machine.** If you have a Time Capsule, you are asked if you want to use it to back up the computer. Chapter 7 has more information on backing up your Mac.

7. **Update the device.** Click Update and Continue to send the settings to AirPort Extreme or Time Capsule.

After about 30 seconds, your AirPort Extreme or Time Capsule restarts, and you can use it. If you ever want to go through this process again, you can choose Base Station ➔ Assist Me from the AirPort Utility menu bar.

WARNING When you first get your AirPort Extreme base station or Time Capsule, it starts without any security. You shouldn't leave it attached to your network without opening AirPort Utility and going through the setup process.

MANAGING WI-FI NETWORKS WITH AIRPORT UTILITY

▶ You can use AirPort Utility to set up and manage only Apple AirPort devices. Non-Apple routers are typically managed in a web interface via a web browser such as Safari.

Once your AirPort device is up and running, you can use AirPort Utility to monitor and manage the device. When you open AirPort Utility, it scans the nearby network for AirPort base stations and displays them in a column on the left side of the window. You choose a Base Station from this column, and the rest of the window displays settings related to this device. You can click Manual Setup to investigate and adjust the individual settings for the base station.

USING TERMINAL TO MANAGE AIRPORT

There's a little-known way of using Terminal to get information and manage AirPort. UNIX geeks will love this hack.

To begin, open Terminal and type the following:

```
/System/Library/PrivateFrameworks/Apple80211.framework/Versions/
Current/Resources/airport
```

You have lots of different options here for managing wireless networks. By appending **-s** to the end of the line of code, you can scan for local networks; by appending **-I**, you can get information about the network you are currently on.

If you use this hack frequently, you can create a shortcut that links to the AirPort app by typing the following code on one line:

```
sudo ln -s  /System/Library/PrivateFrameworks/
Apple80211.framework/Versions/Current/Resources/airport /usr/
sbin/airport
```

After you enter this code and your admin password, you can just type **airport -I** or **airport -s** in Terminal to use those commands. Typing just **airport** brings up a list of available options.

In Manual Setup mode, AirPort Utility offers five icons you can use to adjust settings for the base station:

▶ **AirPort.** This pane displays information related to administration and wireless setup (including SSID names and passwords). You can also adjust access control settings here:

▷ **Summary.** This tab contains information on the name, summary, and wireless functionality of the device.

▷ **Time Capsule.** If you have a Time Capsule, this tab enables you to manage the name and password required to access the disk wirelessly.

▷ **Wireless.** These options determine whether the base station is creating or extending a wireless network. Other options relate to the wireless network name, mode, channel selection, and security. Clicking Wireless Network Options brings up additional selections for creating 5 GHz networks, hidden networks, wide channels, and interference robustness.

▶ **Internet.** This pane displays information used to connect to the Internet. Here you choose how the AirPort base station connects to the Internet (typically via an Ethernet connection to an ADSL router) and how devices on the network are configured (usually using DHCP).

▶ **Printers.** USB printers connected to the AirPort base station appear in this window, where you can manage shared printers on the network.

▶ **Disks.** It is possible to connect a disk to the AirPort base station and share it across the network.

▶ **Advanced.** This pane provides advanced options for logging and statistics. You can also set up MobileMe functionality so you can access the base station remotely.

After you make changes, the AirPort base station must restart. While it is restarting, computers on the network cannot access network functionality or the connection to the Internet.

▶ You can restart an AirPort base station without making changes by choosing Base Station → Restart from the menu bar.

EXPANDING AIRPORT MENU INFORMATION

It's possible to get more information about the network you are currently connected to by holding down the Option key and then clicking the AirPort menu bar icon. The information provided is:

▶ **PHY Mode.** This displays which kind of physical connection is provided by the network. Usually it will be marked 802.11 and then a single letter denoting the type of wireless connection (usually either *g* or *n*). See the "Getting to know WiFi Standards" note for more information.

▶ **BSSID.** The Basic Service Set Identifier is a 48-bit code comprised of six hexadecimal digits (number and letter combinations, such as 00:26:BB:8F:7B:2E). It is used by devices including your Mac to identify each network; although you are more likely to use in Mac OS X the standard SSID (which is typically the name of the network, like MyLocalWiFi).

continues

EXPANDING AIRPORT MENU INFORMATION *(continued)*

▶ **Channel.** Wireless devices can work in up to 14 different channels (depending on the type of wireless network and local regulations—in North America, channels 1 to 11 are allowed).

▶ **Security.** This is the type of wireless security used by the network.

▶ **RSSI.** This is the Received Signal Strength Indicator and is a guide to how strong the signal is. A stronger signal typically provides data at a faster rate.

▶ **Transmit Rate.** This is the rate at which data will be transmitted over the wireless network.

Knowing this information is great for power users with the choice of more than one network to join.

USING THE NETWORK PREFERENCES

It is possible to fine-tune and set up more complex network settings by using the Network preferences pane (in System Preferences). The Network preferences pane sidebar displays all the connections that are set up on your Mac: A green button indicates an active connection, and red signifies inactive. You can use the Add (+) and Remove (-) icons to create or delete connections, and you can use the Actions menu to duplicate, rename, and import and export configurations.

▶ Exporting a working configuration is a good idea if you're planning on tinkering with network preferences.

Customizing network settings is complicated business, and most of these options are beyond the scope of this book. If you're looking to get a good understanding of networking and how to set up networks manually, I recommend either *Networking for Dummies* by Doug Lowe or the *Networking Bible* by Barrie Sosinsky.

The following sections describe a couple of neat tricks related to network settings.

Changing Locations

At the top of the Network preferences pane is a Location drop-down menu that should be set to Automatic by default. You can choose Edit Locations from this menu to bring up a dialog.

You can use the Edit Locations dialog to add multiple locations (for work and home, for example). You click the Add (+) icon to add a new location and click the Remove (-) icon to delete a location. While manually adding and deleting locations can be useful, it means you have to enter all the network information from scratch. Therefore, it's usually easier to highlight the Automatic menu item and choose Duplicate Location from the Actions menu.

When you've created multiple locations, you can choose between them by using the Location drop-down menu.

▶ Different locations can have different settings. For example, work may use Ethernet by default, and home may use AirPort.

Setting the Service Order

Another neat thing you can do in the Network preferences pane is set the service order. If you can connect to a network via multiple methods (typically AirPort and Ethernet), you can decide which of these connection methods takes priority.

To see this in action, you can click the Actions menu below the sidebar and choose Set Service Order. Then, in the dialog that appears, as shown in Figure 8-2, you drag the various services into the order you prefer and click OK.

Finally, you click Apply in the Network preferences pane to save the changes.

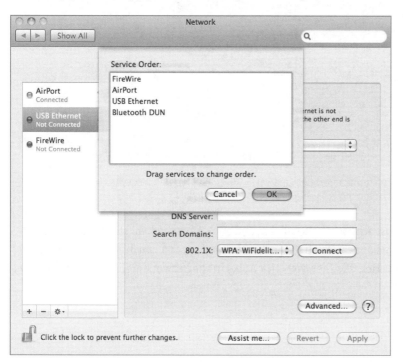

FIGURE 8-2: Changing the service order determines which network connections take priority.

Prioritizing Your Preferred Networks

Another neat trick is to set up your preferred wireless networks. If you have multiple wireless networks available, the Preferred Networks setting lets you choose to connect to your preferred wireless network first, as shown in Figure 8-3. If the first network isn't available, Mac OS X works its way down the list until it finds one that is available.

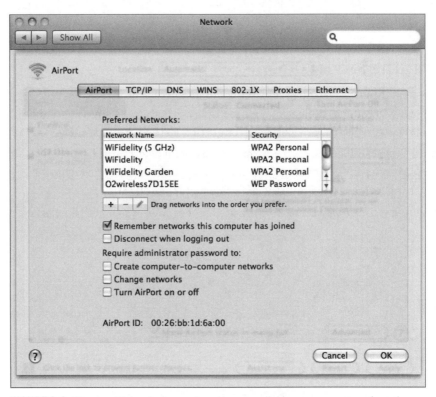

FIGURE 8-3: When multiple wireless networks are available, you can use preferred networks to determine the order in which networks are joined.

▶ You can delete old networks that you aren't going to use again by clicking the Remove (-) button.

If you choose AirPort in the sidebar and click Advanced, all the networks Mac OS X has encountered appear in a list in the main window. You can drag them to the order you prefer and click OK. Then you click Apply in the Network preferences pane to save the changes.

CREATING A COMPUTER-TO-COMPUTER NETWORK

It is possible to use the AirPort functionality on a Mac to create your own wireless network. This is useful if you want to transfer files between two computers or share a wired Internet connection from one computer to another. Here's how you create a network using a Mac:

1. Click on the AirPort menu bar icon and choose Create Network.

2. Give the network a name and choose a channel to use (or stick with the default Automatic option).

3. Click the Require Password check box to require the other computer's user to enter a password to connect to your computer.

4. Choose a Security type from the drop-down menu. You can choose between 40-bit WEP and 128-bit WEP. This will affect the password you create in the next step. The option for 40-bit WEP is generally more compatible with a wider range of devices (especially older devices).

5. Type a password. You'll need to enter the same password into the Password and Verify box. The password will have to be exactly 5 letters (or 10 hexadecimal digits) or 13 letters (or 26 hexadecimal digits) depending on the Security you chose.

6. Click OK.

Other computers will now be able to log on to the wireless network and share files and folders with your computer. Depending on the options in the Sharing preferences pane, they can also share services such as Internet connection and optical drives.

CREATING A NETWORK FROM YOUR ELECTRICAL WIRING

There is an interesting kind of device called the HomePlug Powerline Adapter that uses the electrical wires in your house to transfer data. You attach an Ethernet cable to the adapter and plug it in; then you attach another Ethernet cable to another adapter and plug it in elsewhere in your house. Devices connected to the Ethernet cables can then communicate with each other by sending data over the power lines. More information is available from the HomePlug Powerline Alliance website (`www.homeplug.org`).

USING THE SHARING PREFERENCES

When it comes to networking, it's easy to overlook many of the sharing facilities that are built in to Mac OS X. This is a shame because Mac OS X makes it incredibly easy to share a lot of functionality and data directly between Macs using the Sharing preferences pane. Some of the most useful Sharing preferences settings are described in the following sections.

DVD or CD Sharing

You can enable the DVD or CD Sharing preference to remotely access the optical drive of another computer. This is useful for MacBook Air or Mac mini Server owners because these computer models lack optical drives. Enabling this preference is also useful if the drive on a Mac fails and you want to borrow the drive from another computer.

Screen Sharing

You can select the Screen Sharing check box to enable other users to remotely control the Mac. This option is especially useful for system administrators because it enables them to fix problems without having to leave the office.

▶ To share another Mac's screen, you need to enter an admin name and the password for the Mac you want to control.

You can share the screens of other Macs by locating a Mac in the Shared list located in the Finder window's sidebar. Then you highlight the Mac you want and click Share Screen.

The Desktop for the remotely controlled Mac appears in a window on your Desktop, as shown in Figure 8-4. You can control that Mac just as if you were controlling your own.

> CROSSREF   MobileMe can be used to share screens over the Internet.
> Chapter 20 has more information on MobileMe.

File Sharing

The File Sharing setting enables you to transfer files from one Mac to another. Select File Sharing from the Sharing preferences pane to turn on the feature.

FIGURE 8-4: Screen Sharing is used to remotely control Macs on a network.

By default, only one folder for each user account is accessible via file sharing. This folder, called *Public*, is located in the user account's Home folder. Inside this folder is a folder called *Drop Box*, which other people can use to copy files to your Mac.

Internet Sharing

The Internet Sharing function enables you to share the Internet connection from one Mac to another. A typical setup is to use one Mac connected to the Internet via an Ethernet cable, and share that Internet connection by setting up a wireless network to which other Macs can log on.

Mac Pro models have multiple Ethernet ports and can be used to access and share Internet via linked Ethernet cables. It is also possible to share Internet connections via AirPort, USB Ethernet, FireWire, as well as regular Ethernet.

Internet Sharing has saved my bacon several times over the years, especially when setting up a small network in a hotel room for multiple people to work from.

Networking can be as simple, or as complex, as you want it to be. While it's easy to use AirPort to connect to a Wi-Fi connection, and even easier to hook up your Mac

▶ You cannot connect to the Internet wirelessly and share the Internet connection wirelessly because you only have one AirPort card in your Mac (unless you have installed two cards).

▶ Click AirPort Options if sharing via AirPort and remember to create a password.

directly to a router via Ethernet, you can invest a lot of time and effort into creating more complex, and creative, networking solutions. Just be careful to keep one eye on security when creating networks, you never know who's snooping around.

SUMMARY

With a Mac, there are myriad means to facilitate data sharing. This chapter looks at networks and sharing data between a Mac and a network, a server, the wider Internet, and other Macs on a local network. Typically, you use Ethernet to join a wired network or AirPort to connect to a wireless network. Apple networks are easy to set up and join, especially when you use AirPort Extreme and Time Capsule base station devices to do so. This chapter examined a number of tricks for creating fast and reliable networks. I heartily advise picking up an Apple AirPort or Time Capsule base station to add to your regular home router because it offers a lot of features that go above and beyond those of regular routers. And to further enhance your ability to share data, system preferences such as Network and Sharing let you set up and manage network connections at an extremely fine level. Whether you're the only person using your network or you want to give network access to others, the Mac makes it easy.

CHAPTER 9

Using Disk Utility to Set Up and Control Drives

Disk Utility is a Mac OS X utility that's well worth getting to know. With Disk Utility, you can initialize, or format, hard drives as well as repair and restore them. In addition to creating standard drives, you can use Disk Utility to stitch multiple drives together using RAID, or you can partition a single drive so it appears to be several smaller drives. You can also use Disk Utility to create and manage disk images (files that mount in Finder as volumes when you open them). Or you can use Disk Utility to record optical discs and erase and reuse rewritable discs. This chapter takes you on a tour of some of the neat things you can do with Disk Utility.

GETTING TO KNOW DISK UTILITY

▶ A hard drive typically contains a single volume that stores all the data, but a single hard drive can contain more than one volume, so the terms aren't interchangeable.

Disk Utility is located inside the Utilities folder. You use it to manage *volumes* and disks.

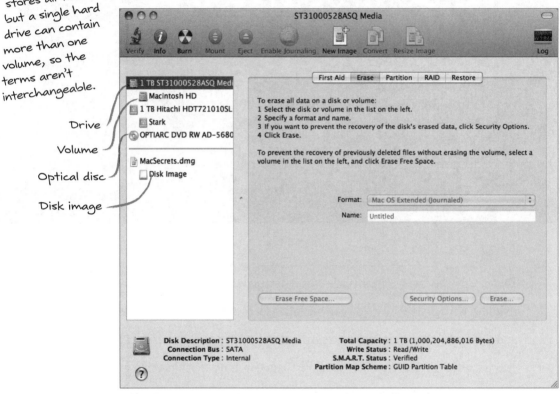

Drive

Volume

Optical disc

Disk image

FIGURE 9-1: Disk Utility is used to format, partition, and verify disks.

▶ Mounted means not just attached to the computer but recognized by Mac OS X and usable in Finder.

The sidebar on the left side of Disk Utility lists the drives that are mounted and the volumes that are accessible by Mac OS X. If a volume displays in grayed-out text, it can be used but isn't currently mounted. Figure 9-1 shows Disk Utility with both mounted and unmounted drives.

When you choose a volume in the Disk Utility window, you get four tabs—and you lose the Partition command. It is still possible to partition a volume—that is, split it into two smaller volumes—but you need to do it while highlighting the whole drive and viewing all partitions.

> **TIP** Disk Utility is a great tool for mounting and unmounting unruly drives. If you attach a hard drive to a Mac and it doesn't automatically mount, you can use Disk Utility to mount the drive. Sometimes when you eject a drive with Finder, the drive quickly reappears before you can safely remove it. This happens a lot with Windows-formatted drives (especially with electronic book readers). When this happens, you can highlight the volume and click Unmount before disconnecting it.

USING DISK UTILITY TO FORMAT DRIVES

When you add a new hard drive to a Mac (by installing a new hard drive inside a Mac Pro, replacing the current drive inside any Mac model, or attaching an external drive), you should format the drive prior to using it.

You can use Disk Utility to format, or initialize, a new drive. To do so, highlight the drive in the sidebar and click the Erase tab. Ensure that Mac OS Extended (Journaled) is selected in the Format drop-down menu and enter a volume title in the Name field. Then click Erase.

▶ Many drives come preformatted to the Windows MS-DOS (FAT) or NTFS standards (both aimed at Windows users). The Mac OS X standard is, unsurprisingly, much better.

> **WARNING** It may sound obvious, but formatting a drive removes all the information from it, so before formatting a drive, ensure that it doesn't contain anything you want to keep. Sometimes brand-new drives contain software and instruction manuals. You should copy any needed information to Mac OS X before performing the format.

The following sections describe how to use Disk Utility to format a drive to a professional level, so data cannot be recovered (which is important if you plan to pass the drive on), as well as how to recover data from a drive in case it has been incorrectly formatted.

Using Secure Erase Options

When you format a drive, you don't necessarily remove all the information from it; instead, you simply erase the information in the directory tree and metadata. Essentially, you delete the part of the drive that points to the data contained on it, and the data is eventually overwritten with new data.

▶ Formatting a drive is a bit like deleting the contents page in a book rather than deleting all the chapters. The rest of the pages are eventually overwritten as new information comes along.

This situation presents a security risk, because the not-yet-overwritten data on the drive remains accessible. To overcome this risk, you can use Disk Utility to securely erase the data. Disk Utility works by removing the filesystem and overwriting the data with new data.

In the Disk Utility window, you click Security Options. Then, on the Secure Erase Options page, you choose the level of security, as shown in Figure 9-2.

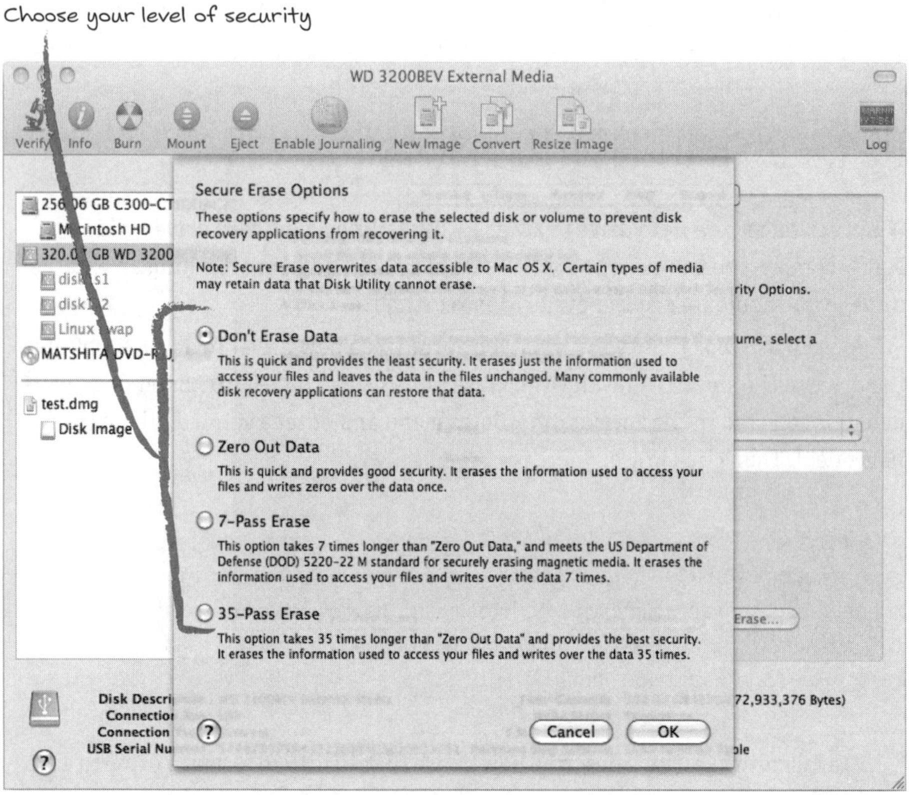

Choose your level of security

FIGURE 9-2: The Secure Erase Options page enables you to completely overwrite the data on a drive so it cannot be recovered easily.

If you have concerns about the security of a drive, I suggest using the 7-Pass Erase. (You'd have to be highly paranoid to spend the time performing a 35-Pass Erase.) Just choose the appropriate level of security, click OK, and then click Erase.

WHY USE THE 35-PASS ERASE?

Like the 7-Pass Erase, the 35-Pass Erase option overwrites all the data with a mixture of different data patterns, some of them random. The 35-Pass Erase secures a drive not just against current attempts to access deleted data but also against a hypothetical future technology that could recover wiped data using the 7-Pass Erase. Peter Gutmann and Colin Plumb suggested that it is theoretically possible to recover data by examining the frequency field of the hard drive. For more information on the Gutmann method, see Wikipedia (`http://en.wikipedia.org/wiki/Gutmann_method`).

Recovering Data from a Formatted Hard Drive

Of course, secure erase options exist because it is possible to recover data from a hard drive that has been erased. In many ways, this is a good thing, especially if you accidentally format a drive or if a filesystem becomes damaged.

Mac OS X doesn't have the capability to recover data itself. Instead, you need to use a program such as Data Rescue (`www.prosofteng.com`), FileSalvage (`http://subrosasoft.com`), or DiskWarrior (`www.alsoft.com/diskwarrior`).

Although it is possible to recover data from a drive that has been formatted, there is no guarantee that you will be able to recover all the data. I simply cannot overstate that nothing is more secure than an effective backup strategy.

> ▶ The more you reuse a drive that has been formatted, the more of the original data will be lost.

It's worth noting that the formatting process takes hours. Generally, it's best to point data recovery software at a hard drive and let it run overnight.

Partitioning Drives

Drives can be partitioned so that they contain multiple volumes, which really comes in handy when you want to install multiple operating systems. However, it's also useful to have different areas on your drive, such as when using multiple operating systems or to provide a single place for large files (such as video clips).

> ▶ Having too many partitions can become confusing. I typically advise using partitions on a single drive unless you are installing multiple operating systems.

To partition a drive, you choose the drive in the Disk Utility window and click the Partition tab. On the left side of the screen, a vertical rectangle known as the *Volume*

Scheme displays the current partition scheme. (Unless the drive has been previously partitioned, the Volume Scheme is a single rectangle.) Then choose the number of partitions, using the Current drop-down menu. You can choose up to 16 partitions in a single volume.

It is possible to add to and remove partitions from a volume by using the Add (+) and Remove (-) icons at the bottom of the Disk Utility window. By using this method, you can highlight a partition and then split it into two smaller partitions.

> **WARNING** If you delete all the partitions on a hard drive (including the first one), you'll need to reformat the drive before you can use it again. You'll also lose all the data on the drive.

RESIZING PARTITIONS

To resize a partition, you click and drag the handle in the gray strip between the partitions. By moving these handles up and down, you can adjust the amount of space offered to each partition.

To size a partition more accurately, you click the name to highlight it. The size of the partition will be displayed in a text field in the Disk Utility window. You can also adjust the size of a highlighted partition by using this text field.

> **NOTE** You can't partition the main Mac OS X volume if Mac OS X is currently running. You need to boot from the Mac OS X installation disc (or another bootable volume) and run the copy of Disk Utility from there. Chapter 5 has more information on booting and running utilities from the installation disc.

NAMING PARTITIONS

By default, each partition is named *Untitled*, with consecutive numbers (*Untitled 1*, *Untitled 2*, and so on). You can give each partition a unique name by highlighting it and typing the new title in the Name text field.

FORMATTING PARTITIONS

It is possible to have different partitions on a drive using different file formats—either Mac OS X Extended (with Journaled and Case-Sensitive options available) or MS-DOS (FAT). Mac OS X Extended (Journaled) is the best option for drives exclusive to Mac, although MS-DOS (FAT) is useful if you want the partition to be available to Windows computers on your network or if you are running a Windows installation on a Mac.

CHANGING THE PARTITION SCHEME

The partition scheme (also known as the *partition table* or *partition map*) is the first sector of a hard drive that maps out the location of partitions on the hard drive, so the operating system knows where one partition ends and another begins. There are several different types of partition schemes to choose from. Mac OS X picks the best format for a partition, depending on its intended use (as a startup volume, a second volume, or a volume designed to run Windows via Boot Camp).

You can manually choose or change the partition scheme by highlighting a partition in the Volume Scheme list and clicking Options. Three types of partition schemes are available:

▶ **GUID Partition Table:** Used by partitions containing startup volumes, typically Mac OS X, running on a Mac with an Intel processor, and also some Linux installations. Typically this is the default format for the main hard drive in an Intel Mac. Note that you won't be able to boot a Windows installation from a GUID partition table.

▶ **Apple Partition Map:** Used by external drives that do not contain a startup Mac OS X installation and by older Macs with PowerPC processors.

▶ **Master Boot Record:** Used by a partition containing a Windows OS (such as a Boot Camp volume). Sometimes external drives that come preformatted with the MS-DOS (FAT) format also use this option.

To change the partition scheme, you choose the appropriate radio button, as shown in Figure 9-3, and click OK.

Unless you're planning to change the designated purpose of a drive, such as installing an operating system on it, I don't typically recommend changing the partition scheme. You can always revert to your original choice by choosing it from the list or by clicking Default.

▶ Both the Apple Partition Map and Master Boot Record options are limited to volumes no larger than 2TB in size (that is, 2,000GB). While this seems pretty large, partitions (especially RAID volumes) can break this limit.

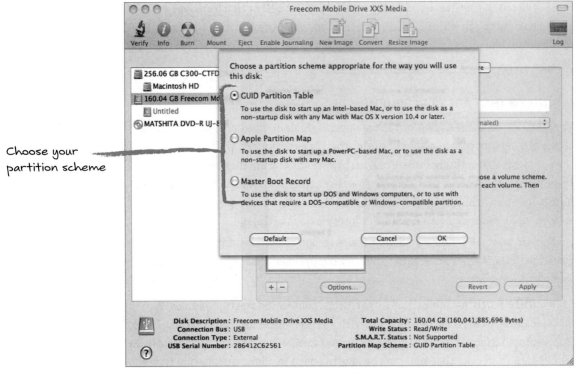

FIGURE 9-3: Disk Utility enables you to choose different partition schemes for a volume.

USING FIRST AID TO FIX AND RESTORE DISKS

A popular use for Disk Utility is to verify and repair disks and permissions, as shown in Figure 9-4. To do this, you click on a volume in the Disk Utility window and then click on the First Aid tab.

The following options are available:

▶ **Verify Disk Permissions:** When you install new applications, disk permissions may change, and poorly written applications can cause problems. These can cause applications not to run, and can scale all the way up to Mac OS X not starting up properly. When you click Verify Disk Permissions, Disk Utility checks the permissions against a list of correct ones and alerts you to any inconsistencies.

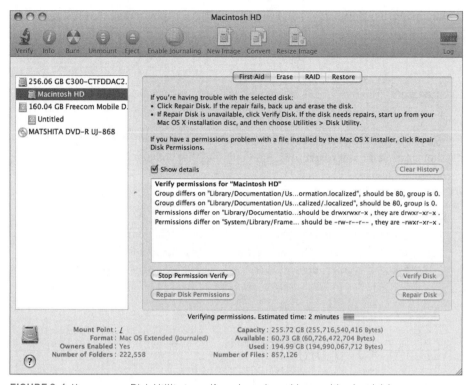

FIGURE 9-4: You can use Disk Utility to verify and repair problems with a hard drive.

▶ **Repair Disk Permissions:** Repairs any inconsistencies between file and folder permissions and corresponding applications. Whereas you often run Repair Disk from the Mac OS X installation disc, you should typically run this option from Disk Utility inside Mac OS X because the correct list of permissions is updated with Software Update.

▶ **Verify Disk:** Works on Mac OS X Extended (Journaled) drives and detects issues such as incorrect file sizes, problems with the volume bitmap, multi-linked files, and more. Mac OS X typically runs quite slowly while disk verification takes place.

▶ **Repair Disk:** Repairs problems found using the Verify Disk option. Note that you cannot use Disk Utility to repair a drive containing the Mac OS X installation that you are running. So, to repair any problems with your main hard drive volume, you need to start up Mac OS X from the installation disc or another bootable OS X volume.

► Since Mac OS X 10.3 (Panther), the operating system has become more stable.

Repairing disk permissions and the disk itself used to be a task that Mac users had to perform quite frequently, but these days you shouldn't have to do it very often.

CROSSREF Chapter 21 has more information on repairing faults on a Mac.

Typically, you discover errors when you run the verification processes, and repairing them is a good habit to get into. But don't feel that you need to do it unless you encounter problems.

NOTE Disk Utility is great for fixing a wide range of problems, but it's not the final word when it comes to data corruption. Two applications offer more complete protection and are worth the investment: Alsoft's DiskWarrior (www.alsoft.com/diskwarrior) and Micromat's TechTool Pro (www.micromat.com).

CREATING RAID DRIVES

RAID drives are the opposite of partitioned drives, in that they create a single volume from several physical drives (or volumes). RAID has two distinct purposes. First, you can use RAID to create a single large drive space from multiple hard drives (known as *striping*). You can do this to create larger volumes than would be possible with a single drive. Second, you can use RAID to add multiple drives that contain identical copies of the same information (known as *mirroring*). With this backup solution, if a hard drive physically fails, you can replace it without problem.

HARDWARE VERSUS SOFTWARE RAID

You can control RAID drives with software or hardware. Unless you're running an Xserve or a Mac Pro with a RAID card installed (or an external drive with a hardware RAID controller built in), you will be running software RAID provided by Mac OS X. If you're serious about RAID, you might want to consider getting a Mac Pro RAID Card (www.apple.com/macpro/features/storage.html), which speeds up performance.

As shown in Table 9-1, several types of RAID configurations are available, and each manages drives differently.

TABLE 9-1: Types of RAID Configurations

RAID LEVEL	DRIVE REQUIREMENTS	DESCRIPTION
RAID 0 (striping)	One to four identical drives	A single volume created from multiple drives. The volume's size is the size of both drives added together.
RAID 1 (mirroring)	Two identical drives	A single volume on one drive, with an identical copy on the second. If one of the drives suffers a problem, it can be replaced without any loss of data.
Concatenated RAID	One to four drives	Similar to RAID 0 but can use drives of different sizes. Typically runs more slowly than RAID 0.
RAID 0+1	Four identical hard drives	A mixture of RAID 0 and RAID 1. The first two drives are striped, and the second two drives mirror the first two.
RAID 5	Three or four identical drives	A new format that creates a single volume, like RAID 0, with redundant backup features. Creates a volume larger than RAID 1

To set up a RAID drive, you need to attach several identical drives to your Mac. If you're using internal drives, you need to be running a Mac Pro, an Xserve, or a Mac mini server. (Chapter 10 has more information on upgrading your Mac.)

If you're running an iMac, a Mac mini, or a Mac notebook, you must use an external drive to create a RAID drive. You can use multiple identical external USB or FireWire hard drives, but it's more common to buy an external RAID drive that either contains multiple hard drives or enables you to insert and remove drives.

If you're interested in creating a RAID drive as a backup solution, you should consider getting a device by Data Robotics called the Drobo (www.drobo.com). This external drive combines up to eight hard drives to create a large volume. The data is spread around so that if one drive fails, the others will keep the data safe while you replace it. The neat twist is that the drives can be different sizes, and you can upgrade by pulling out small drives and inserting big ones.

▶ Strictly speaking, the drives don't have to be exactly the same make and model. They just need to be the same size and speed. But to avoid problems, I advise using completely identical drives.

▶ This is one of the coolest Mac accessories money can buy!

HOT-SWAPPABLE DRIVES

If you're into RAID, you may hear the term *hot-swappable* bandied around; it means that drives can be removed and inserted into the computer while it is turned on. If a RAID drive has mirrored drives (for backing up data) and a drive fails, you can remove that drive and insert a new one without turning off the computer. This is possible only with Xserve systems; the drives in a Mac Pro are not hot-swappable (even with a RAID card installed).

Disk Utility cannot create a RAID array using a volume that is currently running Mac OS X. If you want to create a RAID array by using Disk Utility, you must boot Mac OS X from the installation disc. To create the RAID array, follow these steps:

1. **Select a disk.** Select any of the disks you want to use and click RAID.

2. **Name the RAID.** Enter a name in the text box.

3. **Choose a format.** Select a volume format from the drop-down menu. Typically, you should choose Mac OS X (Journaled).

4. **Choose a RAID type.** Three options are available in Disk Utility: Mirrored RAID Set, Striped RAID Set, and Concatenated RAID Set.

5. **Add the first drive.** Click and drag the first drive from the list to the main window.

6. **Add the remaining drives.** Drag the remaining drives that will be used in the RAID array below the first drive. Each one will be listed as *New member: "disk"* and an identifying number.

7. **Select your options.** Click the Options button and then choose the RAID block size. By default, this is 32K, although your options are 16K, 32K, 64K, 128K, and 256K. Mac OS X advises you to select a block size that matches the kind of data you will be accessing. For example, video may access large blocks of data, and a database will access smaller blocks.

8. **Select to automatically rebuild.** If you are creating a RAID mirrored set, select the Automatically Rebuild RAID Mirrored Set check box.

9. **Create the RAID array.** Click Create to begin building the RAID array. A dialog warns that you will destroy all the information contained on the following disks, and it lists the drives being used in the RAID array. Click Create to confirm that you are willing to wipe the drives and create the RAID array.

SLICES AND SPARES

When you highlight any of the drives in the Disk Utility sidebar, the pull-down menu marked RAID Type turns into Disk Type. This menu now offers two options for each drive: RAID Slice and RAID Spare. By default, the option is set to RAID Slice, which ensures that the drive is being used as part of the RAID array you're using. Choosing the RAID Spare option designates the drive as a spare drive that is used if another drive fails.

This drive will not be used as part of the main RAID volume but will be automatically brought online in the event of the failure of another drive. If you're creating a mirrored RAID set, you can use the RAID Spare option with a third drive to have it automatically substitute one of the other drives in the event of a drive failure.

Creating and managing a RAID array is a challenge, and you should be careful about whether you really need a RAID array, particularly a striped array, before committing to one. But it can be worth it, and most professional computer servers use RAID technology to control drives. The ability to create redundancy, whereby a system can still work in the event of drive failure, is a compelling feature. And Mac OS X makes it as easy as physically possible to create, set up, and manage an array.

CREATING DISK IMAGES

Recall that disk images are files that mount in Finder as volumes when opened. Disk images are digital files that use the .dmg file extension. Typically, these files are used to deliver installation programs in a digital format (such as when downloading new programs from the Internet).

CROSSREF Chapter 4 has more information about using disk images to install applications.

Disk Utility enables you to create disk image files, which you can use to share a volume of files and folders digitally if you want to pass on a volume to other people. Using disk images is also a handy way of creating digital backups of CDs or DVDs. There is also a neat trick you can use with disk images and password protection to create a secure area on your computer; for more information, see the section "Password-Protecting Disk Images," later in this chapter.

Creating a disk image is a fairly straightforward process, as described in the following steps:

1. **Click New Image.** A dialog appears, offering options for the image.

2. **Name the image file.** Enter a name for the image file in the Save As text field. This is the name of the file you open.

3. **Choose a location.** Use the Save dialog to choose a location for the file.

4. **Name the file.** Enter a title for the volume in the Name text box. This is the name of the mounted volume that appears when you double-click the file. It's good practice to have the same title in the Save As and Name fields.

5. **Choose a size for the volume.** By default, disk images are 100MB in size, but you can choose from a variety of presets (including typical CD and DVD sizes) or select a custom size.

6. **Select the format.** Typically, you should leave the format set to Mac OS X Extended (Journaled), although you can choose other Mac OS X formats and MS-DOS (FAT) formats.

7. **Select encryption.** You can choose to encrypt the file by using 128-bit or 256-bit methods. If you choose encryption, you will be prompted to enter a password.

8. **Choose partitions.** You can have only a single partition in a disk image, but you can choose different partition schemes for a volume. Unless you are choosing a custom option for the size, I advise you to stick with the partition used by the preset you chose in Step 5.

9. **Select the image format.** You can choose from the following options:

    ▷ **Read/Write Disk Image.** This is the default and the option I advise you to stick with. This produces .dmg files.

    ▷ **DVD/CD Master.** This produces an .iso file for DVD (or the older .cdr file for CD) that is useful for creating exact copies of optical discs.

    ▷ **Sparse Disk Image.** Unlike a .dmg file that takes up a set amount of space, a sparse disk image takes up only as much space as the data within the volume (up to the maximum amount determined by the installation).

    ▷ **Sparse Bundle.** These files (which Time Machine uses) are similar to sparse image files but use a bundle of files instead of creating a single large block.

10. **Click Create.** The image will be created in the location specified in Step 2. Double-click the .dmg file to ensure that Mac OS X mounts the volume correctly.

Figure 9-5 shows sample settings for creating a disk image.

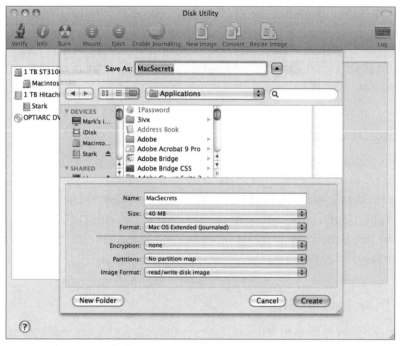

FIGURE 9-5: You can use Disk Utility to create image files.

USING SPARSE IMAGE FILES

For ease of use, I typically recommend creating regular .dmg files. However, sparse image files are pretty neat. They only take up as much space as the data inside the container, and you can resize a container by using Terminal; you un-mount the volume and use the following command:

```
hdiutil resize -size 50g MyFile.sparseimage
```

This command resizes the **MyFile.sparseimage** volume to 50GB. A sparse im-age file that has been expanded but then has had contents removed from it can be compacted with the following command:

```
hdiutil compact MyFile.sparseimage
```

Password-Protecting Disk Images

You can use a cool trick to take advantage of Disk Utility's ability to create password-protected disk images to create secure areas on your computer. This trick is great if

▶ Just remember to eject the volume when you finish working on the files if you want them to stay secure!

you want to keep files safe from prying eyes. You select 128-bit encryption from the Encryption drop-down menu when creating the disk and enter a password during the creation process. You'll need to enter the password whenever you mount the disk image, so the image is a great storage place for sensitive files. (Chapter 15 has more information on Mac security.)

Converting Disk Image Files

Another neat function of Disk Utility is its ability to convert other image files into the .dmg standard that can be mounted in Mac OS X. This is especially useful if you have a file type that ends with .iso (a Windows and Linux equivalent to .dmg).

▶ You can also use Convert to add password protection to image files.

To convert an image file to .dmg format, you highlight it in the Disk Utility window and choose Images ➜ Convert. You need to give the image a new name that ends in .dmg before you click Save.

Burning Disk Image Files

▶ Often these are programs that fix problems with the main Mac OS X volume (such as Disk Utility). To repair problems with the main volume, you need to run these programs outside Mac OS X.

You can use Disk Utility to burn disk image files to optical discs. This method is often useful when an application is delivered electronically, via the Internet, but needs to be run from an optical disc.

Recording a disk image to an optical disc is a straightforward process. First, you double-click the disk image in Finder to mount the volume; then you open Disk Utility. Next, you highlight the disk image in the Disk Utility window and click Burn. You can adjust options for the speed of the burn and whether you want to verify the data afterward. Finally, you click Burn to record the contents to the optical disc.

SUMMARY

Disk Utility is a powerful utility included with Mac OS X to help you set up and manage drives and volumes. You should use Disk Utility to securely format data from a drive so it cannot be accessed when passing on a hard drive. (Keep in mind that a regular format of a drive doesn't remove data from it.) Another use for Disk Utility is to partition drives into multiple segments, or to stitch together multiple drives into single working units called RAID drives. These are pretty advanced options, but a Mac expert can put them to good use. Finally, you can use Disk Utility to create and edit disk images when you want to keep certain files private.

PART II

GETTING MORE OUT OF A MAC

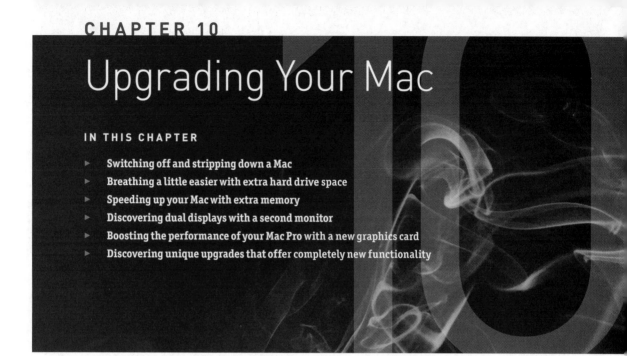

CHAPTER 10

Upgrading Your Mac

IN THIS CHAPTER

▶ Switching off and stripping down a Mac

▶ Breathing a little easier with extra hard drive space

▶ Speeding up your Mac with extra memory

▶ Discovering dual displays with a second monitor

▶ Boosting the performance of your Mac Pro with a new graphics card

▶ Discovering unique upgrades that offer completely new functionality

Sooner or later, the upgrade bug will bite you, and it'll be time to investigate buying some new parts for your shiny Mac. Either you'll run out of hard drive space or decide your Mac should run a little faster, or you'll want to use the latest technology to add a whiz-bang feature to your Mac to take it beyond its original use. In its purest form, upgrading is adding new parts to a computer, or taking parts out and replacing them with newer versions. So get ready to recondition, refurbish, and renovate your Mac.

SWITCHING OFF AND STRIPPING DOWN YOUR MAC

Many upgrades are external—you just attach the new device to a computer using one of the external connections, typically USB or Firewire. Other upgrades require you to insert or replace hardware inside the computer. With Apple computers, internal upgrades can be either extremely easy, or extremely difficult, depending on the model of computer and the type of upgrade in question.

GET TO KNOW IFIXIT

Before you perform any upgrade that requires you to take apart a Mac, pay a visit to iFixit (**www.ifixit.com**). I know these guys, and they've taken apart just about every piece of Apple equipment over the years, taking detailed photographs as they go. iFixit offers free step-by-step guides for upgrading and replacing all kinds of components inside a Mac.

In my experience performing any upgrade in a Mac Pro is reasonably easy, with the exception of upgrading to a graphics card that requires power supplied by a cable. Upgrading the RAM and internal hard drive in MacBook and MacBook Pro computers is only slightly harder, but it's by no means a difficult process. Upgrading the RAM in either an iMac or Mac mini is extremely easy, but any other internal upgrade (including the hard drive) is extremely difficult.

Here are some common things you should know before opening up any Mac:

▶ Keep your screws safe. Use plastic cups to hold each set of screws as you remove them.

- ▶ **Turn off the computer.** You should also wait 5 to 10 minutes for the internal components to cool.

- ▶ **Disconnect all cables.** Make sure you remove all cables before beginning the upgrade process.

- ▶ **Discharge static electricity.** Touch a grounded object to discharge static electricity or wear an anti-static wristband. (On a Mac Pro you can touch the metal PCI access covers on the back of the computer.)

- ▶ **Use a cloth to protect the Mac.** An iMac has to be placed face down, and you should use a towel to protect the screen. You can protect any Mac from scratches by using a towel to protect it from the work surface.

With this advice in mind, let's start upgrading.

ADDING EXTRA HARD DRIVE SPACE

The first stop on the upgrade path is almost always the hard drive. This is typically the most common upgrade because you can never have enough storage space in a computer. Typically, there are two reasons for upgrading your hard drive: size and speed.

▶ You need more storage space to hold data, and you want faster performance from your hard drive.

Replacing the internal hard drive in a Mac notebook or all-in-one-system requires quite a bit of effort, but it's not impossible. And in the right circumstances, it can be highly rewarding. Having said that, when it comes to adding a larger hard drive for space, I typically recommend going for an external option, especially if you're running an iMac or a Mac mini. The internal hard drives in Mac Pros and MacBook notebooks are somewhat easier to upgrade, but upgrading is not as easy as attaching an external drive.

Although the installation process can be difficult, in the right circumstances, an internal hard drive upgrade can be extremely rewarding. One of those circumstances is if you decide to replace the internal hard drive with a newer solid-state disk (SSD).

▶ I performed this upgrade recently, and it was well worth both the effort and money.

Chapter 11 has more information on speeding up your Mac, but there is currently nothing—absolutely nothing—you can do that will have nearly the impact of upgrading your hard drive to a high-quality SSD. It makes Mac OS X fly.

Installing an Internal Hard Drive in a Mac Pro

The Mac Pro has four hard drive bays that can be used to quickly attach and remove multiple hard drives. The only tool you need is a Phillips screwdriver. To replace a hard drive, you follow these steps:

▶ That's the one with a cross-shaped head. You need a reasonably small one for most computer work.

1. Turn off the Mac Pro and use the latch to remove the case.

2. Carefully pull out one of the hard drive carriers.

3. Remove the four screws that mount the drive to the carrier and use them to attach the new hard drive to the carrier.

4. Slide the carrier into the bay in the Mac Pro.

5. Replace the access panel. Push down the latch to close and secure the access panel.

6. Reconnect the computer's cables and turn it on.

> **TIP** Apple has a manual you can download with explicit instructions for inserting a new hard drive into a Mac Pro. See `http://manuals.info.apple.com/en/MacPro_HardDrive_DIY.pdf`.

After you replace a startup disk, you need to start the computer using the Mac OS X CD and reinstall the operating system. If you add a hard drive in addition to your startup drive, the computer should boot up as normal, but you might still need to use Disk Utility to format the drive.

Replacing the Internal Hard Drive in a Mac Notebook

Upgrading the internal hard drive in a Mac notebook isn't nearly as straightforward as doing so in a Mac Pro. Replacing the hard drive inside a Mac notebook is not an easy task, but neither is it impossible. The hard drive inside a MacBook Pro is located in the bottom left of the device and has four screws, as shown in Figure 10-1. To remove it, you'll need a Phillips screwdriver and a T6 Torx screwdriver.

▶ A Torx screwdriver has a six-pointed star-shaped head.

Battery

Hard drive

FIGURE 10-1: The inside of inside a MacBook Pro.

To replace the hard drive, follow these instructions:

1. Place the MacBook lid-side down on a flat surface.

2. Use the Phillips screwdriver to remove the 10 screws on the bottom of the device.

▶ Note the position of the three screws in the top-right corner; these are longer than the other screws.

3. Remove the single screw on the plastic bracket that holds the hard drive in place and remove the bracket.

4. Gently lift the hard drive out of the case, being careful of the cable that attaches the hard drive to the computer.

5. Remove the cable from the hard drive by gently pulling it directly away from the drive.

6. Use the Torx screwdriver to remove the four screws from the side of the hard drive. These are used to position the drive into the hard drive slot.

7. Use the Torx screwdriver to place the four screws into the matching slots of your new hard drive.

8. Attach the cable from the MacBook Pro to the new hard drive.

9. Gently place the hard drive into position in the MacBook Pro, ensuring that the four screws line up correctly.

10. Re-attach the bracket and use the Phillips screwdriver to secure it.

11. Re-attach the bottom of the notebook, using the Phillips screwdriver to replace the 10 screws. Make sure the three longer screws go into the right slots.

▶ It's best to replace these screws first, because they won't fit into the wrong slots.

After you replace your hard drive, you need to reformat it and reinstall Mac OS X. You may also need to use Time Machine to restore the hard drive. Chapter 9 has more information on formatting drives, Chapter 2 has more information on setting up Mac OS X, and Chapter 7 has more information on backing up a Mac.

HARD DRIVE UPGRADES ON OTHER MAC MODELS

Hard drive upgrades on the Mac mini, MacBook Air, and iMac all require you to strip down much of the machine to locate the hard drive. Brave upgraders can find out more information at iFixit:

▶ **Mac mini:** www.ifixit.com/Guide/Repair/Installing-Mac-mini-Model-A1347-Hard-Drive-Replacement/3113/1

▶ **iMac:** www.ifixit.com/Guide/Repair/Installing-iMac-Intel-20-Inch-EMC-2266-Hard-Drive-Replacement/919/2

▶ **MacBook Air:** www.ifixit.com/Guide/Repair/Installing-MacBook-Air-Hard-Drive-Replacement/860/1

I suggest avoiding performing upgrades for any of the preceding models unless you're experienced and the upgrade is absolutely necessary.

ADDING EXTRA MEMORY

▶ RAM is short for random access memory. It's what people refer to when they talk about a computer's memory. ROM (read-only memory) is also used by computers, but you don't upgrade that.

Aside from increasing hard drive space, the next most popular upgrade for a computer is to increase the amount of memory, or RAM. Increasing the memory in a computer enables it to function better—for several reasons. Increasing the memory enables a computer to hold more data in memory before having to write the data out to a swap file on the hard drive. In addition, increasing memory improves both the speed of Mac OS X and any applications you're running. It's especially useful if you work with large video files or want to run other operating systems within a virtual environment.

How much RAM you put into a machine depends on how much money you want to spend and what sort of requirements you have. Because the price of RAM tends to fall over time, don't overdo it too early. Try to get the amount you need and plan to upgrade over time.

▶ I run 8GB of RAM in each of my two main work machines, an iMac and a MacBook Pro.

Most Macs come with either 2GB or 4GB of RAM installed, which runs Mac OS X and most applications just fine. Upgrading to 4GB will give your Mac a bit more pep and is what most people have. Upgrading to 8GB is great for running intensive applications such as Final Cut Pro and Adobe After Effects, as well as virtual operating systems. Anything beyond that (the Mac Pro can happily accommodate up to 32GB) is overkill.

RAM comes in chips, known as *DIMMs* (dual in-line memory modules), typically in 1GB, 2GB, 4GB, or 8GB configurations. Most Macs (with the exception of the Mac Pro) use a variation called *SO-DIMM* (small outline DIMM). SO-DIMMs are typically used in laptops, but the iMac and Mac mini are encased like a laptop, and Apple uses smaller memory modules in them to save space. Usually it's cheapest to combine more RAM chips with lower amounts of memory. So, for example, you would want to install two 4GB chips to create 8GB of memory rather than install one 8GB chip.

> **TIP** It's much less expensive to pick up RAM from a supplier such as Crucial.com than it is to buy it pre-installed in a Mac. Crucial also has a neat program called System Scanner (www.crucial.com/systemscanner/MacOS.aspx) that inspects the RAM in your Mac and outlines what upgrades will work. It's also pretty handy for figuring out the maximum amount of RAM that can be installed in your machine.

The RAM chips slide out of and clip into corresponding slots on the motherboard, as shown in Figure 10-2.

> **WARNING** Never force a RAM chip into or out of a slot. It should come out gently and pop firmly back in. If you have to push it, then it's not lined up correctly.

FIGURE 10-2: When you pull out the tabs next to RAM, the chip ejects from the slot. You place the chip back in and click it into place.

Upgrading the RAM in a Mac mini

The Mac mini is Apple's smallest computer, and upgrade options are somewhat limited. However, as with all other Macs (except the MacBook Air), it's possible to upgrade the RAM. To upgrade the RAM in a Mac mini, you follow these steps:

1. Turn the Mac mini upside-down and locate the circular black cover, as shown in Figure 10-3. Place your thumbs in the depressions on the cover and rotate the cover counter-clockwise until the white dot on the cover lines up with the ring on the case.

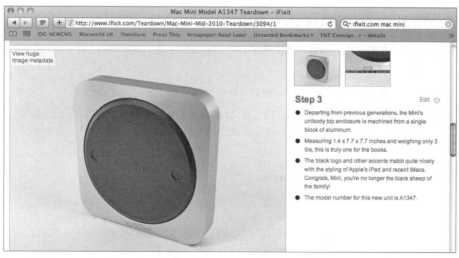

FIGURE 10-3: The Mac mini has a large circular cover underneath that you rotate to access the internal components.

2. Tilt the mini so the cover comes off and set the cover aside.

3. Locate the RAM chips at the bottom and remove each one by simultaneously pushing away the tabs on each side of the slot. The RAM chip should pop out. Gently pull it out of its slot and put it to one side.

4. Insert a new RAM chip into each slot. An indentation in the chip guides you to insert it with the correct orientation. Gently push the RAM chip into the slot. (The tabs should click into place to secure it.)

5. Replace the bottom cover by rotating it with both thumbs to lock it into place.

When you reconnect the computer's cables and turn on the Mac, you can choose Apple ➜ About This Mac to make sure Mac OS X recognizes the newly installed RAM.

WORKING WITH OLDER MAC MINI MODELS

Prior to 2009, a Mac mini wasn't easy to take apart. On the older models, owners often used a putty knife to pop the case apart. A 1.5-inch putty knife works well, but you should grind the edge down so as not to damage the case. Rub the putty knife's short edge back and forth on 100 grit sandpaper until it attains a beveled edge. For more information, see `www.ifixit.com/Guide/Repair/Installing-Mac-mini-Model-A1283-Top-Housing/1073/1`.

Upgrading the RAM in a Mac Pro

As with most other upgrades in the Mac Pro, upgrading the memory is a fairly straightforward process:

1. Turn off the Mac Pro, disconnect the cables, and open the case.

2. Pull out the processor tray. This is located at the bottom of the machine and has two latches. You press on the latches to unlock the tray and lift it out.

3. Put the RAM in the slots.

4. Re-insert the processor tray.

NOTE If you have an earlier 2008 model of Mac Pro, you install the memory by removing a RAM board at the bottom of the computer instead of removing the whole processor board. You can find more information at `http://manuals.info.apple.com/en/MacPro_Early2008_MemoryDIMM_DIY.pdf`.

The order in which you place the RAM in the slots in a Mac Pro affects its performance. To the side of each slot, on the board, is a number that identifies the slot. Table 10-1 describes which slots to use for RAM in a quad-core machine, and Table 10-2 describes which slots to use for RAM in an eight-core machine.

▶ You should have four slots in a quad-core machine and eight slots in an eight-core machine.

TABLE 10-1: RAM Placement in a Quad-Core Mac Pro

NUMBER OF RAM CHIPS	SLOTS USED
2	1 and 2
3	1, 2, and 3
4	1, 2, 3, and 4

TABLE 10-2: RAM Placement in an Eight-Core Mac Pro

NUMBER OF RAM CHIPS	SLOTS USED
2	1 and 2
3	1,2, and 3
4	1, 2, 5, and 6
6	1, 2, 3, 5, 6, and 7
8	1, 2, 3, 4, 5, 6, 7, and 8

After you insert the RAM, you can put your Mac back together and use About This Mac to check whether the RAM is installed properly.

The Mac Pro also has small LED lights next to the RAM chips that you can use to identify problems. You need to have the case open and the power on to use the LEDs. If one of the LEDs lights up red, the memory bank may not be fitted properly and should be checked. More detailed information on upgrading the RAM in a Mac Pro can be found online at http://manuals.info.apple.com/en_US/Mac_Pro_Early2009_Memory_DIMM_DIY.pdf.

> **TIP** Mac OS X has an application you can use to identify that you have RAM chips installed in the correct slots in a Mac Pro (for maximum performance). This program, called Memory Slot Utility, resides in System/Library/Core Services.

Upgrading the RAM in a MacBook or MacBook Pro

As with the Mac Pro, upgrading the RAM in a MacBook or MacBook Pro notebook is a straightforward procedure. To begin, you remove the bottom of the Mac. (See the section "Replacing the Internal Hard Drive in a Mac Notebook," earlier in this chapter, for details.)

Next, you use the tabs on each side of the RAM slot to remove the RAM chip. Then you ensure that you slot in the upgraded chips correctly by lining up the indentations on each chip.

More detailed information on upgrading the memory in a MacBook Pro is available at Apple's support site, at `http://support.apple.com/kb/ht1270`.

▶ You cannot upgrade the RAM in the MacBook Air. The memory is welded into the circuitry.

Upgrading the RAM in an iMac

Although it's incredibly difficult to upgrade just about anything else internally on an iMac, upgrading the RAM is a piece of cake. A dedicated access door at the bottom of the machine provides quick access to the RAM slots, as shown in Figure 10-4.

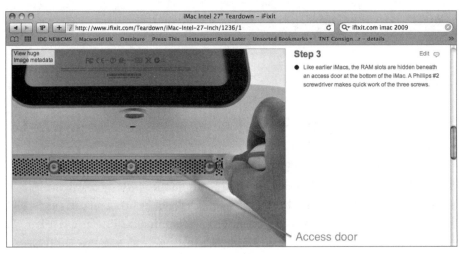

FIGURE 10-4: The access door at the bottom of an iMac.

To upgrade the RAM in an iMac, you need a Phillips screwdriver and a cloth or towel (seriously). To upgrade the RAM in an iMac, you follow these steps:

1. Lay a towel or blanket on the workspace. Slowly place the iMac on the towel face down, to protect the screen from scratches.

2. Unscrew the access door, which is located on the bottom part of the iMac.

3. Untuck the tabs from inside the compartment. Pull the tabs gently to remove the RAM chips from the machine.

4. Place the new RAM chips into the slots. Be sure to gently push them in; you should not need to force them.

5. Tuck in the tabs so that they are inside the compartment.

6. Replace the access door.

When you have attached all the cables and turned on the Mac, you can select About This Mac to see the RAM information.

> **WARNING** iMacs with i5 and i7 processors cannot start up if only a single RAM chip is installed in the bottom slots (the ones closest to the stand and farthest away from the display).

Upgrading the RAM is one of the cheapest and most rewarding ways to boost the performance of a Mac. You should investigate upgrading to the maximum amount of RAM over time, because the price of memory falls quite rapidly.

ADDING A SECOND MONITOR

Adding a second monitor to a Mac is a great way to expand the amount of available desktop real estate available. Adding another monitor makes you much more productive and improves your Mac experience.

You can use a second monitor to display video, while working on a program in the main display. And programmers, for example, often display code on one monitor and run programs on the other. Even users of more lightweight programs can have important work on one display, with the more fun applications (iTunes, QuickTime, and so on) on the second display. In the case of Mac notebooks, a second display is typically larger than the main display, allowing for a more comfortable viewing experience.

Attaching a second monitor to a Mac is a simple case of using the monitor cable to attach the display to the Mini DisplayPort connection. This port is located on the left-hand side of the MacBook and MacBook Pro, and it's on the right-hand side of a MacBook Air. On the Mac Pro, Mac mini, and iMac, the port is on the back.

The Mac Pro differs from all the other Mac computers in that it offers two connections for connecting external displays: a Mini DisplayPort and a DVI Dual Link port.

▶ Add a keyboard and mouse to a display and you can turn a Mac notebook into a desktop.

▶ The only Mac to which you cannot attach a second monitor is the Mac mini. This model has two ports (one Mini DisplayPort and one HDMI), but only one can be used at a time.

There are many different ports out there, and you need to ensure that the connection between your Mac and your monitor is correct. (See the following sidebar, "Getting to Know Different Display Connectors," for more information).

Depending on what monitor you attach to your Mac (as well as what Mac you are using), you might need to purchase an adapter. The following adapters are available from Apple:

▶ Mini DisplayPort-to-VGA adapter

▶ Mini DisplayPort-to-DVI adapter

▶ Apple MiniDVI-to-VGA adapter

▶ Apple DVI-to-VGA adapter

▶ Mini DisplayPort-to-HDMI adapter

By using the right connector, you should be able to attach a display to any Mac.

GETTING TO KNOW DIFFERENT DISPLAY CONNECTORS

Different displays use different ports to connect to your computer. Here are some of the common ports you'll encounter:

▶ **Mini DisplayPort.** This is the connector typically available on all current Macs. Outside of Apple, it's a fairly rare connection, though, and it is typically used only with certain Apple displays, such as the Apple LED Cinema Display. Other display types require use of an adapter.

▶ **DVI Single Link.** This is the most common type of connection between a monitor and a Mac. DVI is used on the Mac Pro and most older Macs.

▶ **DVI Dual Link.** This connector is the same shape as DVI Single Link, but the connector uses twice as many pins. This enables it to power larger displays. (Monitors 30 inches and larger typically use DVI Dual Link.) Don't mistake Dual Link for using dual displays; this type of connector is used to power a single large display. Also note that DVI Dual Link cables can be used to connect DVI Single Link monitors, but DVI Single Link cables do not have enough pins to power DVI Dual Link monitors.

▶ **Mini DVI.** This format was used only once by Apple, on the first-generation MacBook Air. It is the same as DVI Single Link but with a smaller adapter.

▶ **VGA.** This older format was used on many monitors, and you might still come across it on older monitors. It's also popular with projector manufacturers, so those who like to show presentations might need to consider VGA compatibility. You need an adapter to connect any modern Mac to a VGA device.

▶ **HDMI.** This modern format is typically used on high-definition televisions, although some entertainment-oriented monitors also use HDMI. HDMI is based on the same standard as DVI but carries sound as well as the display signal. The connector is different from HDMI, although DVI-to-HDMI cables are available.

This is by no means an exhaustive list. For example, S-Video, Component, and SCART connectors are typically used only in relation to video editing and rarely used outside specialist areas.

UPGRADING THE GRAPHICS CARD IN A MAC PRO

On a Mac Pro, the graphics card is a separate card attached to the motherboard. Its sole function is to generate and output images to the display. Typically, a graphics card has its own processor and RAM, and graphics cards with faster clock speeds and increased memory offer higher performance.

Only the Mac Pro has a graphics card that can be upgraded. On all other Macs, the graphics card is either integrated with the main CPU or is permanently soldered to the motherboard. In a Mac Pro, the graphics card fits into one of three PCI Express 2.0 slots inside the computer.

▶ PCI stands for Peripheral Component Interconnect. It's used for other internal cards, not just graphics cards.

To install a new graphics card into a PCI Express 2.0 slot, you follow these instructions:

1. Open the computer and locate the metal bracket that holds in the current graphics card. Loosen the screws holding the metal bracket to the card and remove it.

2. Pull out the graphics card. If you are installing a second graphics card, however, leave the graphics card in its place but remove the metal strip covering the slot so the card can be placed in the new slot.

3. Insert the new graphics card gently into the PCI Express 2.0 slot.

4. Attach the power cable to the power port on the graphics card and to the power port on the logic board. The cable should be supplied with the graphics card. See the following note regarding the power cable.

5. Replace the metal bracket that holds the PCI Express 2.0 card.

6. Replace the Mac Pro access panel and connect all cables, including the display cable, to the new graphics card.

7. Turn on the computer. Mac OS X should appear on the display through the new graphics card.

Upgrading the graphics card on a Mac Pro is by no means a simple process, and it's unlikely to go as smoothly as the steps just outlined. Information on graphics card upgrades is rare, so you should carefully consult the manual and documentation that comes with your graphics card. Pay particular attention to the point at which you need to load the graphics card driver software.

► Make sure to back up your Mac and be prepared to replace the old graphics card if the installation doesn't work.

> **NOTE** On some Mac Pro units, attaching the power cable can be tricky because the power port on the motherboard is hidden behind the front fan, and there is only a narrow access point between the two. Be prepared for some twisted-finger prodding to access the power port on the motherboard. The last time I tried this, I took apart the first hard drive bay to get more space for my fingers to guide the cable to the port.

DISCOVERING UNIQUE UPGRADES

Upgrading a Mac is a rewarding process that can improve the performance of your Mac. You can also upgrade a Mac to enhance its functionality with new capabilities. There are countless upgrades out there, but the following is a list of some of the most useful upgrades you can perform on a Mac:

► **Watch and record television.** You can attach USB adapters that enable you to watch and record live television. My money is on a company called Elgato (www.elgato.com), which makes a wide range of Mac-specific tuners and produces highly regarded software called EyeTV.

► Every creative designer and photographer should try a graphics tablet. Many people swear by them.

► **Graphics tablet.** A graphics tablet is a unique alternative to a mouse that enables you to draw with a pen on a tablet. As well as offering a more natural form of input for designers and artists, a graphics tablet enables pressure sensitivity, creating different brush strokes depending on how hard you push the pen. The main company to look at is Wacom (www.wacom.com).

► **Turbo.264 HD.** This is another device by Elgato (www.elgato.com), but I'm putting it in this list because it's pretty unique. The Turbo.264 HD adapter enables you to quickly convert video clips into a Mac-friendly format because it is a dedicated graphics card that plugs in via USB. If you use a lot of video or own an Apple TV, iPhone, iPad, or iPod touch, this is a great upgrade.

▶ **Bluetooth headset.** You can sync a Bluetooth headset with your Mac to use it instead of the built-in speaker. This is great if you use iChat or Skype (www.skype.com) to communicate.

▶ **Echo smartpen.** This is a really neat product for students and other note takers. The Echo smartpen and LiveScribe software (www.livescribe.com) combine an electronic pen with an infrared camera that records every pen stroke and audio. This is then transferred to your Mac. You can even tap notes in your paper pad to hear the audio that was played at that time.

▶ **Musical connections.** Musicians can plug just about any instruments into a Mac with the Apogee's Duet (www.apogeedigital.com/products/duet.php) and use it with Apple's GarageBand or Logic's software, as shown in Figure 10-5. Electric guitarists should also look at Apogee's GiO guitar interface with built-in pedal controllers (www.apogeedigital.com/products/gio.php).

FIGURE 10-5: The Apogee GiO and Duet devices enable you to attach any kind of electronic musical instrument to a Mac. They are especially good for electronic guitars.

There's no shortage of cool Mac accessories and upgrades to try out, and this is just a short list of some of my personal favorites. With a bit of investigation and some effort, you can enhance your Mac experience beyond recognition.

SUMMARY

The two upgrades you are most likely to investigate with a Mac involve the hard drive and memory. To add extra hard drive space, it's usually easiest to attach an external hard drive to a Mac. In the case of the Mac Pro, however, you can install up to four hard drives internally. The other upgrade you will probably want to consider at some point is RAM. This upgrade is fairly easy on most Macs. If you have a MacBook Air, however, you're out of luck; it's the only Mac whose RAM you can't upgrade. One upgrade is only for Mac Pro owners: the graphics card. This can offer some serious performance boosting, but isn't always easy. Typically the easiest and most fun upgrades are external. At the end of this chapter, I described some of the coolest upgrades I've come across. All are heartily recommended.

CHAPTER 11

Speeding Up Your Mac

A question computer buffs often hear is "How can I make my computer run faster?" You can never get enough speed. Any slow-down—from those tiny pauses between clicks to long delays between tasks—is annoying. If a Mac tries to bite off more than it can chew, it becomes slow and unresponsive, and you might wonder whether it's completing a difficult task or whether something serious has gone awry. In this chapter we'll look at tried-and-true techniques for getting a Mac to run faster, smoother, and more reliably. This chapter is seriously good for your Mac—and your sanity. So let's crank things up a notch and ensure that Mac OS X never irritates you ever again.

CLEANING UP MAC OS X

When tuning up your Mac, the first place to turn is Mac OS X itself because the operating system controls everything else. If you want to make your Mac run as fast as possible, you need to speed up Mac OS X. Getting Mac OS X to run more efficiently isn't difficult. It just requires a bit of tidying up, sorting out, and either deleting or turning off various settings or files, as described in the following sections.

▶ Always be sure you're running the latest version of Mac OS X.

Shutting Down Unused Applications

Having too many applications running simultaneously slows down Mac OS X. All the applications jostle for memory and processor attention. Quitting unused programs—especially processor intensive applications such as Adobe Photoshop—speeds up your computer. To quit an application, open the Dock, Ctrl+click the icon for the program you aren't using, and choose Quit.

To see how many applications your Mac is currently running look at the Dock. An open application has a small white dot below its icon.

▶ You can also use the Application Switcher to see what apps are open by pressing ⌘+Tab.

SHUTTING DOWN MENU BAR APPLICATIONS

Not every running program displays in the Dock. Some of these applications, which typically are services that run in the background, display instead in the menu bar at the top right of the desktop. Therefore, it's easy to overlook these applications. Quitting them speeds up background processing. To quit an application, you click its menu bar icon and choose Quit, as shown in Figure 11-1.

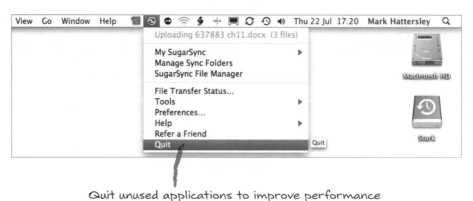

Quit unused applications to improve performance

FIGURE 11-1: It's a good idea to check the menu bar for unneeded applications running in the background.

Some applications that display as menu bar icons relate to Mac OS X functions (for example, AirPort, Time Machine, and MobileMe Sync). These don't have a Quit option, so you can't close them.

GETTING RID OF LOGIN ITEMS

You should also check for programs that load during login. These applications slow down the initial startup process and take up space in memory while you use the computer.

If you want to see a list of items that open automatically when Mac OS X starts, open System Preferences (by selecting ⌘ ➔ System Preferences), click Accounts, and click Login Items. The dialog shown in Figure 11-2 appears.

To prevent an item from loading during startup, you highlight it and click the remove icon.

▶ You can remove some Mac OS X menu bar icons by holding down ⌘ while you drag them out of the menu bar. These are shortcuts to System Preference panes rather than programs.

▶ You should keep iTunesHelper as a login item. It's not vital, but it keeps an eye open for iPods, iPads, and iPhones that you plug in to Mac OS X.

FIGURE 11-2: You can prevent unwanted programs from running during startup by using the Accounts window.

> **TIP** Not sure what an item in the Login Items list is? Simply ⌘+click it and choose Reveal in Finder, which takes you to the location of the application in Finder. If you're still none the wiser, try copying and pasting the application name into your favorite search engine.

Cleaning Out Unused System Preferences

Sometimes when you install new programs, new options appear in System Preferences. Programs running in System Preferences often work in the background, rather than as visible applications working in the Dock. You can gain a performance boost by turning off or removing unused preferences.

Open System Preferences (by selecting ✿ ➔ System Preferences) and take a look at the Other section. This section lists the applications you have added to Mac OS X.

To remove a system preference, ⌘+click the icon and choose Remove *name of application* Preference Pane, as shown in Figure 11-3. You will need to enter an administrator password to remove items from System Preferences.

▶ You can remove items from System Preferences only in this Other section. All other preferences are part of Mac OS X and cannot be deleted.

FIGURE 11-3: You can remove unwanted items from System Preferences to improve performance.

> **NOTE** You can only remove items from the Other section of System Preferences; the items that are included by default with Mac OS X cannot be removed. Because of this it's usually pretty safe to remove items from the Other section, although you will, of course, no longer be able to use the functionality of that item.

Slimming Down the Hard Drive

The less clutter you have on your hard drive, the faster it'll run. It sounds fairly straightforward, and it is, so go spring cleaning. Deleting any programs, files, folders, and other items you don't need will speed up your machine.

> CROSSREF Chapter 6 has more information on tidying up your hard drive.

After you clean up your hard drive, don't forget to empty the Trash by ⌘+clicking the Trash icon and choosing Empty Trash. But this isn't all you can do; you can use the tricks described in the following sections to slim down Mac OS X even further.

▶ You can move rarely used files and folders to an external hard drive instead of deleting them.

REMOVING OLD CODE

When Apple moved from PowerPC computers to the modern Intel ones, it created programs known as *Universal applications* that could run on both types of computers. Universal applications contain two sets of code (one for PowerPC and another for Intel), but you need only one—the right one for your Mac.

Help is at hand, thanks to a program called Xslimmer (www.xslimmer.com), as shown in Figure 11-4. This application analyzes installed programs and removes any unnecessary code.

FIGURE 11-4: Xslimmer is a neat application that removes unused code from applications installed in Mac OS X.

To use Xslimmer, you drag applications from the Applications folder to the main window and click the Slim! button.

REMOVING LANGUAGES

Languages are another area you can investigate to slim down the size of Mac OS X. Mac OS X installs multiple languages, all of which take up space. But you're only really likely to ever use one language, so why not get rid of all the unused ones? Monolingual (http://monolingual.sourceforge.net) is a free program that enables you to remove unwanted languages.

> **WARNING** Both Xslimmer and Monolingual are pretty reliable. But even so, they nonetheless remove code. Be sure back up Mac OS X before using these programs.

GETTING RID OF PROBLEM FONTS

Mac OS X and various applications use fonts to control the display of text. However, duplicate fonts can cause problems. Therefore, although cleaning out your fonts saves only a small amount of space, keeping only trouble-free fonts ensures that your applications run smoothly.

Mac OS X has a built-in application for managing fonts called Font Book (located in the Applications folder). Font Book identifies duplicate fonts with a small yellow triangle. To remove these fonts, you highlight them and choose Edit ➜ Resolve Duplicates, as shown in Figure 11-5.

> **TIP** The Resolve Duplicates command doesn't always fix the problem. If it doesn't solve your problem, you can highlight the duplicate fonts and choose Edit ➜ Disable.

▶ Font Book can identify problem fonts, but it can't fix them. To fix problem fonts, take a look at FontAgent Pro by Insider Software (www.insidersoftware.com).

You can also validate fonts to see if any are corrupted. To do so, you choose Edit ➜ Select All and then select File ➜ Validate Fonts. Fonts with problems appear in the list with a yellow exclamation mark icon. To remove a problem font, you select its check box and click Remove Checked.

FIGURE 11-5: You can ensure that all your fonts are free from problems and duplicates to speed up Mac OS X.

SHOULD YOU CLEAR THE CACHE?

Programs improve performance by storing data on a hard drive in an area called a *cache*. The concept of clearing out the caches often crops up in Mac speed tips, but it shouldn't be part of regular maintenance. While a faulty cache can bring a program to a halt, caches are used, by and large, to speed up a system, so deleting them without purpose defeats the objective. The program OnyX (www.titanium.free.fr) enables you to clear a wide range of caches, but my advice is to keep caches unless Mac OS X is having problems.

STAYING UP TO DATE

As programs evolve, developers distribute performance enhancements and general bug fixes as *updates*. Keeping Mac OS X and the applications you commonly use up to date is one of the best ways to get the most performance out of your system.

USING SOFTWARE UPDATE

Apple includes a software update feature with Mac OS X that updates the operating system and key Apple software. By default, Software Update is set to run once a week, but you can run it at any time by choosing → Software Update.

You can adjust the update schedule by using the Software Update pane in System Preferences. I find weekly updates to be enough, but you can choose daily or monthly settings if you like. You can also choose Download Updates Automatically to download the updates in the background and be notified when they are ready to be installed.

UPDATING NON-APPLE APPLICATIONS

Software Update works with Apple applications only. Other programs have their own systems for delivering software updates. Typically a Check for Updates option appears in a non-Apple application's menu, under either the application name menu or the Help menu. Some applications also check for updates automatically when you start them (or at defined periods).

Some companies create programs that manage the download and installation of software updates. These are installed along with the programs themselves. Two common ones are Microsoft AutoUpdate and Adobe Update. These programs check for updates to all Microsoft and Adobe applications in Mac OS X.

▶ Many application installations offer the option of automatically checking for updates. I always click yes.

SPEEDING UP APPLICATIONS

Speeding up Mac OS X is one thing, but you can also do a lot to speed up applications. As well as ensuring that you're running the most up-to-date version of each program, you can use the tips described in the following sections to speed up some common applications.

Improving Safari and Other Web Browsers

It's possible to spend a lot of time looking at the computing world through the window of a web browser. Ensuring that your web browser runs quickly is one of the best ways to gain an overall faster experience.

REMOVING UNUSED EXTENSIONS

Extensions add additional functionality to a program. Web browsers—particularly Firefox—have supported extensions for a while, but this support is relatively new to

Apple's Safari software. Safari 5 includes extensions in its preferences. You add them by downloading files from the Internet.

You can manage extensions by using the Safari Preferences menu. To do so, you choose Safari ➜ Preferences and click Extensions. You can disable individual plug-ins by deselecting the Enable check box, or you can remove them completely by clicking Uninstall. The Off/On switch at the top right of the Extensions preference pane is used to control all extensions. Switching it to Off ensures that no extensions are running.

Firefox is another popular web browser that features extensions. To manage these extensions, you choose Tools ➜ Add-ons and click Extensions. All installed extensions appear in the Add-ons window, and you use the Disable and Uninstall buttons to control them.

► Safari plug-in files end with .safariextz.

REMOVING PLUG-INS

Plug-ins are similar to extensions. However, you typically install and remove plug-ins from applications by adding them to folders in Finder. To remove plug-ins from Safari, you choose Help ➜ Installed Plug-ins. If you want to remove a file, you have to look for it in Finder and drag it to the Trash. Then you should be sure to close and restart Safari.

RESETTING SAFARI

Safari retains a lot of data—from caches, to the Web history and Autofill information. Deleting all this information can contribute to Safari slowdown. To wipe information from Safari, you choose Safari ➜ Reset Safari, select the check boxes for information you want to remove, and click Reset. Alternatively, you can clear the cache by choosing Safari ➜ Clear Cache.

► This is the bit where Safari automatically fills in the URL as you type. It also retains information on forms you've filled out and passwords you've entered.

Speeding Up Mail

Mail is another application that can suffer from bloat. Large quantities of e-mail can soon clog up a system. If Mail is running slowly, you can try some of the following solutions:

- ► **Clean out your Inbox and your Sent folder.** Highlight messages in your Inbox and your Sent folder, and delete any unnecessary messages.

- ► **Archive your messages.** You can drag messages from a Mailbox to an archive. This is useful if you have messages on a server. Create a new mailbox called

Archive by choosing Mailbox ➜ New Mailbox. Give it a name (like *Archive*) and drag all your messages to it.

▶ **Split Mailboxes.** If you have more than a thousand messages in a Mailbox but want to keep them, you can create two mailboxes and move some of the messages into the new mailbox.

▶ **Check less frequently.** Checking for new e-mail takes time. Checking less frequently enables Mail to perform faster. Choose Mail ➜ Preferences and click General. Then use the Check for New Messages drop-down menu to check for email every 30 minutes or longer.

▶ **Remove previous recipients.** By default, Mail remembers every e-mail address you enter, and after a while this can get clunky. You can choose Window ➜ Previous Recipients, highlight any names you don't need, and click Remove from List.

These tips will help you speed up Mail immensely.

IMAP VERSUS POP FOR SPEED

There are two main types of e-mail system: IMAP (Internet Message Access Protocol) and POP (Post Office Protocol). The key difference is that with IMAP, all e-mails are usually stored remotely on the server; on POP, they are typically downloaded from the server and stored on your computer.

POP has a speed advantage in that once messages are downloaded, they can be accessed instantly; IMAP depends on how fast your network and server are running. IMAP is useful if you are accessing e-mail from more than one device, because it makes changes remotely. This ensures that messages are synchronized across multiple devices (Macs, iPhones, iPads, and so on).

GETTING RID OF SLOWDOWNS AND MEMORY HOGS

So far in this chapter, we've looked at ways to fine-tune Mac OS X and applications so they perform the same functions as normal but more efficiently. If this isn't enough—perhaps because you're running an old machine—you might want to consider turning off certain Mac OS X functions. In some ways, this limits the usefulness of the operating system, but an operating system that runs quickly with fewer features may well be better than one that runs slowly or not at all.

Here are three memory hogs you should turn off: Universal Access, Bluetooth, and Internet Sharing. Unless you're using these features, you should turn them off. Make sure you're not using a wireless mouse or keyboard before turning off Bluetooth, and note that some applications use universal access even if you don't require it.

Getting Rid of Widgets

Widgets are small applications that appear in Dashboard. They are great to use, but they take up a surprising amount of memory. What's more, widgets take up RAM even when you're not using Dashboard, so it's best not to run them if you don't need them.

To remove widgets, you open Dashboard (by pressing F4 or clicking the Dashboard icon in the Dock), as shown in Figure 11-6. Then you click the small plus icon in the bottom left of the screen to manage the widgets. You click the X icon in the top left of each widget to remove it.

You can add widgets again by using the widget shelf at the bottom of Dashboard.

> ▶ Don't forget to occasionally restart your Mac. Even though you don't need to restart it every day, if you don't shut down at night you should occasionally perform a restart.

> ▶ When you remove a widget, it isn't deleted from the computer; it's just removed from Dashboard.

Remove unnecessary widgets

Click to remove widgets

FIGURE 11-6: Widgets take up a surprising amount of memory. Removing them from Dashboard can help speed up Mac OS X.

Removing Dock Animations

The animated Dock is a marquee feature of Mac OS X. But as with any other complex visual interface, it can cause quite a bit of processor slowdown, especially in an old Mac. You can help keep things running smoothly by turning off Dock animations. To do so, you open System Preferences and click Dock. Then you deselect the Magnification and Animate Opening Applications check boxes and set Minimize Windows Using to Scale Effect. This should help minimize the effect of the animated Dock on your Mac.

COOLING DOWN YOUR MAC

Every computer runs a little faster when it is cooler. I'm not suggesting that you run your Mac in a refrigerator, but it isn't surprising that Macs, especially the notebook models, that run in hot environments suffer from a little slowdown.

Aside from moving to a cooler environment, there are devices that can help you keep a Mac notebook running cooler. Bytecc sells a range of notebook coolers (www .byteccusa.com) that place additional fans underneath your Mac notebook. If you don't want additional noisy fans, you can also try using stands such as Rain Design's iLap (www.raindesigninc.com/ilap.html), which lifts the notebook from a flat surface and enables air to circulate underneath.

> **TIP** If you want to keep a closer eye on the amount of heat being emitted by your Mac notebook, you can use an application called Fan Control (**www.lobotomo .com/products/FanControl**). Fan Control enables you to increase the speed of a MacBook's internal fans. This is great if you regularly need to use a Mac in a hot environment and can't use an external cooler.

Another way to cool your Mac is to turn down the screen brightness. This reduces the amount of power being drawn, which reduces the amount of heat being dissipated.

MAXING OUT YOUR MAC

If you've tried all the tips in this chapter, and your Mac still isn't running up to speed, you should consider either upgrading your internal components or perhaps upgrading to a new or more powerful Mac.

Two upgrade components will impact the speed of your Mac more than any others:

▶ **RAM.** Having more RAM ensures that programs have enough space to run without having to cache information to the hard drive.

▶ **SSD hard drive.** These hard drives offer significant speed advantages over traditional hard drives.

Putting these components in any Mac will improve its ability to quickly perform complex tasks. And this is exactly what you want.

> CROSSREF Chapter 10 has more information on upgrading a Mac.

SUMMARY

Sooner or later, all Mac users want their machines to run faster. Speed and efficiency sit in the same boat, and some of the best ways to speed up a Mac are to clean off the hard drive, empty the Trash, and remove unwanted applications. This is a great start, but if you're running an older Mac, you might need to get more surgical and start removing unwanted languages, login items, preferences, and even unwanted code. This chapter has some great advice on stripping Mac OS X back to the bare minimum. Finally, don't forget to take a look at how hot your Mac is running (especially if you're running a Mac notebook in a warm environment). If all that fails, it's time to hit the upgrade trail.

Finding and Organizing Your Stuff

Filing stuff, making notes, writing labels. Sounds like a

total chore, and why bother? Isn't it all just a big waste of time, right? Surprisingly, the

answer might be "yes." There is a myth that being highly organized makes you more

productive, but it's not necessarily true. You might just spend more time organizing.

There are an awful lot of people in the world who are incredibly well organized yet

never seem to create anything. Conversely, some of the most actively creative people

have computer desktops that match their real-life desktops, which look like an explo-

sion in a stationery store. In this chapter we'll look at organizing your workspace, but

really this is more about finding stuff quickly. Mac OS X has tons of features for sorting

and searching through all your data, based on propriety technologies such as Spotlight,

Spaces, Exposé, and Quick Look. With a bit of practice, you'll find files faster than ever.

ORGANIZING THE MAC OS X WORKSPACE

Like a new sheet of paper, a brand-new installation of Mac OS X is a blank slate, waiting for you to make your mark; and make your mark you certainly will. Files, folders, documents, downloads—all this and more will end up cluttering your desktop and being dispersed throughout Finder. And there's nothing wrong with this, because Apple makes it easy to find documents. With Spotlight, you can hunt down files without having to religiously file them away, but this method can make working your way around Mac OS X a chore.

> ▶ Technically the Finder doesn't contain anything. It just points to the data on the file system.

> **TIP** If you're looking for advice on how to organize your computer, e-mail, and life in general, read up on David Allen's Getting Things Done (GTD) method (www.davidco.com). He's worshipped almost as a deity in busy tech circles. A good place to learn more about GTD is 43 Folders (www.43folders.com).

Straightening Out the Desktop

One trick that many people use is to drag all the miscellaneous files and folders from the desktop to one folder, typically called something like *Junk* or *Old Desktop*. They keep this folder hanging around until months later, when they finally decide it can't possibly contain anything of worth, and they drag it unceremoniously to Trash.

Contrary to popular belief, there's nothing really wrong with this method. The files are no untidier in a folder than they are clogging up your desktop. And you're just as likely, or unlikely, to find them in this folder as you are on the desktop. But if you're hankering for a little more structure, you should try out the tips in the following sections.

CLEANING UP THE DESKTOP

You can clean up the desktop in Mac OS X by choosing View ➜ Clean Up (or by Ctrl+clicking on the desktop and choosing Clean Up). This aligns all the icons in a grid format. Figure 12-1 shows the difference between a desktop before and after using the Clean Up function.

Before using
Clean Up

After using
Clean Up

FIGURE 12-1: The same desktop before and after using the Clean Up function.

You can also set up Mac OS X to automatically clean up icons as you add them to and move them around the desktop, ensuring that they line up neatly. To do this, you right-click the desktop and choose View ➔ Show View Options. The following options enable you to keep the desktop tidy:

▶ **Icon Size:** Larger icons help keep the clutter on the desktop to a minimum and ensure that things are easier to find.

▶ **Grid Spacing:** This option increases the amount of space between items when they are cleaned up.

▶ **Arrange By:** This option automatically arranges icons on the desktop. You can arrange items automatically by aligning them to an invisible grid, by the date and time an item was last saved, by the date an item was created, or by size or file type (or kind). You can also arrange icons by any labels you've added to files.

Automatically arranging items on the desktop prevents it from cluttering up, and the grid structure enables you to find items much faster.

▶ Arranging items by kind is the fastest way to find the things you need. Selecting the Kind option also automatically keeps the desktop neat.

USING FOLDERS AND ALIASES

If you really want to keep a desktop tidy, one way to do it is to use good, old-fashioned folders and then uses aliases to bounce items to these folders. For example, I create folders for each project that I work on and keep them in a folder called *Active Projects* in the Documents folder, as shown in Figure 12-2. I then use aliases to these folders located in the Places area in a Finder window sidebar, but you can also create aliases and keep them on the desktop.

Here are a couple of good places to put aliases:

▶ **Create an Alias in a Finder sidebar.** Drag a file or folder from the Finder to Places in the Sidebar. Then click on the alias to navigate to that folder and drag items to the alias in the Sidebar to move them to that folder in Finder.

▶ **Create an Alias on the desktop.** Locate a folder or item in the Finder and hold down Ctrl+⌘. Then drag the item or folder to the desktop to create an alias there.

▶ The alias will look like the regular folder, but it will display a small black arrow in the bottom-left corner.

Now, instead of leaving a file on the desktop, you can drag it to one of the aliases, and it'll be bounced to that folder. The great thing about aliases is that you can keep them on the desktop to quickly access folders, and you can delete them with impunity. You simply drag the aliases on the desktop to Trash and drag them out of Places to delete them from the Sidebar.

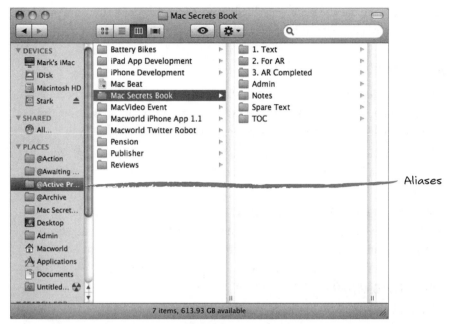

FIGURE 12-2: Aliases can be contained in the Places area of the Finder window's sidebar or placed within Finder itself.

TIP I sort things not by what they are but by what state they're in. I use these four folders: Action, Active Projects, Awaiting Others, and Archive:

▶ Action is for stuff I'm working on right now.

▶ Active Projects is for things that I'm working on (just not at the moment), organized by project name.

▶ Archive is for projects that I've finished but want to keep a record of.

▶ Awaiting Others is for items that I'm working on but for which other people need to get back to me.

This way, I can keep my projects on hand but organized for ease of access.

Cleaning Out the Dock

The Dock is a wonderful tool for organization but, as with the desktop, it's far too easy to end up with a cluttered Dock. My advice is to get rid of icons in the Dock for programs that you don't use regularly.

▶ I define regularly as at least a couple times an hour. Anything less frequent, and you might as well use the Applications folder.

Once you clean out the Dock, you should consider adding items to it that will help you locate and organize items in the Finder, as described in the next sections.

ADDING STACKS

You can add folders to the right side of the Dock, where you can expand them to reveal the contents by using Stacks. Stacks is a great feature but, as with applications, you should only create a stack for items you frequently use.

By default, Mac OS X includes two stacks: Applications and Downloads. You can take folders from Finder and add them to the Dock, where they will act as shortcuts (like aliases).

I prefer to use the Dock for applications and Places in Finder for shortcuts, but this is just a personal preference. Stacks is a great way to access shortcuts, because you can click and navigate through them directly from the omnipresent Dock.

▶ It's possible to store files in the Dock and launch them with one click, but I think it's better to keep the Dock clean and free from documents.

USING DOCK DIVIDERS

If you have a lot of items in the Dock, you can use Dock dividers to separate the items. Dock dividers are small applications that do nothing but sit in the Dock, as shown in Figure 12-3. You can get some nice Dock dividers from Brandon Kelly's website (http://brandon-kelly.com/dock-dividers).

▶ If you try to open a Dock divider, it launches a nonexistent application that closes immediately.

FIGURE 12-3: Using Dock dividers is a great way to arrange items in the Dock.

USING DRAGTHING INSTEAD OF THE DOCK

My advice is to pare down the Dock to the bare minimum and use it to launch applications you use all the time. However, many Mac fans go in the opposite direction and use the Dock all the time; in fact, some don't think the Dock goes far enough. If you're one of the latter users, you should investigate a program called DragThing (www.dragthing.com). DragThing was actually around way before Mac OS X introduced the Dock, and it has a lot of great functionality. DragThing enables you to divide items into tabs (Applications, Documents, Folders, URLs, and so on), and it has a Dock for each open application, volume, and window. DragThing also creates a new Dock based on the items already in the Mac OS X Dock, so it's easy to move from using the Dock to DragThing.

Organizing Work by Using Spaces

Spaces is a virtual desktop feature that enables you to switch from one desktop area to another. This enables you to fit application windows in different spaces, for example, and then jump from one space to another.

Because Spaces multiplies the number of desktops available, it's easy to lose applications and windows across multiple desktops, which is counterproductive. If you're going to use Spaces, you should consider assigning applications to different screens so they always open in the same area. For example, you can group your spaces by type of application (office productivity in Space 1, web tools in Space 2, communication apps in Space 3, and so on). Then you can use shortcuts or application icons in the Dock to move to the space you need.

> **TIP** A neat trick is to line up your Dock icons from left to right, according to which space they are in, and use Dock dividers to match up the Dock with spaces.

You assign applications to spaces by using the Exposé & Spaces pane in System Preferences, as shown in Figure 12-4. You get to this pane by choosing Apple System Preferences, clicking Exposé & Spaces, and then clicking the Spaces tab. In the top of the window, you see a visual layout of the number of spaces available. The default is 4, but you can add rows and columns to create up to 16 spaces.

You start by opening all the applications you use daily. Then you click the Add (+) icon below the Application Assignments list. A drop-down menu appears, showing all the open applications. Next, you choose a program to add to the Application Assignments list. Then you use the drop-down menu to the right of the application to assign it to a space. You can also add applications that aren't running by choosing Other from the drop-down menu that appears when you click the Add (+) icon.

▶ It's best to stick with four spaces to start with and build up as you become more familiar with the Spaces feature.

> **CROSSREF** Chapter 13 has information on customizing spaces so each space displays a different desktop background.

Now, whenever you use an application, it will open in that space. It's possible to get an overview of all the screens used by clicking the Spaces icon in the Dock (or by opening Spaces in the Applications folder or by pressing F8). You can also move between Spaces by using Ctrl and the arrow keys.

Safari assigned
to space 2

Microsoft Word
assigned to space 1

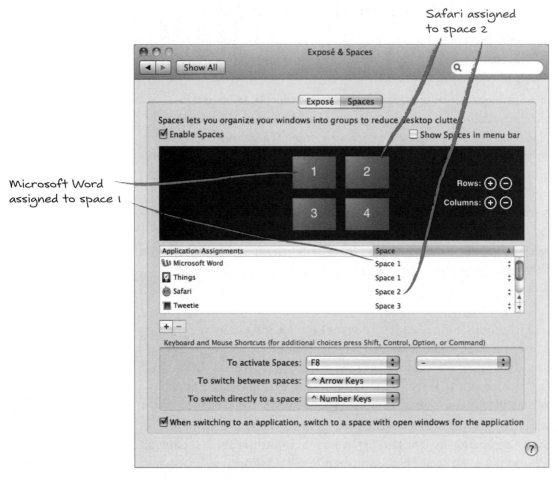

FIGURE 12-4: Assigning applications to specific areas using the Spaces feature prevents you from wasting time looking through multiple desktop areas.

Using Exposé to Navigate Windows

▶ Hidden windows don't appear in Exposé even if they're performing a function, such as iTunes playing music.

Exposé is a pretty neat technology that enables you to get a quick overview of every window. Most Apple keyboards have an Exposé button (it shares the F3 key) that you can press to zoom out and display all the windows in a grid. Active windows appear in the top the screen, and minimized windows appear smaller near the bottom, below a faint dividing line.

In addition, Mac OS X 10.6 Snow Leopard enables you to get an Exposé view of just the windows from a single application. To do this, you click and hold any application icon in the Dock.

> **TIP** Hold down ⌘ while opening Exposé to clear all the windows and display just the desktop.

One more really neat trick with Exposé enables you to drag items from one application to another quickly and easily. When you're dragging an item in Finder and want to use it in an application that's hidden (dragging a file into a Mail message, for example), you can drag the item to the application icon in the Dock and then hold it over the icon to use Exposé to display all the windows. Then you drag the item to the window of the application you want to use and press the spacebar. This brings that window to the foreground, and you can drop the item straight into it.

> **TIP** You can combine Spaces with Exposé to get a complete overview of every window that Mac OS X is using.

Using Quick Look to Spy Inside Files

Quick Look is a technology developed by Apple and first introduced in Mac OS X 10.5 Leopard. It enables you to quickly view the contents of a file without having to open a program. What's really cool is that it works with most files—even music and video files—playing or displaying the contents in a small transparent window.

Using Quick Look instead of opening programs to check the contents of a file is a good habit to get into. Many people don't use Quick Look because they try to access it through the menu bar or by right-clicking and choosing Quick Look. Both of these work, but the shortcut is to select a file and press the spacebar.

A great trick is to put a Finder window into Cover Flow mode (by choosing View → As Cover Flow). You can then use the arrow keys to move through files, and you can press the spacebar to use Quick Look to expand a file and view its contents.

Making Files with Labels and Tags

It is possible to label files and folders in Mac OS X with seven different colors. These labels highlight the files, enabling you to quickly recognize them. You typically use labels to assign status to files or folders. It's a fairly common for users to label files green when they're ready, for example, or red if they've been rejected. These designations are not explicitly declared within Mac OS X; only the color, not the meaning of the color, is added to the icon.

▶ You can use a program called Labels X (http://unsanity.com/haxies/labels) to add a wider range of colors and tints.

▶ Be careful not to spend more time tagging up items than you'd spend just looking for them.

To label a file or folder, you Ctrl+click the file in Finder and choose one of the colored squares in the Label section. Or you can choose the x icon under Label to remove a label.

If you want to move beyond using labels, you should investigate tags. Websites frequently use tags to group similar articles, and photo programs such as Aperture and iPhoto use them to add information to images. Applications such as Tags (www.gravityapps.com/tags) enable you to extend the ability to tag items in Mac OS X. Unlike with labels, with tags you add short text descriptions to files and folders. You can then use these tags to browse, search, and group items. By using the Tags application, you can add tags to mail messages, photos, bookmarks, and lots of other aspects of Mac OS X. This personalization enables you to group items using tags, and search for those grouped items by tagging—which some people find more accurate than using Spotlight.

For myself, I find that a combination of keeping a clear desktop and tucking away files into folders in the Finder, combined with some pretty clever usage of Spotlight (which we'll get to next), is the best way to store and find things.

SEARCHING SMARTER WITH SPOTLIGHT

▶ This is information usually added to a file to help you organize it, such as the artist, album, and genre info added to music files by iTunes.

Spotlight is a system-wide search tool designed to hunt down files, folders, applications, information...in fact, just about everything in Mac OS X. Spotlight searches through the data in files and through the information contained within applications, as well as for filenames and any metadata associated with files. In short, it can find pretty much everything and anything in Mac OS X. If you become adept with Spotlight, you won't need to spend much time sorting your files. You can just hunt for what you need.

It's possible to access Spotlight by using the text fields located in the top right of the Finder window, as well as in supporting applications (notably Mail, Address Book, iCal, and Preview).

> **TIP** System Preferences uses Spotlight. You can type the name of any preference or function located within a preference in the text field in the top right of System Preferences, and the appropriate icon is highlighted, with other unrelated icons dimming away.

Using Spotlight Shortcuts

You should get used to using the shortcut combination to access the Spotlight text field in the top right of the desktop. By default, it is ⌘+spacebar. You can press this key combination and start typing to find what you want. By default, the most likely result is deemed the top hit, and pressing Return takes you straight to it. Alternatively, you can use the ↑ and ↓ keys to navigate through the list of items.

▶ You can also open Spotlight in a window by pressing Option+⌘+spacebar or by choosing Show All from the Spotlight menu).

Table 12-1 lists some shortcuts for the Spotlight menu, and Table 12-2 lists some shortcuts for the Spotlight window.

TABLE 12-1: Spotlight Menu Shortcuts

KEYBOARD SHORTCUT	EFFECT
⌘+spacebar	Access the Spotlight menu from Finder.
Option+Enter	Select Show All from the Spotlight list.
⌘+Return	Open a folder containing the selected item in the Spotlight list.
⌘+↑ ⌘+↓	Go to the previous or next category in the Spotlight list.

TABLE 12-2: Spotlight Window Shortcuts

KEYBOARD SHORTCUT	EFFECT
Option+⌘+spacebar	Open Spotlight window from Finder.
⌘+1	Open Icon view.
⌘+2	Open List view.
⌘+4	Open Cover Flow view.
⌘+A	Select all.
⌘+Y or spacebar	Open Quick Look.
Option+⌘+Y	Run a full-screen slideshow of the selected items.

By learning even just a few of these shortcuts, you'll become more adept at finding whatever you need, wherever it may be.

Discovering Powerful Spotlight Searches

Most people use Spotlight in a straightforward manner, entering just one search term at a time and then selecting items from the results. This is fine, but there are ways to get more out of Spotlight. One technique is to use specific keywords to search for specific file types (images, music, contacts, and so on). You do this by using the kind: command with a keyword and a search term. For example, to search for images, you can type kind:image: into Spotlight, along with the search term. Table 12-3 lists some of the keywords you can use in Spotlight. You can find more keywords at www.macworld.com/article/132788.

TABLE 12-3: Spotlight Keywords

KEYWORDS	FILE ASSOCIATION
Kind: application, applications, app	Applications
Kind: audio, music	Audio and music files
Kind: email, emails, mail	E-mail messages
Created: date	Files created on a particular date, in the format mm/dd/yy (for example, created:10/1/2012 for October 1, 2012). The date format may vary, depending on your Date & Time settings. It can also accept Today, Yesterday, and Tomorrow (for iCal events).
Created:>; created:<	Files created before and after the date specified
Kind: event, events	iCal events
to do, to dos, todo, todos	iCal to-dos
Kind: image, images	Images
Kind: pdf, pdfs	PDF documents
Kind: word	Word documents

Using Logic in Spotlight

Spotlight power users will want to learn to use logical expressions and Boolean operators to narrow search results. You must enter Boolean operators in all uppercase

▶ Boolean logic is the basis of computer programming and is named after George Boole, the inventor of this form of logic.

letters; otherwise, Spotlight uses them as search terms. Spotlight then uses these operators to refine searches. The commands are as follows:

▶ **NOT:** This specifies that the result shouldn't contain the item. For example, *Mark NOT Hattersley* returns results for occurrences of *Mark* on my Mac that aren't me.

▶ **AND:** This is the default between two items, although you can enter it as a command. For example, *Mark AND Hattersley* returns results all occurrences of *Mark Hattersley* but not occurrences of *Mark Walter* or *Susan Hattersley*.

▶ **OR:** This returns results that have both items specified. For example, *Mark OR Hattersley* returns all items that have either *Mark* or *Hattersley* mentioned in them.

▶ **" ":** Entering terms inside quotation marks finds the term instead of looking for both terms occurring independently.

By default, the priority of the logical operations is NOT, then AND, and then OR, regardless of which way you enter the terms. You can use parentheses to specify a different order. For example, *"(Mark AND macworld) NOT Hattersley"* searches for occurrences of *Mark* that appear in conjunction with *Macworld*, but not occurrences that include *Hattersley*.

Some people understand Boolean logic instinctively, which is great because getting a simplistic overview of Boolean logic can be difficult. Most descriptions go into too much depth and make it more complicated than it needs to be. Rockwell Schrock's Boolean Machine website (http://kathyschrock.net/rbs3k/boolean) gives a visual explanation of Boolean operators on keywords. Google also has a cheat sheet that explains using Boolean logic in web searches (www.google.com/help/cheatsheet.html).

▶ You can use Boolean logic in search engines, but they use a different syntax. For example, Google uses the pipe (|) symbol instead of OR, the plus symbol (+) instead of AND, and the minus symbol (-) instead of NOT.

Adjusting Spotlight Search Results

You can control Spotlight results by using the Spotlight preference pane (which you open by choosing ➜ System Preferences and clicking Spotlight). You use the check boxes shown in Figure 12-5 to determine which items Spotlight should include in its search results. Removing items (such as presentations or fonts) makes a search faster and shortens the results. Removing items from a Spotlight search isn't necessarily a good thing because it limits Spotlight's functionality.

▶ You can rearrange the order in which results are displayed in the Spotlight menu by dragging the items around.

FIGURE 12-5: You use the Spotlight preference pane to disable and enable search results and to rearrange the order of results.

> **TIP** In Spotlight's search results, drag Documents to the top of the list, above Applications and System Preferences. If you type in the exact term of an application or a preference, it'll appear in the Top Hit section anyway.

You can also prevent Spotlight from searching certain folders or volumes attached to Mac OS X by using the Privacy settings. To do this, you click the Privacy tab and drag items from Finder to the window (or use the Add (+) button to add items via a dialog). You can make Spotlight run faster and return more accurate results by adding folders and volumes you don't need to search. For example, I exclude external volumes and the Movies folder. Some people also exclude the Music folder, but I like to be able to search for my audio through Spotlight.

▶ The Movies folder contains large files that take a long time to index, but I don't have many of them, and I don't really need Spotlight to locate them.

THREE COOL SPOTLIGHT TIPS

As well as searching for files, applications, and other items, Spotlight has a few other tricks up its sleeve. Here are three to try out:

▶ **Calculator:** You can type math equations into Spotlight, and the Calculator search result displays both the equation and the answer. You can type in simple commands, such as 2*2, or more complex ones, such as pi*10*10 or sqrt(128).

▶ **Dictionary:** If you type a word, Spotlight displays the definition. You can then select it to open the Dictionary utility at that definition.

▶ **Program launcher:** One of the most common Spotlight tricks is to use it to launch programs. You can press ⌘+spacebar, type a program name, and press Enter to launch the program. This can be even faster than using the Dock.

With these tricks, you'll get more out of Spotlight than you ever thought possible.

Adding Spotlight Comments to Files

A final tip for using Spotlight is to add Spotlight comments to files and folders. By doing this, you can ensure that certain items are returned in Spotlight searches, even if they don't otherwise contain the specified search term within them. For example, I tag files for my books with the publisher's name, Wiley Publishing. This way, I can search through everything I've done for that company, even if the files don't include the term.

To add a Spotlight comment to a file, highlight it in Finder, and press ⌘+I to bring up its Info window, as shown in Figure 12-6. Then you can add a search term to the Spotlight Comments text field.

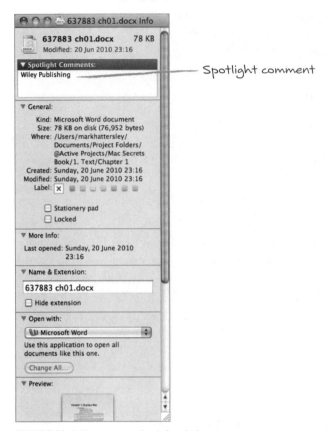

Spotlight comment

FIGURE 12-6: You can use the Info window to add Spotlight comments to files.

Adding Spotlight comments manually can be something of a drain, and you should balance the time you spend sorting something against the amount of time you spend searching for it. Fortunately, you can use an application called Automator that comes with Mac OS X. You can use Automator to create a quick application that enables you to quickly add Spotlight comments to multiple files. To begin, you open Automator and follow these simple steps:

1. Select the Application template and click Choose.

2. Drag the Set Spotlight Comments for Finder Items from the list of Actions (the second column) to the main window.

3. Click Options and select Show This Action When Workflow Runs check box.

4. Choose File ➔ Save As and save the application to Finder, giving it the title Add Spotlight Comments.

Congratulations! As shown in Figure 12-7, you've just made an application.

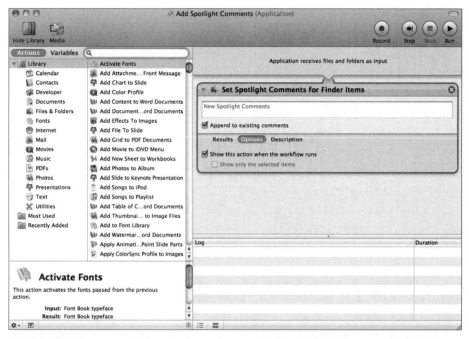

FIGURE 12-7: You can use Automator to create an application that adds the same Spotlight comment to multiple files at once.

You can save the application anywhere—it's an application—but it probably should live in the Applications or Utilities folders. You can add it to the Dock as you would any other program.

CROSSREF Chapter 23 has more information on creating applications using Automator.

Now when you drag files to this app, a dialog appears, asking you to enter the Spotlight comments. You can enter the term you want associated with the files and then click Continue. The Spotlight comment will be added to all those files.

FINDING FILES WITH SMART FOLDERS

Smart Folders look like regular folders, but instead of containing items, they display Spotlight search results. When you open a Smart Folder, you don't view the contents inside the folder; instead, you view items elsewhere in the directory structure.

▶ You can identify Smart Folders by their purple color and cog icon.

Because of this, you can't add items to Smart Folders, but you can use them to search for items elsewhere on your system.

You can use the Spotlight search box in Smart Folders to narrow searches even further. Smart search technology exists within Finder, and also in some Mac OS X applications (such as Mail and iTunes) although they are often named differently: Smart Mailboxes, Smart Playlists, and so on.

Making Smart Folders is pretty easy. In fact, Mac OS X comes preloaded with a number of Smart Folders. To see this, open a new Finder window and look in the sidebar for the Search For area. Here you'll see Today, Yesterday, Past Week, All Images, All Movies, and All Documents. All of these are Smart Folders.

To create a new Smart Folder, you choose File ➜ New Smart Folder from the Finder menu bar. Then you use the first drop-down menu option to choose a category, such as Kind, Last Opened, or Created Date.

CHECK OUT THE OTHER OPTION

When creating Smart Folders, be sure to look at the Other option. This opens a huge list of options that can be added to the drop-down menu—everything from aperture values used to take photographs to video bit rates of movie files. It's worth taking time to investigate these offerings.

You can also use the Add (+) button to add multiple search terms to narrow the results even further. For example, you can create folders that display images created in the last week.

When you've finished, you can save the Smart Folder and access it in Finder. You click the Save button on the right side of the New Smart Folder window, as shown in Figure 12-8.

Select the Add To Sidebar check box in the save dialog to add the Smart Folder to the Search For area in the Finder window's sidebar.

Using a combination of Smart Folders for frequent searches with clever Spotlight searching can make organizing files and folders in the Finder almost redundant.

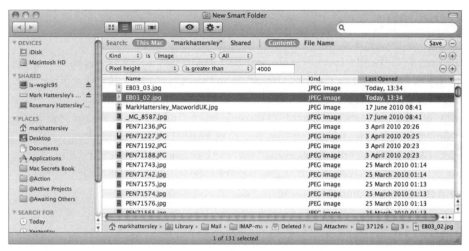

FIGURE 12-8: You create a Smart Folder by using the drop-down menus to choose search options.

SMART FOLDER INSPIRATION

Here are some ideas for Smart Folders you might want to create:

▶ **Kind is Microsoft Word:** This searches for Microsoft Word documents.

▶ **Kind is PDF:** This displays PDF files.

▶ **Kind is Image and Pixel Height Is Greater Than 2000:** This searches for large images, enabling you to skip over icons and other small images.

▶ **Kind is Document and Last Modified is Today:** This searches for documents you've worked on today.

▶ **Location:** Increasingly, cameras (especially the iPhone) are adding location information to images. By using this option, you can search for where a file was created.

▶ **Device Make:** This searches for photographs taken with certain cameras, such as Device Make is Fuji or Device Make is Canon.

By looking through the Other folder, you can find lots of inspiration for different Smart Folders.

SUMMARY

Organizing files and folders isn't always a barrel of laughs, which is why so few people do it. But using a few neat tricks for storing and searching can make a big difference. Mac OS X offers some great technology, such as Stacks, Places, and aliases, which can help you quickly locate and move files around. Spaces and Exposé are two of Mac OS X's flashiest interface features, and they're also powerful tools for arranging your workspace. With your desktop straightened out, you can use Spotlight to find files, folders, and just about everything else in Mac OS X. Spotlight is much, much more powerful than you probably realize.

CHAPTER 13

Personalizing Your Mac

It's true that Mac OS X looks beautiful the moment you switch it on. Every Mac looks the same when it first starts up, though, and this isn't just any old Mac; it's your Mac, so why not have it your way? A ton of customization tricks enable you to jazz up a Mac in a number of ways. Just about every part of Mac OS X can be configured either within the operating system itself or through judicious use of extra programs and the odd hack. Taking advantage of a few tricks and tips goes a long way toward making a Mac act like your machine. In this chapter, you'll learn how to put your personal stamp all over your Mac.

VIEWING AMAZING DESKTOP IMAGES

▶ Confusingly, one folder is called Desktop Pictures, but it contains a selection of fairly old images used in previous operating systems.

Probably the first place most people start customizing their Mac is with the desktop image, which is easy enough. You simply Ctrl+click the desktop and choose Change Desktop Background for a shortcut to the desktop preferences pane, as shown in Figure 13-1. Apple provides a great selection of stock images in folders such as Nature, Art, Black & White, and so on. You can also pick images from the iPhoto library or the Pictures folder.

New desktop image

Right-click to change the desktop

FIGURE 13-1: You can use any picture as a desktop image.

ADDING DIFFERENT DESKTOP IMAGES TO SPACES

If you use Spaces, you may find it useful to add a different desktop image to each individual space to further differentiate your spaces. Mac OS X does not allow you to adjust the desktop image for each different space; however, it is possible to add this functionality by using a free program called SpaceSuit (www.docklandsoft.com/spacesuit).

You can also have Mac OS X change the picture periodically by using the Change Picture check box and pop-up menu.

Here are some great places to look for customized desktop images:

http://wallpaperstock.net

www.desktopwallpapers.co.uk

www.digitalblasphemy.com

www.flickr.com/groups/wallpapers

Or you can use image searches such as Google Images (www.google.com/imghp) or Bing Images (www.bing.com/images) to look for images in subjects or styles you like. If you're a fan of a movie, TV show, musician, or band, you might want to check out their respective websites. These are another great source of desktop images.

Adding Trash to the Desktop

Older Mac fans might remember the presence of Trash on the desktop from pre-Mac OS X days (at which point it was moved to the Dock). Trash exists as an invisible folder in your home folder, and it's possible to use some Terminal trickery to create a shortcut to it.

Simply launch Terminal and type the following code:

```
ln -s ~/.Trash ~/Desktop/Trash
```

Presto! You have a Trash shortcut on the desktop. It looks like a regular shortcut, but you can replace the icon with a Trash-like one to complete the effect.

▶ Hidden folders have a period (.) before them, and the Trash is a collection of all the .trash folders (there are multiple in Mac OS X) you can access with your account.

Moving the Dock

By default, the Dock appears at the bottom of the screen, and most people never think to move it. By positioning the Dock on the left or right, however, you free up space for windows to expand down to the bottom of the display. Because the Dock reflects windows and the desktop, it also has a vastly different appearance when positioned at the side of the screen, as shown in Figure 13-2. You can move the position of the Dock using the Dock preferences pane, or by Ctrl+clicking the Dock divider and choosing Position On Screen from the contextual menu. You can also choose ➝ Dock to access the different options directly.

▶ You can use the Dock preferences pane to adjust the magnification, size, minimize window effect, and animation of the Dock, as well as automatically show and hide the Dock.

FIGURE 13-2: The Dock positioned on the side of the Mac OS X desktop.

Now that you've personalized your desktop, let's take a moment to check out screen savers.

GETTING PERSONAL WITH SCREEN SAVERS

Screen savers are another part of Mac OS X that you can use to customize the look and feel of your Mac. A screen saver is an animated effect that typically appears when you haven't been using your Mac for a short period. Screen savers were initially developed to prevent screen burn.

▶ This is a problem where static images would physically burn into a CRT display if left on the screen constantly. Today's LCDs and LEDs make this issue virtually obsolete.

Many screen savers have options you can use to customize the look and feel of the animation. If this is the case, the Options button underneath the preview pane is enabled. Clicking Options brings up a different set of controls for each screen saver, as shown in Figure 13-3. The Streams screen saver, for example, offers a pop-up menu to adjust the color cycle and a number of sliders to adjust the number, thickness, and speed of the streams.

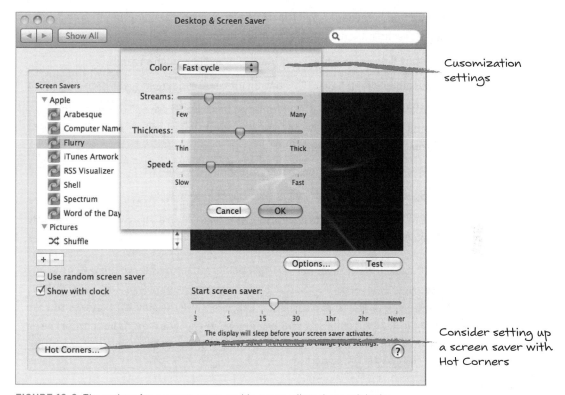

FIGURE 13-3: The options for a screen saver enable you to adjust the way it looks.

One way to activate your screen saver is to set it up with Hot Corners. This features enables you to activate a screen saver on demand, without having to wait for it to start.

Using Hot Corners

You can use Hot Corners to activate functionality—such as launching your screen saver—when your mouse moves into one of the four corners of the screen. To set up Mac OS X so that moving the mouse into a Hot Corner activates the screen saver, you follow these steps:

1. Open the Screen Saver preferences pane and click the Hot Corners button.

2. Click one of the four pop-up menus for each corner, choose Start Screen Saver, and click OK.

3. Move the mouse into the corner you set up and let go of it to activate the screen saver. You can then move the mouse or touch a key to halt the screen saver.

▶ You can also access Hot Corners in the Exposé & Spaces preferences pane.

Hot Corners offer additional functionality. Some of this functionality applies to the screen saver, and some applies to other functions, as follows:

▶ **Start Screen Saver:** This option activates the screen saver.

▶ **Disable Screen Saver:** This option prevents the screen saver from activating.

▶ **All Windows, Application Windows, Desktop:** These options relate to Exposé and display different windows (or the desktop) when you move the mouse to the different Hot Corners.

▶ **Dashboard:** This option displays Dashboard widgets.

▶ **Spaces:** This option displays all the available spaces.

▶ **Put Display to Sleep:** This option switches off the display when you move the mouse to the appropriate Hot Corner.

The Disable Screen Saver option is particularly useful when you're watching a movie on your Mac. Because you don't interact with the mouse or keyboard while watching a movie, the screen saver may activate while the movie is playing. You can set a Hot Corner to Disable Screen Saver and move the mouse into that part of the screen after you've started the movie running to prevent the animation from interrupting the feature presentation.

Creating Screen Savers from Pictures

It is possible to use a desktop image or photos from iPhoto to create screen savers. When you use a still image in a screen saver, Mac OS X can animate the image in a variety of ways.

▶ Ken Burns is famous for creating movie documentaries using archival photographs and video, and for perfecting a style of pan and zoom movement that brings still images to life.

To create a screen saver from a still image, from the Screen Saver preferences pane, you choose a collection from the Pictures section of the list, as shown in Figure 13-4. By default, this animates the pictures using a slideshow zoom technique known as the Ken Burns effect. However, you can choose any of three options: Slideshow, Collage, and Mosaic.

Using your own pictures to create animated screen savers is a great way to personalize your Mac, but you can also install new screen savers, as discussed next.

FIGURE 13-4: You can create an animated screen saver by using your own photograph collection.

Installing New Screen Savers

While Mac OS X comes with a range of pretty good screen savers, you may want to install new ones. From the Screen Saver preferences pane, you click the small Add (+) icon and choose Browse Screen Savers to see a variety of screen savers.

Screen savers are typically files with the .saver extension, although they can also be .app or .dmg files that you install as you would any other program. Occasionally, screen savers also come as completely independent preferences panes.

Installing a .saver file to Mac OS X places it in the Other section at the bottom of the list of screen savers. Like the built-in screen savers, installed screen savers typically have their own options.

> TIP You can also add pictures from a Finder folder, a MobileMe gallery, or an RSS feed by using the Add (+) button.

▶ Another great place to find screen savers is www.apple.com/downloads/macosx/icons_screensavers.

▶ To delete a screen saver that you installed, you highlight it in the list and click the Remove (-) button.

Here are some cool screen savers for you to check out:

▸ **LotsaWater:** This makes your desktop appear to be on the bottom of a pool of water with ripples. See `http://wakaba.c3.cx/s/lotsablankers/lotsawater.html`.

▸ **Holding Pattern Coach Class:** This displays the view from an airplane as it slowly moves across a variety of aerial landscapes. See `www.idletimesoftware.com/screensavers`.

▸ **Marine Aquarium 3:** One of the world's most popular screen savers, this turns your desktop display into a virtual fish tank. See `www.serenescreen.com`.

▸ **Fireflies:** This is similar to the popular Flurry screen saver included with Mac OS X but with more flurries. See `http://s.sudre.free.fr/Software/Fireflies.html`.

Be aware that some screen savers you find won't work in Mac OS X 10.6 Snow Leopard. If that's the case, the screen saver will be grayed out in the list, and selecting it will produce a dialog that offers to move it to Trash.

Combining Screen Savers with Desktop Backgrounds

A neat customization trick is to use an animated screen saver as your desktop background, as shown in Figure 13-5.

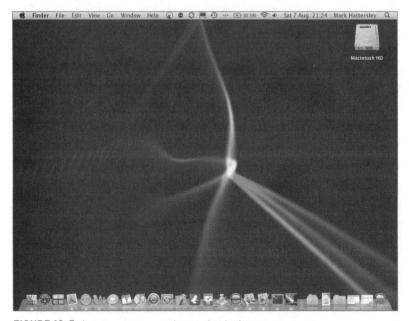

FIGURE 13-5: A screen saver running on the desktop.

To do this, you pick a screen saver using the Screen Saver preferences pane and open Terminal. Then type this command all on one line:

```
/System/Library/Frameworks/ScreenSaver.framework/Resources/
ScreenSaverEngine.app/Contents/MacOS/
ScreenSaverEngine -background
```

When you press Return, the screen saver appears on the desktop. You can move icons around and work as normal. To halt the effect, you return to Terminal and press Ctrl+C.

▶ If typing this code is too much, you can download a program called Wallsaver that does the same thing (www.nwwnetwork.net).

INVESTIGATING COMPLEX DESKTOPS

While it's possible to pick your own desktop and even turn screen savers into desktop backgrounds, you can go even further. Quite a few programs enable you to create interactive animated desktops that use a variety of visual effects.

Two programs are particular favorites of mine for creating spectacular desktop results. The first is My Living Desktop (www.mylivingdesktop.com), which enables you to run video clips on the desktop, either from a provided collection or your own video files. You can combine this with animations to create subtle (or not so subtle) desktop effects.

My other favorite desktop program, EarthDesk (www.xericdesign.com/earthdesk.php), turns your desktop display into a visualization of the Earth, as taken from space. It's a real-time dynamic image that portrays the effect of daylight as it passes across the planet and includes more than 10,000 cities.

Now that you know how to set up cool screen savers, let's take a look at how to change the look of your icons and folders.

CUSTOMIZING ICONS AND FOLDERS

Beyond the desktop and screen saver, the most obvious parts of Mac OS X to change are the other parts of Finder, in particular icons and folders. The first thing you can adjust is what icons and folders appear on the desktop. To do this, you choose Finder ➜ Preferences and click the General tab. Then you use the Show These Items On The Desktop check boxes to specify what items (for example, hard disks, external disks, CDs, DVDs and iPods, or connected servers) appear on the desktop.

By default, Mac OS X uses a particular set of graphics with each type of item displayed on the desktop and in Finder windows. However, it is possible to change these icons by cutting and pasting icon types from one icon preview to another, as shown in Figure 13-6. This is a great way to extend your personalization beyond the desktop imagery and into the Finder itself.

To change icon graphics, you complete the following steps:

1. Highlight the item (file or folder) you want to change on the desktop or in Finder.

2. Open the item's Info window by pressing ⌘+I (or by choosing File ➜ Get Info).

3. Highlight the small icon image at the top of the Info window (not the main preview image) and press ⌘+C to copy the icon.

4. Highlight a second item on the desktop or in Finder.

5. Open a new Info window by pressing ⌘+I.

6. Highlight the small icon image at the top of the new Info window and paste the icon image by pressing ⌘+V.

When you cut and paste the icon image from the Info window, you also change the icon image in Finder and on the desktop.

FIGURE 13-6: New icon styles are distributed as empty folders, and you can use the Info window to cut and paste them from one item in Finder to another.

Of course, this only enables you to cut and paste icon types from one type of default icon to another.

To move beyond the regular look, you can download from the Internet new icons that are typically distributed as a set of empty folders with custom icons. Here are some good places to get icon collections:

- http://iconfactory.com/freeware

- http://browse.deviantart.com/customization/icons/

- www.apple.com/downloads/macosx/icons_screensavers

- http://pixelgirlpresents.com/icons/48

It can be awkward to use the Info window to cut and paste icons, so you might want to get a program that does it for you. One such program is FolderBrander (www .yellowmug.com/folderbrander). This program enables you to drag and drop folders onto its preview pane and then apply different folder styles. In addition to changing icon styles, you can add glows and drop shadows to folders.

And now that you've changed your icons, you might want to customize the folders that contain them. The next section looks at modifying Finder windows.

▶ Be careful. If you just move the default icons around, you'll end up mixing up Mac OS X and making a mess of the Finder.

MODIFYING MAC OS X WINDOWS

One final part of the Finder that you can adjust is Finder windows. By default, these windows contain a plain white background, but it is possible to add a number of custom patterns and images. Changing the background is a great way to liven up Finder, and it's also practical because it enables you to identify active Finder windows. Here's how you do it:

1. Open a folder in Finder and make sure you are in Icon view (choose View → As Icons) so you can see its contents.

2. Ctrl+click (or right-click) a blank area inside the folder and choose Show View Options, as shown in Figure 13-7.

3. Choose the Picture button from the Background options.

4. Double-click the Drag Image Here preview to choose an image file from Finder. Alternatively you can drag an image from within the Finder window (or desktop) direct to the preview.

▶ You can also use the Color option to change the background color of a window.

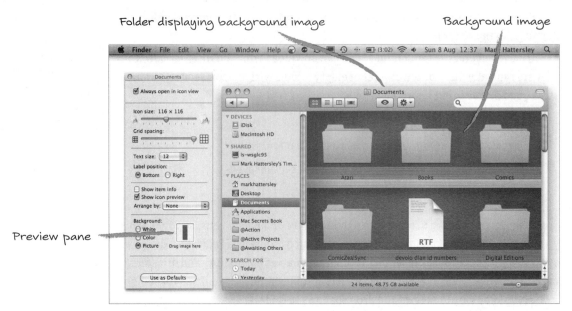

Folder displaying background image

Background image

Preview pane

FIGURE 13-7: You can use the View Options window to add a background image to a folder.

The image appears in the background of that window. To remove the image, you can select White as the background.

TURN FOLDERS INTO SHELVES

You can add any images you want to the backgrounds of your folders, and there are plenty of styles on the Internet. One of my favorites is a background image that turns Finder windows into wooden shelves, as shown in Figure 13-7. You can download this theme from www.macthemes.net/forum/viewtopic .php?id=16792664. Note that for the effect to work properly, you need to use the icon size slider to match up the folder icons with the shelves.

Of course, the way Mac OS X looks isn't the whole story. You can also change the way it sounds, thanks to a wide range of sound effects and audible alerts; we'll look at these next.

GETTING NOISY: SOUND EFFECTS AND AUDIBLE ALERTS

By default, Mac OS X is a fairly unobtrusive operating system. It makes noises when errors occur and to alert you to messages from Mail and iChat. In addition, some user interface sounds occur when you copy files, empty the Trash, and so on. Most of this audio can be customized, or at least ~~turned on or off~~. And with a few neat tricks, you can add custom audio clips or even create your own audio sounds.

> ▶ Of course, you can just use the audio mute button to turn off sound, but this mutes all sounds, including any audio you might be playing.

Changing the Alert Sound

Mac OS X ships with a range of alert noises, as shown in Figure 13-8. There are 14 different effects to choose from, and most are variations of short and reasonably subtle noises.

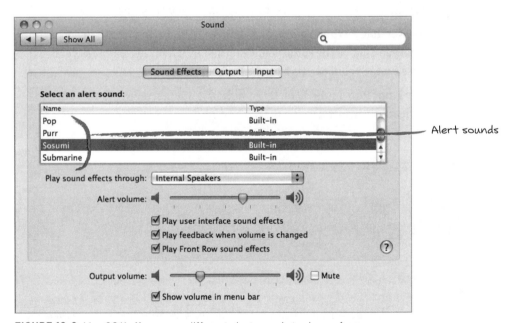

FIGURE 13-8: Mac OS X offers many different alert sounds to choose from.

To customize your sound effects, you use the following steps:

1. Choose Apple ➜ System Preferences and click Sound to open the Sound preferences pane.

2. Click Sound Effects and choose an option from the Select an Alert Sound list. As you click the different items in the list, examples play.

3. Adjust the volume of the alert sound, using the Alert Volume slider.

The alert sound changes as soon as you select it in the Sound preferences pane. When you close the preferences pane, it remains in effect.

NOTE Apple folklore has it that the Sosumi sound effect was a cheeky response to the Apple Computer vs. Apple Corps (the music label of The Beatles) legal conflict in the 1990s. Originally it was called Let It Beep, but when somebody told the musician Jim Reekes that it wouldn't get through Apple's legal department, he changed it to Sosumi (a homophone of So Sue Me) and told the legal department that it was Japanese.

You might want to investigate some of the other options in the Sound preferences pane:

▶ **Play User Interface Sound Effects:** This option switches on or off user interface audio, such as the noises that play when you copy files.

▶ **Play Feedback When Volume Is Changed:** This option provides feedback when you change the audio volume (either by using the volume slider or by pressing the volume button on the keyboard).

▶ **Play Front Row Sound Effects:** Front Row is a full-screen interface used to navigate and control media files.

Using these check boxes, you can determine what type of sound effects, alongside the audio alerts, play in Mac OS X.

FLASHING SCREEN ALERTS

Some people prefer to use visual alerts rather than the audio alerts used by default. Mac OS X has a visual alert option that quickly flashes the screen. It's designed principally for people with hearing difficulties, although many sound engineers use it because they don't want Mac OS X creating any audio outside of what they are working on. It's also used extensively in communal settings like classrooms and libraries where the noise from multiple Macs would be distracting.

To set up screen alerts, you open the Universal Access preferences pane and click the Hearing tab. Then you choose the Flash the Screen When an Alert Sound Occurs check box to create a visual alert. This still occurs if you set the Alert Volume slider in the Sound preferences pane to silent (the far left).

Creating Custom Alert Sounds

It is possible to add any sounds you want and have them play in Mac OS X as alerts. To do this, you simply add AIFF (Audio Interchange File Format) audio files (with the .aif extension) to the Sounds folder (located in the Library folder in your Home folder). When you add AIFF files to this folder, they appear in the Sound preferences pane.

Unfortunately, not many sound clips are distributed as AIFF files. They instead come in a variety of formats: WAV, MP3, AAC, and so on. However, it's really easy to convert audio files from one type to another by using a trick in iTunes:

1. Open iTunes and choose iTunes ➜ Preferences from the menu bar.

2. Click the General tab and then click Import Settings to open the Import Settings dialog, shown in Figure 13-9.

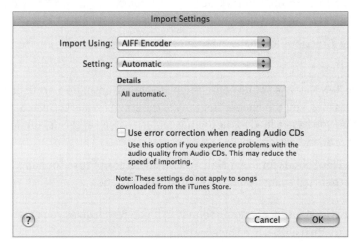

FIGURE 13-9: You can use the Import Settings dialog in iTunes to convert any compatible music file to that audio type.

3. Choose AIFF Encoder from the Import Using pop-up menu and click OK to close the Import Settings dialog.

4. Click OK to close the iTunes preferences window.

5. Choose File ➜ Add to Library in iTunes and use the Finder dialog to locate the audio file. Then click Choose.

6. Locate the file in the iTunes Library and choose Advanced ➜ Create AIFF Version.

7. Drag the created AIFF file from the iTunes library to the Home/Library/Sounds folder.

▶ You can also use a free tool like ffmpebX (www.ffmpegx.com) or Movie Tools (http://ecamm.com/mac/free) to convert audio files. These are free tools and can save you from converting iTunes settings back and forth.

You can use iTunes to convert any audio file playable in iTunes into the new default import format.

> **WARNING**   You should set iTunes preferences to import music to either AAC or MP3 after you finish using it to convert files. Otherwise, it will import all new music using the AIFF format (which creates much larger files than AAC or MP3).

Many applications also provide sound effects in Mac OS X, and you can further customize the operating system by adjusting the programs within it.

Changing Mail and iChat Sounds

Two applications are notorious for making their own sounds: Mail and iChat. You can change the sounds in both of these applications.

Here are the directions for changing sounds in Mail:

1. Choose Mail ➜ Preferences.
2. Use the New Message Sound pop-up menu to choose an audio alert to go with new messages. You can choose from any of the standard alerts (including any AIFF files you have added to the Sounds folder) instead of the default New Messages Sound option.
3. Use the Play Sounds for Other Mail Actions check box to turn sounds on and off for other Mail events, such as sending new messages.

And here are the steps for changing sounds in iChat, which gives you greater control over the individual noises used on events:

1. Choose iChat ➜ Preferences and click Alerts.
2. Use the Event pop-up menu to choose from all the different events that can occur in iChat.
3. Use the Play a Sound pop-up menu to choose a corresponding audio sound. As with Mail, you can choose from the default iChat sounds and alert sounds, including any audio files you have added to the Sounds folder.

Customizing these two programs along with Mac OS X alerts can make your Mac's audio highly personable. While many Mac users like to keep their machines silent, others like to customize Mac OS X to be as loud as possible—just be sure not to annoy those working nearby.

CUSTOMIZING YOUR MAC'S IDENTITY

A final customization trick is to change the way Mac OS X appears during startup and login. These are neat areas of customization that really enable you to make a Mac your own. Some of these are pretty in-depth hacks, though, and you need to be comfortable with using Terminal before you try them. Let's look at how to change both the login screen and the login panel.

CROSSREF Chapter 22 has more information on using Terminal to enter UNIX commands.

Changing the Login Screen

Using Terminal, you can customize the screen that appears behind the login information when you log in to Mac OS X. To do this, you need an image to replace the desktop background. It should be a JPG file that is the same resolution as your screen. To make the following code easier to follow, you should call it NewImage.jpg and place it on your desktop. Then you open Terminal and type the following:

```
cd /System/Library/CoreServices
sudo mv DefaultDesktop.jpg DefaultDesktop_old.jpg
sudo cp ~/Desktop/NewImage.jpg DefaultDesktop.jpg
```

▶ Sudo stands for Super User Do, and it enables you to enter commands that would normally require you to be logged in as a root user.

When you enter the second command, Terminal will prompt you to enter an administrator password. Type the password, press Return, and then enter the third command.

This process duplicates the DefaultDesktop.jpg image in the CoreServices folder to DefaultDesktop_old.jpg, which you can use to reverse the process and regain the original Desktop image.

The second command beginning with sudo copies the NewImage.jpg file from the desktop to the CoreServices folder and renames it DefaultDesktop.jpg. In Terminal, the ~ symbol is the Home folder of the current user, so ~/Desktop always points to your desktop.

Changing the Login Panel

If you want to get more control over the Mac OS X launch process, including changing more information on the login panel, you should investigate a program called
Visage (http://keakaj.com/visage.htm). Visage installs as a preferences pane and
enables you to adjust several areas of Mac OS X, including the login panel, as shown
in Figure 13-10.

FIGURE 13-10: You can replace the images displayed on the login panel by using Visage.

▶ A quick way
to create an
image of text is
to use TextEdit
to create the
text and then use
Shift+⌘+4 to do a
screen grab. Drag
the crosshairs
around the text
to create an image
on the desktop.

   Both the computer icon and the displayed name are image files. The replacements
you provide should be JPG images. The icon should be 90 × 90 pixels, and the name
should be 210 × 135 pixels.

You follow these steps to replace the icon:

1. Open the Visage preferences pane and click Login Panel.
2. Click Import underneath Manage Login Logo Collection. Locate the desired icon file and click Choose.
3. Choose the imported icon from the Current Login Panel Logo pop-up menu.
4. Enter your administrator password and click Apply Changes.

When you next log out, the login screen displays the icon. The process is exactly the same for the login panel title, which is an image, even though it typically displays the text Mac OS X.

You can also add a login panel text message in the text box below the panels. This text appears below the login panel title image.

You can use the Visage preferences pane to return the login icon back to the original Mac logo. To do so, you choose Apple Default from the Current Login Panel Logo pop-up menu and click Apply Changes.

▶ The Visage preferences pane is a 32-bit application, and System Preferences will have to quit and restart before you can open it.

▶ Visage also enables you to set a screen saver as a background (as outlined earlier in the chapter) and create personalized alerts.

SUMMARY

Mac OS X is the most beautiful operating system in existence, and you have every right to be happy with the way it looks out of the box. But that doesn't mean you have to stick with the same experience that every other Mac owner has. You can change the look, feel, and sound of Mac OS X to create a Mac that is truly yours. You can make some of these changes in Mac OS X itself, using various options such as desktop images and screen savers in System Preferences. However, you can get into a lot more depth in Mac OS X by changing the style of icons, folders, and audio alerts to create a more personal experience. If you want to go even further, it's even possible to hack changes, such as playing screen savers as desktop backgrounds or changing the login display. These changes require a bit of confidence, though, and you should be sure you know not just how to make changes but also how to put things back the way they were, if needed.

CHAPTER 14

Making the Most of Your Mouse, Keyboard, and Trackpad

IN THIS CHAPTER

▶ **Getting more out of a Magic Mouse** with scrolling and multi-finger gestures

▶ **Extending the capabilities of Magic Mouse** gestures with MagicPrefs

▶ **Putting amazing multi-touch** trackpad tricks to use

▶ **Harnessing the power of the keyboard** for speedy navigation

Input is incredibly important to Apple, and the company has lots of original ideas when it comes to the way users interact with computers. Aside from the keyboard, there are typically two ways computer users interact with machines: using either a mouse or a trackpad. This chapter looks at some of the options with the mouse on a Mac and then discusses the trackpad and multi-touch gestures. Even though multi-touch is fairly intuitive, you may not know about some of the neat gestures and tricks available; with the right information, you can take multi-touch to a whole different level. Finally, the keyboard is the input device you use the most, so this chapter also looks at some keyboard tricks and shortcuts that enable you to get the most from Mac OS X.

GETTING MORE OUT OF A MAGIC MOUSE

Apple has spearheaded a new kind of input called *multi-touch*, which enables users to control the Mac using gestures with one or more fingers on a trackpad or a Magic Mouse. (These gestures are familiar to owners of Apple's touch-screen devices, such as the iPhone, iPad, and iPod Touch.) Most current desktop Macs come with a wireless Magic Mouse, which has a multi-touch surface, and all Mac notebooks have large trackpads built in. Mac users can also buy a trackpad to go with a desktop Mac called the Magic Trackpad.

By default, the whole surface of the mouse acts as a single left-click. But it is possible—and indeed preferable—to set the right-hand side of the Magic Mouse to act as a right-click. You do this in the Mouse preferences pane in System Preferences by selecting the Secondary Click check box. You can use the pop-up menu next to Secondary Click to set the secondary click to either left or right, adjusting the mouse for left- or right-handed users.

▶ This is probably one of the first things you should do when setting up a new Mac.

Adjusting Inertial Scrolling

The Magic Mouse and trackpads include a technology called *inertial scrolling*. With this technology, when you slide your finger down the mouse, the window keeps moving after you finish the swipe gesture, before it slows down and comes to a halt. If you want to instantly stop a window midscroll, you touch the mouse surface again.

While inertial scrolling is intuitive, some people just don't like it. If that's you, then head over to the Mouse preferences pane and change the Scroll pop-up menu to Without Inertia. You can also turn off scrolling completely by unchecking the Scroll check box.

Using Two-Finger Navigation

The Magic Mouse enables you to navigate using a two-finger swipe gesture, where you place two fingers on the surface of the mouse and quickly move them left or right. The most common use for this gesture is in web browsing software, where you can use the two-finger swipe to navigate forward and backward through web pages. However, you can also use it in Preview, iPhoto, or any other program that has been developed to support multi-touch in Mac OS X.

▶ You swipe with three fingers to navigate on a trackpad.

Using Screen Zoom

A neat navigation option is Screen Zoom, which you can find as a check box in the Mouse preferences pane. Selecting the Screen Zoom check box enables you to zoom in on the display, as shown in Figure 14-1, by holding down the Ctrl key and using the single-finger scrolling gesture on the mouse (Ctrl+slide up to zoom in or Ctrl+slide down to zoom out).

Screen zoomed in

FIGURE 14-1: Screen Zoom enables you to zoom in on parts of the screen.

MAKING PRESENTATIONS GREAT

Screen Zoom is a fantastic tool to use when doing demonstrations or tutorials in Mac OS X. It enables you to highlight certain areas of the screen and show details of the display up close.

To view some controls for zooming, you click Options. You can change the modifier key and determine how you move around the zoomed in screen (either continuously with the pointer, when the pointer reaches the edge of the screen, or so the pointer remains near the center of the screen). A final Smooth Images check box (enabled by default) smoothes the pixels of the image as you zoom in.

Extending Magic Mouse Gestures

Owners of the highly versatile multi-touch Magic Trackpad and Mac notebook users are aware that the number and complexity of gestures available on the trackpad far exceed those of the Magic Mouse. In some ways, this makes sense; after all, the large surface area of Apple trackpads makes it easy to use two-, three-, or even four-fingered gestures. Conversely the small, thin stature of the Magic Mouse limits you to just two-fingered gestures. And even then, you can't use the two-fingered pinch-to-zoom function available to trackpad owners.

You can use a free program called MagicPrefs (http://magicprefs.com) to expand and customize the gestures available on a Magic Mouse, making it even more versatile than the unaltered multi-touch trackpad. The MagicPrefs preferences pane (accessed through System Preferences or the MagicPrefs icon in the menu bar) offers a graphical display of the mouse and three tabs, as shown in Figure 14-2.

▶ MagicPrefs is installed as a preferences pane in System Preferences, along with another preferences pane called MagicMenu.

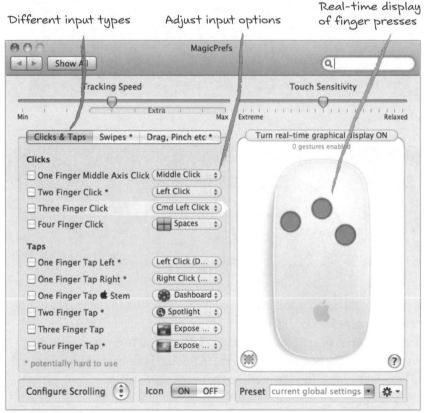

FIGURE 14-2: MagicPrefs enables you to customize the multi-touch gestures used on a Magic Mouse.

Each tab provides a variety of check boxes that enables new gestures. You can use corresponding pop-up menus to assign system functions to those gestures:

> **WARNING** Be careful when adjusting two-finger taps because Mac OS X assigns this as a left-click by default, and you might find it difficult to perform left-clicks accurately.

It's easy to get carried away with all the different options available in MagicPrefs, so it's important to keep some sense of control over your mouse. Adding too many complex gestures is a sure way to become frustrated. Add new gestures sparingly, and wait until you're used to them before adding more. You can use the real-time graphical display to test out finger movements while setting up gestures.

USING MAGICMENU

MagicMenu is an additional preferences pane placed alongside MagicPrefs that offers shortcuts to four actions. By default, these are set to Cut, Copy, Hide All Other Windows, and Unhide All. However, as with MagicPrefs, you can assign all kinds of Mac OS X features to the four slots.

So far we've looked at multi-touch on a mouse, and while this is cool, it's nowhere near as cool as the multi-touch gestures you can perform on the large glass Apple trackpads. This is what comes next.

AMAZING MULTI-TOUCH TRACKPAD TRICKS

Apple's multi-touch trackpad enables you to perform complex gestures using up to four fingers. All current Apple notebooks, with the exception of the MacBook Air, possess a single large glass trackpad. Depressing the surface of this trackpad causes a single click. To move the pointer and perform other gestures, you can lightly tap the trackpad's surface. Even if you have a desktop Mac, you can join in with the multi-touch activity by using a Magic Trackpad, which is a wireless trackpad device that sits on your desk.

▶ The MacBook Air has a more traditional trackpad with a separate button at the bottom, but it offers the same four-finger gesture function as the other notebook trackpads.

You can view and adjust the gestures available in Mac OS X by using the Trackpad preferences pane in System Preferences, as shown in Figure 14-3.

FIGURE 14-3: You can activate and adjust multi-touch gestures by using the Trackpad preferences pane.

By using the Trackpad preferences pane, you can adjust a variety of gestures, using a different number of fingers. These gestures are described in the following sections.

One-Finger Gestures

By default, all single-finger gestures are turned off, and using just one finger on the trackpad moves the pointer around the display. However, on a Mac notebook with a glass trackpad (or using a Magic Trackpad) you also have these options:

▶ **Tap to Click:** This option lets you lightly tap the trackpad to perform a left-click.

▶ **Dragging and Drag Lock:** This setting lets you double-click a window's toolbar to drag it around. With the Drag Lock check box activated, you can double-click a second time to return to moving just the pointer.

▶ **Secondary Click:** By default, the way to access a right-click with a trackpad is via the two-finger secondary click method or to Ctrl+click. The Secondary Click option divides the trackpad in half, with the lower-right half providing a secondary click; this option will be more familiar to owners of Windows PC laptops.

▶ The Secondary Click pop-up menu enables you to assign the secondary click to the bottom left or bottom right of the trackpad.

After you master one-finger gestures, you can explore more complex gestures.

Two-Finger Gestures

The two-finger gestures are all active by default. The following gestures are available:

▶ **Scroll:** This option enables you to move two fingers up and down to scroll windows.

▶ **Rotate:** This option enables you to move two fingers clockwise or counter-clockwise to rotate images and documents in supporting applications.

▶ iPhoto and Preview, for example.

▶ **Pinch Open & Close:** This option enables you to move two fingers in or out to zoom in or out of supporting documents.

▶ **Screen Zoom:** This option enables you to hold down Ctrl and move two fingers up to zoom in the screen. You can select Options to choose a different modifier key.

▶ **Secondary Click:** This option enables you to hold two fingers on the trackpad and click with your thumb (or any other convenient finger) to perform a secondary (or right-) click.

Most of these settings are fine set to their defaults, although some people might prefer to turn them off.

Three-Finger Gestures

There is only one three-finger gesture check box, but its pop-up menu provides two distinct options:

▶ **Swipe to Navigate:** This default option enables you to perform navigation tasks in supporting applications by placing three fingers on the trackpad and moving them quickly left or right.

▶ In the Safari web browser, for example, you can navigate to the previous page and next page using this option.

▶ **Dragging:** This option lets you drag a window by holding three fingers over the window's toolbar.

Both of these are useful functions, and you might have some difficulty choosing between them. Personally, I stick with Swipe to Navigate, but you should try them both to see which works best for you.

Four-Finger Gestures

Using four-finger gestures may seem somewhat overkill, but you'd be surprised how incredibly useful these gestures are. Because using four fingers in a complicated gesture would be tricky, the gestures are fairly simple: Basically, you just swipe horizontally or vertically. By using these gestures, you can perform the following tricks:

▶ **Swipe Up/Down for Exposé:** This option enables you to put all four fingers on the trackpad and push up to move all windows out of the way and reveal the Desktop. You can slide your fingers down to reveal all windows using Exposé.

▶ **Swipe Left/Right to Switch Applications:** Swiping all four fingers left or right brings up the Application Switcher. You can use the pointer or press Tab to move along the applications and press Enter to select one.

▶ Application Switcher is an opaque overlay with icons for all active applications. You can also open it by pressing ⌘+Tab.

These are two of my favorite gestures in Mac OS X, and the four-finger up and down move for Exposé alone is worth the price of a Magic Trackpad.

Multi-Touch Trackpad Gestures

Although Mac OS X offers a range of options for trackpad gestures, it's possible to extend them even further by using a program called Jitouch (http://www.jitouch.com). Jitouch installs as a preferences pane and enables a wide range of gestures, as shown in Figure 14-4.

Some of these gestures can be quite intricate. For example, you can place one finger on the trackpad and move another two fingers down to close a window. If you hover the pointer over a gesture in the list, a small preview window appears that uses red dots to demonstrate the appropriate finger gestures. Double-clicking a gesture in the list brings up a dialog that enables you to change the action caused by the gesture.

Now that you have explored multi-touch gestures with a mouse and trackpad, it's time to take a look at what is possible with the keyboard.

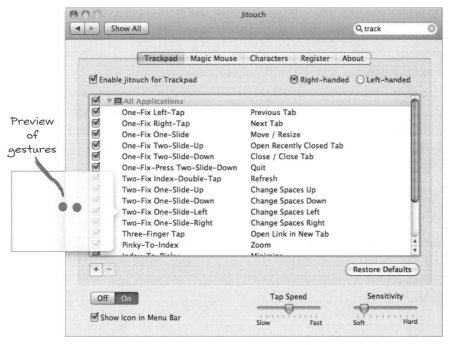

Preview
of
gestures

FIGURE 14-4: Jitouch vastly expands the number and complexity of multi-touch gestures.

LEARNING KEYBOARD TIPS AND SHORTCUTS

When it comes to input, most computer users massively underestimate the keyboard. Talking about the humble keyboard is like describing water to a fish; it's so omnipresent most of us don't think much about it. But it needn't be this way. While you're unlikely to need any instruction on using a keyboard, a few tricks and tips will help you get more out of it. You can start this exploration by firing up the Keyboard preferences pane in System Preferences and taking a look at the options under the Keyboard tab, described next.

Controlling Function Keys

By default, most Mac keyboards use the function keys for Mac OS X–specific control keys, such as volume, screen brightness, Exposé and Dashboard, and so on. To access the function key, you hold down the fn button on the keyboard (located above the

Delete button on an Apple Keyboard with Numerical Buttons, or to the left of the Ctrl key on a smaller Apple Wireless Keyboard).

▶ You use the fn key to select the alternate choice, either a function key or Mac OS X-specific control key, depending on the chosen setting.

Selecting the Use All F1, F2, Etc. Keys As Standard Function Keys check box enables the function keys to be the default instead.

Many applications map shortcuts to function keys, so if you use a certain application a lot, it may be more useful to have quick access to function keys instead of the Mac OS X–specific control key shortcuts. Plus, Mac OS X uses function keys to provide different types of shortcuts than the Mac OS X–specific control keys, so you may find it more useful to use the function key shortcuts than the regular shortcuts.

Using the Keyboard and Character Viewer

The Keyboard preferences pane provides the option Show Keyboard & Character Viewer in Menu Bar. Selecting this check box places an icon in the menu bar that enables you to access the Keyboard Viewer and Character Viewer, which are described in the following sections.

USING THE KEYBOARD VIEWER

To open the Keyboard Viewer, from the menu bar, you click the Show Keyboard Viewer from the Keyboard and Character Viewer icon. The Keyboard Viewer is a window that displays all the keys on your keyboard, as shown in Figure 14-5.

FIGURE 14-5: You can use the Keyboard Viewer to enter keystrokes and get a visual overview of the keyboard.

As you type on the keyboard, the keys on the Keyboard Viewer flash to indicate key presses. In addition, you can use Keyboard Viewer to input characters at the point of the cursor (in a text document or in a filename, for example) by clicking the virtual keys onscreen. You can use this method as if you were pressing the keys on the keyboard. Although this might sound a little odd (why not use the actual keyboard?), it comes in handy if a key on the keyboard fails or if you want to get a visual overview, and usage, of a keyboard from another language.

ACCESSING A FOREIGN KEYBOARD

You can use the Keyboard Viewer to access keyboard layouts from different languages by using the Input Sources preference pane. Choose Apple ➔ System Preferences and click Language & Text and then Input Sources. Input Sources lists all the available keyboard layouts. Select the ones you want from the list, and they will appear as an option underneath the Keyboard & Text menu bar icon.

When you choose more than one layout, the Keyboard & Text menu bar icon turns into a flag denoting the current language. Choosing a different language from the menu bar causes both the flag and the keyboard layout to change. You can use the Keyboard Viewer to see the new keyboard layout, as shown in Figure 14-6.

FIGURE 14-6: You can use the Keyboard Viewer to see the keyboard layouts from different languages, such as Arabic.

> **TIP** Holding down the modifier keys (particularly Option and Shift+Option) with the Keyboard Viewer visible displays the characters associated with the different keys. This is a great trick if you need to find an obscure character (such as ∑, °, or) or simply want to learn the keyboard layout in more detail.

You can change the keyboard layout on your physical keyboard as well as on the Keyboard Viewer, so all your key presses will correspond to that language.

INSERTING SYMBOLS WITH THE CHARACTER VIEWER

The Character Viewer enables you to browse all the different characters and symbols available to Mac OS X, as shown in Figure 14-7, and insert them into documents. To open Character Viewer, choose Show Character Viewer from the Keyboard & Character Viewer menu.

▶ You can also access the Character Viewer from the Finder menu by choosing Edit ➔ Special Characters.

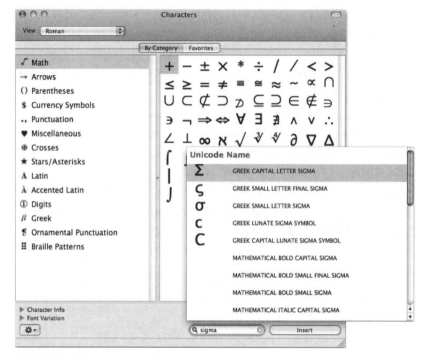

FIGURE 14-7: The Character Viewer enables you to search, browse, and insert characters into documents.

The View pop-up menu enables you to choose from different types of character sets, based on the alphabet: Roman, Japanese, Traditional Chinese, Korean, and Simplified Chinese. You can also choose Code Tables, PI Fonts, and Glyphs.

You double-click a character to insert it into the document at the position of the cursor; alternatively, you can drag and drop symbols from the Character Viewer to Mac OS X windows.

▶ You can also choose All Characters if you really want to browse the thousands available.

> **TIP** It is possible to search for particular symbols using the search text box at the bottom of the Character Viewer window. A lot of characters have descriptive terms, and you'll find this method useful if you're looking for a character whose name you know. So if you know that Σ means "sigma," searching for "sigma" brings up the Σ character, although some, like pi, don't appear.

To the left of the window is a list of groups—Math, Arrows, Currency Symbols, and so on—that can help you narrow your search.

Working with Keyboard Shortcuts

Most users are intimately familiar with keyboard shortcuts, perhaps even to the point of not realizing they're using them. By using these key combinations to perform menu commands, you can save a lot of trouble related to navigating through the menu structure. Many shortcuts (such as ⌘+S for Save) are virtually universal, used in every application that has a save function.

FINDING SHORTCUTS

You can get a fairly comprehensive overview of the keyboard shortcuts used in Mac OS X, and most of its applications, by using Mac OS X's built-in Help viewer. For example, in Safari, you can choose Help → Safari Help and type *shortcuts* into the search text box. The Help results will contain a reference for all the shortcuts available to that application, as shown in Figure 14-8.

Another technique for learning keyboard shortcuts is to keep an eye on the menu bar. If a keyboard shortcut is available for a menu bar item, it appears next to the item.

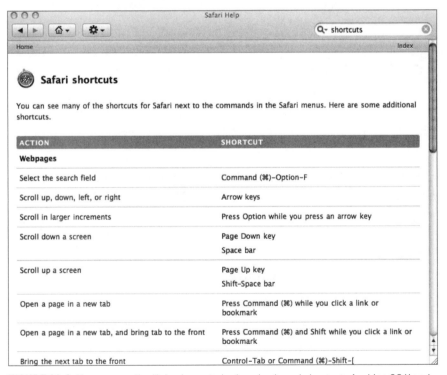

FIGURE 14-8: You can use the Help viewer to look up keyboard shortcuts for Mac OS X and just about every application.

CREATING SHORTCUTS

It is possible to create your own keyboard shortcuts for menu bar items by using the Keyboard preferences pane, as shown in Figure 14-9.

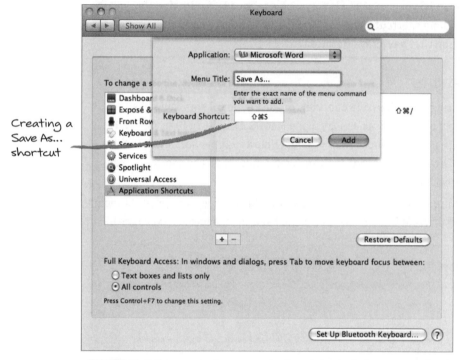

Creating a
Save As...
shortcut

FIGURE 14-9: You can create your own keyboard shortcuts for every application in Mac OS X.

For some inexplicable reason, Microsoft Word 2008 doesn't have a Save As short-cut (which in many applications is mapped to Shift+⌘+S). To set up a Save As shortcut in Word, you do the following:

1. Choose Apple ➜ System Preferences, click Keyboard, and select the Keyboard Shortcuts tab.

2. Click the Add (+) button at the bottom of the window.

3. Scroll down the list of applications and choose Other.

4. Navigate to the Microsoft Word application, using Finder, and click Add.

5. Type **Save As...** in the Menu Title shortcut bar. Note that this must match the menu item exactly, including the ellipsis, which forms part of the name.

6. Highlight the Keyboard Shortcut text field and press the key combination that you want to use for the shortcut. Click Add.

> **WARNING** Changing a keyboard shortcut will overwrite the existing shortcut in the Application. You can use the Remove (-) button to remove the new shortcut, which will revert to the original or press Restore Defaults to restore the original settings in Keyboard Shortcuts.

The shortcut is now added to the Microsoft Word menu bar. When you use Microsoft Word, you can now save documents and specify the filename using the keyboard shortcut you just created.

Navigating Mac OS X with the Keyboard

Did you know that by using some common keyboard shortcuts that work across all applications, you can perform much—although not all—of the navigation you need without ever touching the mouse or trackpad? Table 14-1 lists the keyboard shortcuts you can use to navigate around Finder and windows, all without using the mouse.

TABLE 14-1: Keyboard and Text Input Shortcuts

KEYBOARD SHORTCUT	COMMAND
↑ ↓ ← →	Move around highlighted items (Desktop icons, dock icons, Exposé windows, and so on)
F9 Exposé	Display all Windows with Exposé
F10 Ctrl+Exposé	Display Application Windows with Exposé
F11 ⌘+Exposé	Display the Desktop with Exposé
F5	Access spaces
F12 Dashboard	Move to the Dashboard
Apple+Esc	Open Front row
Ctrl+F7	Change the Tab focus
Ctrl+F2	Move the focus to the menu bar
Ctrl+F3	Move the focus to the Dock

continues

TABLE 14-1: Keyboard and Text Input Shortcuts *(continued)*

KEYBOARD SHORTCUT	COMMAND
Ctrl+F4	Move the focus to the next window
Ctrl+F5	Move the focus to the floating window toolbar
Ctrl+F6	Move the focus to the next floating window
⌘+`	Move the focus to the previous window in the application
Shift+⌘+`	Move to the next window in the application
Option+⌘+`	Move the focus to the window drawer
Ctrl+F8	Move the focus to status menus
Tab	Move focus to the next item
⌘+Tab	Open Application Switcher (and on subsequent presses, move to the next application)

CROSSREF Chapter 2 has more information on working ergonomically to avoid problems with RSI and other computer-related injuries.

TIP Holding down Option and pressing any of the Mac OS X–specific control keys (Dashboard, Screen Brightness, and so on) opens System Preferences at the preferences pane that shows controls for that function. Pressing Alt+Screen Brightness opens the Display preferences pane, for example.

Learning these keyboard shortcuts will help you move around Mac OS X much faster and with less effort than using a mouse. There are also good ergonomic reasons for using the keyboard more than using the mouse.

Navigating with Quicksilver

An application worth mentioning for keyboard buffs is called Quicksilver (http://blacktree.com/?quicksilver). This application lays a translucent interface over the top of Mac OS X, enabling you to perform just about every task in Mac OS X without once touching the mouse.

Quicksilver works is via a keyboard shortcut trigger (by default, Ctrl+spacebar). Pressing this shortcut brings up a control box that displays two squares. The first square is for an item (for example, an application, a folder, or a document), and the second square is for a command. You start typing to locate the item for the first square, and then press Tab and type the command. For example, to open iTunes, you'd activate Quicksilver, type **itunes**, press Tab, and type **open**; to quit iTunes, you'd type **itunes**, press Tab, and type **quit**.

> **NOTE** As with Spotlight, you don't have to type the full command name. You can shorten iTunes to just **it** and quit to just **q**.

With a bit of practice, you can use Quicksilver to perform all kinds of tasks. For example, you can create a folder called *letters* on the Desktop by typing *desktop*, *new*, *folder*, *letters* (pressing tab between each item).

Control is often something that is performed on the mouse, or trackpad, with data entry restricted to the keyboard. But with a few tweaks and some practice, you can gain a remarkable level of control in Mac OS X without ever letting your hands leave the keyboard. This is a much faster way of working, and is beloved by many developers and programmers. Personally, I like using the Magic Mouse and multi-touch features on a trackpad too much to spend all my time on the keyboard, but a few shortcuts here and there make using a Mac much more fun.

> ▶ Quicksilver is incredibly popular, although the original creator of the program no longer works on it. Google hosts the code at http://code.google.com/p/blacktree-alchemy. Because of this, it may not always be supported.

SUMMARY

How you interact with your computer is incredibly important, and Apple makes it a high priority by creating superb devices like the Magic Mouse and multi-touch track-pads. Apple is keen on multi-touch, but you might find using a multi-touch Magic Mouse or trackpad strange at first. Even seasoned Mac fans may not know every input trick. The time you'll save is well worth becoming familiar with multi-touch and using programs such as MagicPrefs and Jitouch to customize the available gestures. The keyboard is another area that often goes overlooked, but it's possible to gain a lot of control of Mac OS X without taking your fingers off the keys. If you want to get the most out of Mac OS X, it's a great idea to discover and personalize keyboard shortcuts. And if you really want to take keyboard control to the next level, you should take the time to learn the built-in keyboard controls and investigate the fantastic Quicksilver application.

Why Security Matters on a Mac

Take pity on the poor PC fools with their expensive security software! Seriously, you can have a good chortle because, compared to Windows users, you've really got it easy on the Mac. Infectious viruses are virtually nonexistent, and other types of malicious software—such as spyware, malware, and adware—are far less common on the Mac OS X platform. But you shouldn't be completely cavalier with regard to security. There are plenty of malicious people out there with clever plans to part you from your data and money, and not every scheme they have requires hacking into Mac OS X. Good security isn't just about the Internet. You also need to think about keeping your information safe in case somebody physically accesses your Mac, either when you're not around or if your notebook goes missing. It's possible to lock down Mac OS X tighter than a bank vault, but with a bit of sense, you can find a great compromise between keeping your data safe and using Mac OS X easily. But first you need to know what kind of threats are out there.

IDENTIFYING MAC THREATS

When learning about security, it's easy to become bamboozled by the variety of terms, such as *malware*, *spyware*, *adware*, or *rootkits*. All are mysterious-sounding terms that can strike fear into the hearts of computer users.

Threats to modern computer users come in two main forms: malicious software and Internet scams. Here's a guide to some of the most common terms being bandied around:

▶ **Malware:** This is a catch-all term for any kind of malicious software. As with any other computer program, the design and purpose of malware can be quite varied. The following are some of the possibilities:

   ▷ **Infectious virus:** This is designed to hide on a computer and pass itself from one computer to another via local networks and by hijacking e-mail programs to send messages containing the virus to people in your address book.

   ▷ **Trojan horse:** This is a malicious program that hides inside another program that you may intentionally install. The genuine program may have been designed to hold the Trojan, or the Trojan may have been inserted into a genuine program and distributed via the Internet.

   ▷ **Rootkit:** This is a tool that is designed to take over the administrator-level access of a computer.

   ▷ **Adware:** Like a Trojan horse, this is installed alongside a more innocuous program but is designed to surreptitiously deliver advertisements.

▶ **Internet scams:** Due to the cross-platform nature of the Internet, scams are somewhat more relevant than viruses to Mac users. Internet scams may include the following:

   ▷ **Password phishing:** This is a common scam that fools you into visiting a fake website that looks like a real website (such as eBay or PayPal) and gets you to enter your login and password details. The phishers then use your account to order goods or send messages from your account to other users in an attempt to scam them. The fake sites are also referred to as *pharming sites*.

   ▷ **Identity theft:** Essentially, with identity theft, websites try to get your personal information so they can use it for nefarious purposes. Of course, people can also try to steal your identity by other methods, such as via email or by stealing paper documents.

▶ Part of the paranoia is a result of security firms trying to convince users that they really need security software. But paranoia or not, there are still real threats out there.

▶ For a list of the sort of threats you could come across, see www.iantivirus.com/threats.

▶ According to the Federal Trade Commission, nine million Americans suffer identity theft each year (www.ftc.gov/bcp/edu/microsites/idtheft).

▷ **Money scam:** You're likely to see everything from Nigerian billionaires to free holidays and free iPads. All this and more will be waiting for you once the scammers get your e-mail address. Nothing is free on the Internet, and if it sounds too good to be true, it's almost certainly a lie.

▷ **Security breach:** This is a relatively new problem that first affected iPhone owners, but it now seems to be moving to Mac OS X. A website exploits a flaw (typically in Adobe's PDF or Flash technology) to install software directly in Mac OS X. Apple and Adobe are fixing these problems as they arise, but they have the potential to be quite serious.

So this is what you're up against. Although some of these threats are more problematic to Mac OS X users than to others, you're highly unlikely to come across an infectious virus or any form of malware. However, phishing and identity theft are problems that affect everybody, and the security breaches are seemingly on the rise.

TIP Be sure to use Software Update frequently. Apple frequently delivers updates that protect against a range of security breach threats.

The following sections include some tips for protecting yourself against such threats.

Installing Security Software

There's a whole "should you or shouldn't you?" decision to be made when it comes to security software, and it's clear that this is a hot topic among Mac owners. Very little malicious software affects Mac OS X, and you are unlikely to encounter malware, viruses, rootkits, and adware on the Mac. Never say never, though; it might happen one day. So you still might want the peace of mind that security software offers.

▶ Many Mac owners remain convinced that security software for the Mac is the technological equivalent of snake oil.

Even if you never find yourself the target of malicious software, you may be unwittingly receiving malware from Windows users and passing it on to your Windows-using friends. While the "they should buy a proper computer" argument may seem logical, it doesn't excuse you from the social faux pas of passing on malware to other users.

Here are four programs you might want to look at:

▶ **iAntiVirus (www.iantivirus.com):** This free program, shown in Figure 15-1, protects against the few malware programs that have been developed for the Mac. (iAntivirus lists 113 potential threats at the time of this writing.)

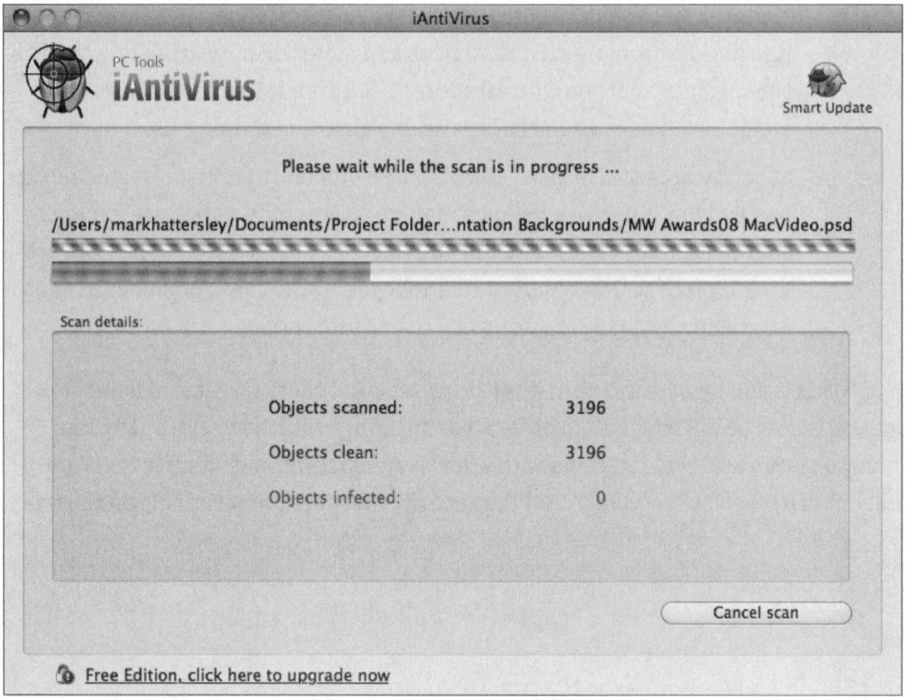

FIGURE 15-1: You can use antivirus software to check files and folders in Mac OS X for contaminated items.

It offers relatively little protection against other threats but is free and lightweight, running in the background with little impact on Mac OS X performance.

▶ **ClamX AV (www.clamxav.com):** This is another free virus checker of considerable repute. Apple includes ClamX AV with its Mac OS X Server software.

▶ **McAfee VirusScan for Mac (www.mcafee.com):** McAfee VirusScan is a comprehensive commercial solution that scans files and folders as they are accessed and identifies any emerging malware.

▶ **Intego Internet Security Barrier (www.intego.com):** Intego specializes in Mac security, and Security Barrier is a commercial program that contains antivirus and malware technology for both Mac OS X and Windows running on a Mac. It also offers enhanced parental controls, anti-spam, and firewall technology.

Whether or not you decide to install antivirus software is very much a personal choice. Viruses aren't quite the problem for Mac users as they are for Windows users, as explained in the sidebar "Why Are Macs Safer Than PCs?"

WHY ARE MACS SAFER THAN PCS?

The battle about whether security is as serious for Mac owners as for Windows users has raged for years. One argument is that the Windows market is simply bigger than the Mac market and that it makes commercial sense for malicious developers to focus on Windows.

One thing's for sure: There are no infectious viruses in the wild for Mac OS X, but there does seem to be a rise in malware. Two Trojans have hit the headlines in recent years (OSX.Trojan.iServices versions A and B). However, in order to install these Trojans, you had to have installed pirated versions of iWork '09 or Adobe Photoshop CS4.

Some malware is also distributed with video codecs (files added to QuickTime and other video players to play specific video types). So if you're looking at sites hosting pirated or otherwise dubious video, it's wise to install antivirus software and do not install the codecs that those sites recommend.

To be safe—and legal—don't use pirated software. Trust me, you'll be better off in the long run.

▶ I have little doubt that Macs are more secure than Windows PCs. With its UNIX foundation, Mac OS X has serious security features built in: Password-protected installation and sandboxed memory make life difficult for those with malicious intent.

Turning Off Administrator Access

By default, the account you use in Mac OS X has administrator rights. This gives you the power to install software, modify accounts, and modify files and folders system-wide. These aren't things you do all the time, so you shouldn't use an administrator account for day-to-day work.

Instead, you should create a second administrator account and remove administrator rights from your current account. To do so, follow these steps:

1. Choose Apple ➜ System Preferences and click Accounts.

2. Click the small lock icon in the bottom left of the window and enter your administrator details.

▶ Alternatively, create a second standard account and use that as a day-to-day account. If you do that, all your files (documents, iTunes music, and so on) will be in the admin account.

3. Click the Add (+) button to create a new account. Choose Administrator from the New Account drop-down menu and fill out the Name, Account Name, Password, and Verify text fields.

4. Click Create Account.

5. Highlight your current account in the My Account list and deselect the Allow User to Administer This Computer check box.

6. A dialog appears, warning you to restart your computer. Click OK and choose Apple → Restart.

▶ You don't need to log out and back in to use the administrator account. You can simply enter those account details when prompted.

Now you can log in using your regular account for day-to-day work and use the administrator account to perform additional functions.

Setting General Security Preferences

The Security preferences pane includes a number of options that you can use to add more security to your Mac. Open the Security preferences pane and click the General tab. Consider the following options:

▶ **Require Password:** You select this check box to require a password after Mac OS X goes to sleep or activates a screen saver.

▶ **Disable Automatic Login:** You select this check box to require a password whenever you log in.

▶ **Require a Password to Unlock Each System Preferences Pane:** You select this check box to require a password to access and change any preferences.

▶ **Log Out After:** This option lets you enter a period of time after which Mac OS X will automatically log out. You'll need to enter a password to log back in, which is useful if you leave your computer unattended.

▶ **Use Secure Virtual Memory:** This option protects sensitive data as it gets swapped from RAM to virtual memory.

▶ **Disable Location Services:** This option lets Mac OS X determine your position in relationship to nearby networks. Select this check box to turn off this feature.

▶ **Disable Remote Control Infrared Services:** It is possible to control a Mac by using an Apple remote to access Front Row and to control Keynote presentations. You can select this check box to prevent other people from using remote controls with your Mac.

> **TIP** You can pair an Apple remote control by clicking Pair in the Security preferences pane. This is handy if you are going to be making presentations in a public arena, such as a trade show. Mischievous Mac fans have been known to use Apple remotes to mess around with Macs during presentations.

Which of these preferences you decide to implement or turn off is largely a personal preference, based on how easily you want to be able to use your Mac versus how protective you are of your data. I suggest turning on password protection and secure virtual memory and disabling automatic login. However, I find having to enter a password for each preferences pane—instead of just important ones like Accounts and Security—to be overkill. Location services and infrared services are both useful to me, but your mileage may vary.

SECURING YOUR NETWORK

Modern computers are great, and one of the best things that ever happened to computing is networking: the linking together of computers to share data with each other. It's also the worst thing that ever happened to security, because it enables computers to remotely access data, even data that you might not want to share. You can help keep your Mac secure by setting up a firewall and keeping an eye on the Sharing preferences pane.

▶ A firewall blocks unauthorized connections from a local network and the wider Internet.

Setting Up a Firewall in Mac OS X

Mac OS X comes with built-in firewall software that can be turned on in the Security preferences pane. Follow these instructions to turn on the firewall:

1. Choose Apple ➜ System Preferences, click Security, and then click Firewall.

2. Click Start to turn on the firewall.

3. Click Advanced to fine-tune the firewall, and set the following, as shown in Figure 15-2:

   ▷ **Block All Incoming Connections:** You can select this check box have the firewall block all incoming connections.

   ▷ **Choose connections:** The main window lists all applications and file sharing and screen sharing functions. You can determine which ones should allow or deny incoming connections by using the menu next to each application or function.

▶ Exceptions are made for DHCP, Bonjour, and IPSec, so basic Internet functions such as web access and e-mail still work.

▷ **Add/remove application:** You can add or remove applications to and from the main window by using the Add (+) and Remove (-) icons.

▷ **Automatically Allow Signed Software to Receive Incoming Connections:** If you select this check box, Mac OS X allows exceptions for signed software.

▷ **Enable Stealth Mode:** Hackers sometimes locate computers by sending a query to every network port. You can select the Enable Stealth Mode check box to get Mac OS X to ignore such requests.

▶ Signed software has been validated and digitally signed by a trusted certificate authority, such as VeriSign (www.verisign.com).

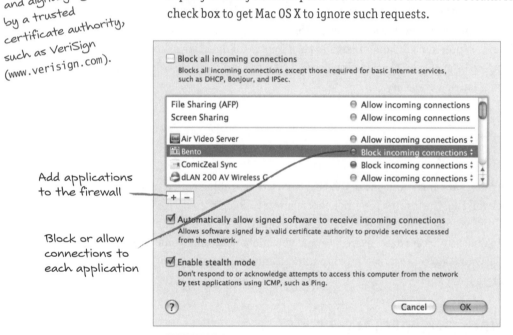

Add applications to the firewall

Block or allow connections to each application

FIGURE 15-2: You use the Mac OS X firewall to protect your computer from malicious incoming connections.

It's important to note that the firewall in Mac OS X is relatively light on features compared to professional options, such as NetBarrier (part of the VirusBarrier X6 suite of applications, www.intego.com/virusbarrier) and Little Snitch (www.obdev.at/products/littlesnitch). The Mac OS X built-in firewall doesn't provide any information on traffic and only prevents incoming connections. It doesn't monitor or prevent unwanted outgoing traffic. So if your Mac has been compromised and is sending out malicious code to other computers, the Mac OS X firewall will not prevent it.

Stopping Sharing

By default, the Mac OS X firewall doesn't prevent problems related to using Sharing preferences, as shown in Figure 15-3. Therefore, you should remove any sharing services you aren't frequently using.

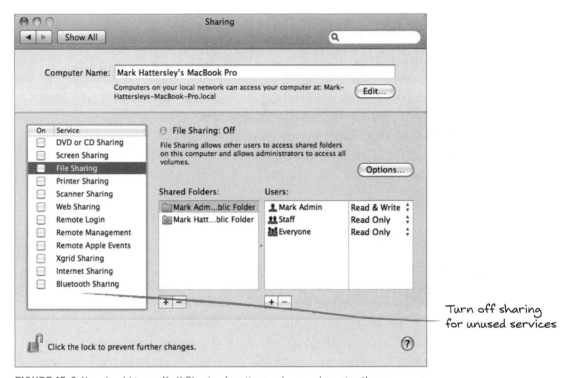

Turn off sharing for unused services

FIGURE 15-3: You should turn off all Sharing functions unless you're using them.

You follow these steps to turn off sharing services:

1. Choose Apple ➔ System Preferences and click Sharing to access the Sharing preferences pane.

2. Click the lock icon in the bottom of the Sharing preferences pane and enter an administrator name and password.

3. All the different services are in a list on the left side of the Sharing preferences pane. Use the check boxes to deactivate any preferences that aren't currently being used.

4. Click the lock icon to prevent any further changes from being made and close System Preferences.

Some sharing options, such as file sharing and screen sharing, can be very useful, and you might want to consider whether you'll need these functions before turning them off. And remote access functions—by their very nature—can't be turned on when you're not near your Mac, so remember to turn them on if you must remotely access Mac OS X.

KEEPING FILES SAFE FROM PRYING EYES

It's one thing to protect your Mac from network intrusions, but you should also consider keeping the data on your Mac safe from physical access. Using the Account preferences pane to require login whenever the screen saver appears and to log you out automatically after a period of inactivity are both good moves. But if you have sensitive data on your Mac, you should consider further security measures, as described next.

Turning On FileVault

There is a performance hit, but it's typically not big enough for you to notice.

FileVault is a Mac OS X technology that encrypts and decrypts files as you use them. It does this seamlessly in the background, and you almost certainly won't notice it at work. FileVault works by turning your entire home folder into a large single encrypted file. You need to set and use a master password (which is independent from your account login) to turn FileVault on, as shown in Figure 15-4.

You really should perform a full backup prior to using FileVault. Although you can back up post-FileVault, there are some challenges. You can use backup software such as Time Machine, but be aware that Time Machine can only be used to backup a FileVault volume when you are logged out from the account, so you will need to set up a separate account for performing backups. Also, Time Machine can restore only the entire FileVault file, not individual files.

> **WARNING** Because FileVault turns the entire folder into a single file, you need to be careful when using backup software other than Time Machine. Some backup software records the entire file every time it changes (which is every time you use it), and because the file is generally large, the backups take a long time and fill up hard drive space quickly. Time Machine is able to work with FileVault—at least on operating systems post Mac OS X v10.5—but other programs such as EMC Retrospect include options to ignore backup of FileVault files.

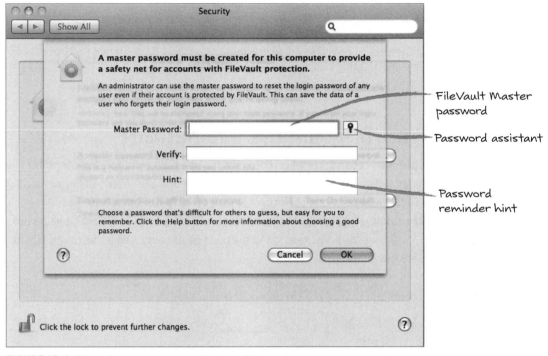

FileVault Master
password

Password assistant

Password
reminder hint

FIGURE 15-4: FileVault encrypts your entire home folder using a master password.

You follow these steps to turn on FileVault:

1. Open the Security preferences pane by choosing Apple ➔ System Preferences. Then click Security and FileVault.

2. Click Set Master Password. You are prompted for your administrator account and password. After entering them, enter a master password for FileVault.

3. Click Turn On FileVault. FileVault can take a long time to set up, so it's best to leave your Mac running overnight.

> **TIP** When using FileVault to encrypt an account, I recommend setting up a second account with administrator privileges. You can then use this account to access and manage the FileVault-protected account if any problems arise.

FileVault is quite a serious data protection solution, and you should consider whether you really require it.

WARNING Your master password should be memorable, and you should write it down and keep it in a safe place. Do not forget or lose your master password because without it, you may lose the data on your Mac OS X system completely. We discuss memorable passwords later in the chapter.

Protecting Individual Files with Passwords

If encrypting an entire drive feels like overkill, you might want to consider protecting individual files. There are a few programs out there that enable you to password-protect individual files. One of the best is Crypt (www.dekorte.com/projects/shareware/Crypt). Crypt copies a file or folder into an encrypted file with a password, as shown in Figure 15-5. The encrypted file must be unencrypted using Crypt, which then re-creates the original file.

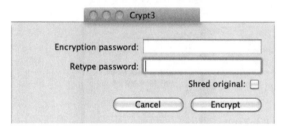

FIGURE 15-5: You can use Crypt to create password-protected files.

TIP Crypt duplicates files rather than encrypting the originals. Make sure you select the Shred Original check box to remove the original file or drag it to the Trash and use Secure Empty Trash.

You can also use Disk Utility to create a password-protected disk image. You choose 128-bit or 256-bit from the Encryption drop-down menu when creating a disk image, and then you enter a password. This way, you can create a disk image that opens as a volume in Finder but requires a password for access. You can use this image to contain any sensitive files or folders.

CROSSREF Chapter 9 has more information on using Disk Utility to create encrypted disk images.

Browsing Privately in Safari

In this increasingly online world, it's worth remembering that all the websites you've visited are recorded in Safari's History folder. It's possible to prevent this record by using Private Browsing.

To turn on Private Browsing, you choose Safari ➜ Private Browsing. If you forget to turn on Private Browsing but want to clear your online history, you choose Safari ➜ Reset Safari. The dialog shown in Figure 15-6 appears. It contains a series of check boxes that enable you to remove information cached in Safari. You simply choose the information you want to remove and click OK.

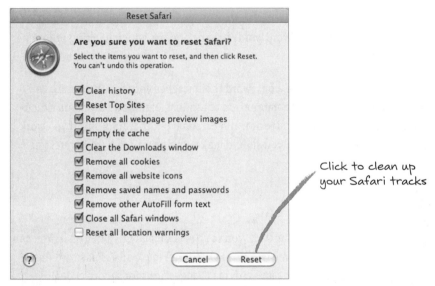

Click to clean up your Safari tracks

FIGURE 15-6: You can use the Reset Safari function to clear information Safari stores about your web activity.

A lot of the security measures we've discussed have included password protection of some form or other, and next we'll take a closer look at these.

CREATING SECURE PASSWORDS

One thing you'll notice when you take security seriously is the need for good passwords. A password has to be easy enough for you to memorize, and it needs to be quick and easy to type; but it also has to be difficult for somebody who knows you to guess, and it should be obscure enough to prevent hacking using a brute-force method.

▶ In brute-force hacking, an automated program guesses until it gets a password right. The speed with which these programs can enter passwords makes brute-force hacking extremely effective with short passwords.

Here are some tips for choosing a secure password:

▶ **Make it as long as possible.** Use a memorable quote from a movie or book instead of a single word. Inserting spaces between the words makes it more secure.

▶ **Use as many characters as possible.** Insert numbers and punctuation characters, and mix uppercase and lowercase characters.

▶ **Don't use passwords that are easy to observe.** Think about how easy it is for others to spot a password (such as *qwerty* or *12345*) as you type it.

▶ **Avoid personal information.** Don't use the name of your spouse, children, or pets.

▶ **Avoid standard words.** Avoid words in a dictionary, which hacking programs often use.

Obviously, you should choose a password that matches your requirements. You might find using a 20-character combination of random letters and numbers ridiculous for protecting your iTunes collection and personal photographs, but if you work in a data-sensitive environment, you should make your password hard to guess or crack.

Using Password Assistant

When you create a password in Mac OS X, you see a small icon with a key on it. You can click this icon to open Password Assistant, as shown in Figure 15-7. Password Assistant rates the quality of passwords and provides suggestions for secure codes.

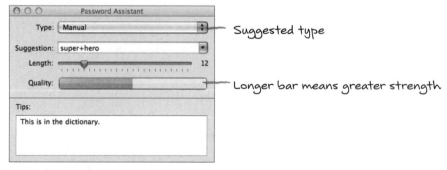

FIGURE 15-7: Password Assistant checks password strength and provides suggestions for good passwords.

A drop-down menu titled Type enables you to choose from a variety of different password types:

- ► **Manual:** This lets you enter your own password.

- ► **Memorable:** These passwords tend to be whole words mixed with punctuation that are designed to be easy to remember.

- ► **Letters and Numbers:** This is a random string of letters and numbers.

- ► **Numbers Only:** This is a random string of numbers.

- ► **Random:** This is a random collection of letters, numbers, and punctuation.

- ► **FIPS-181 Compliant:** FIPS stands for Federal Information Processing Standard, and FIPS-181 creates solid passwords based on pronounceable sounds.

> **TIP** A neat trick is to use two words with a plus (+) sign between them, such as super+hero. This creates a reasonably secure but easy-to-remember password.

Select the type of password you want and use the length slider to extend or reduce the number of letters in the password. The Quality bar at the bottom of the Password Assistant shows you how strong the password will be.

Using 1Password

A neat program to investigate is 1Password (http://agilewebsolutions.com). This application stores information on all your different passwords. You can integrate it with Safari and other web browsers and have it insert your passwords into websites as you browse. You do this by setting a master password, which is used to unlock the passwords contained within 1Password.

Hang on, I hear you say. What happens if somebody gets your master password? That person would have access to all your passwords. But to gain access to 1Password, a person has to be using your Mac (because all the data is locked up in a highly secure local file). So the chances of that happening are pretty remote.

And there are reasons 1Password is a fantastic application that will make your life much more secure and simple:

- ► **Multiple passwords:** Let's face it: Your head isn't going to be full of different passwords for every website. Instead, you're likely to have one or two passwords and use them whenever you sign up. So if an unscrupulous website

► Firefox, Safari, and Mac OS X's built-in Keychain app all store passwords, but 1Password enables you to keep them in a single, secure, password-protected location.

uses the password you've entered into it with other online services, it may get lucky. With 1Password, you can create a different password for each site.

▶ **Longer passwords:** With 1Password, you can enter large, complicated passwords because you don't have to worry about keeping them in your head.

▶ **Phishing proof:** When you use 1Password to enter a password into a site, it checks the URL against its database. If the URL is different (because you're not actually on the website but a phishing site mimicking it), 1Password will give you an error message.

1Password is an excellent program that I highly recommend. While it takes a leap of confidence to store passwords in a program on your Mac, once you find yourself managing multiple complex passwords with ease, you'll find it invaluable.

SUMMARY

Security is serious business, and Mac OS X offers a huge range of security features out of the box, designed to protect you and your information. It's important to recognize that Mac OS X's UNIX base is far more secure than other operating systems, but it's not wholly impregnable, and network attacks are increasingly becoming a concern for Mac users. Therefore, you should consider investigating security software. You should also think about creating a second account purely for administration and turning off administration functionality on the account you use. It's also a good idea to investigate Mac OS X's built-in security features, such as the firewall, FileVault, and Sharing. Finally, you should probably get a bit more serious about picking good passwords. If you want to create lots of effective passwords, be sure to investigate 1Password, which is a highly regarded program that enables you to manage multiple passwords from one place.

PART III

BECOMING A DIGITAL GENIUS

Managing Digital Music and Audio

Managing music and audio, along with digital video and photographs, is a major part of the modern computing experience. Much of this is now managed in Mac OS X with iTunes. iTunes is a fantastically powerful and increasingly complex program, and it's likely that you've missed some—if not many—of its nuances. As well as managing music, iTunes also manages video and the applications and other data used in Apple's iPod, iPhone, and iPad devices. We'll take a look at Apple's "iDevices" in Chapter 19, but it's worth knowing some really neat tricks for getting the most out of iTunes—especially with regard to its original purpose: managing music and audio.

MANAGING THE ITUNES MUSIC LIBRARY

In many ways, iTunes is a great application because it enables you to manage and tag music files, and browse and organize them in a much better way than Finder allows.

The flipside of this is that you interact with your music through iTunes, not through Finder, which can make managing the original files a complicated process. It also makes moving and managing the files in Finder tricky, because changes made in iTunes may not always have the desired effect in Finder, and changes made in Finder may interfere with the operation in iTunes.

iTunes stores music and all the associated tags and other files (such as album artwork) in a folder called iTunes, located within the Music folder in your Home folder, as shown in Figure 16-1. Depending on your iTunes preference settings, your music will either be all in the iTunes Media folder or scattered around Finder, with iTunes referencing the original files.

▶ All information associated with a file beyond the filename—such as artist info, song name, rating, and genre—is referred to as a tag.

▶ Prior to iTunes 9, the iTunes Media folder was called iTunes Music. Your folder may still use this name if you upgraded from a previous version.

iTunes folder

FIGURE 16-1: The iTunes folder contains all your audio files, plus all the data used to support the files.

▶ If iTunes can't locate a music file, it displays a small triangle warning icon.

When you import music into iTunes, you should copy the music to the iTunes folder. This method makes your music easier to manage and makes it less likely that you'll end up with missing music files.

Before you import music into iTunes, you should check the iTunes preferences, as shown in Figure 16-2, by choosing iTunes → Preferences and clicking Advanced. Ensure that both of these check boxes are selected:

▶ **Keep iTunes Media Folder Organized:** When you select this option, iTunes renames files according to the disc number, track number, and song title and places them in an album folder, within an artist, compilations, or composer folder.

▶ **Copy Files to iTunes Media Folder When Adding to Library:** This option copies media files from their location in Finder to the iTunes Media folder.

▶ Hold down the Option key when adding files to iTunes to reference the file without copying the file to the iTunes Library folder.

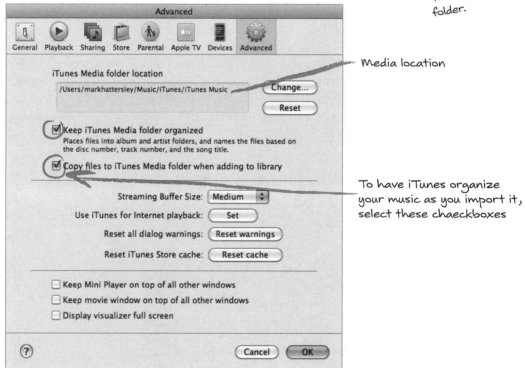

Media location

To have iTunes organize your music as you import it, select these chaeckboxes

FIGURE 16-2: You should enable iTunes to organize your music to prevent organizational problems further down the line.

With both of these items selected, iTunes will copy and organize your music within the iTunes Media folder as you import it.

But what about the music that iTunes is already using? It might be located all over Finder, and if it becomes accidently deleted or moved, iTunes may not be able to use it. Fortunately, help is at hand with the Organize Library command. You choose File ➔ Library ➔ Organize Library to bring up the Organize Library dialog.

I advise that you select both of the check boxes in this dialog:

▶ **Consolidate Files:** This option transfers all the audio file references in iTunes from their current position in Finder to the iTunes Media folder.

▶ **Upgrade to iTunes Media Organization:** If you upgraded iTunes from a version prior to iTunes 9, your iTunes folder will be organized slightly differently. iTunes works fine with the older folder layout, but this option reorganizes the iTunes folder to the newer structure.

▶ If the Upgrade to iTunes Media Organization option is grayed out, you are already using the newer folder structure.

After you select these check boxes and click OK, iTunes reorganizes its files in the newer structure.

> **TIP** When you upgrade to the new structure, iTunes may leave lots of folders containing artwork in the old iTunes Music folder, which may clutter up your iTunes Music folder. Feel free to delete these folders (because they've now been copied to the Artwork folder), but be careful not to delete any folders used by iTunes, including these:
>
> ▶ Audiobooks
>
> ▶ Automatically Add to iTunes
>
> ▶ iPod Games
>
> ▶ Mobile Applications
>
> ▶ Movies
>
> ▶ Music
>
> ▶ Podcasts
>
> ▶ Ringtones
>
> ▶ TV Shows
>
> ▶ Voice Memos
>
> Not all of these folders will be present if you don't have any of that type of content in iTunes.

Although iTunes restructures all your media into the new folder structure, it's worth noting that it doesn't change the name of the folder from *iTunes Music* to *iTunes Media*. However, you can change this folder name manually in Finder, and iTunes will still recognize the folder, as long as you don't move its location. (More information regarding moving the Library safely can be found later in the chapter.)

TIDYING UP ITUNES

Once you have iTunes set up to manage your music properly, you should take a look at organizing the files in it. A neatly organized iTunes Library with complete info and artwork is much easier to work with, and it looks great whether you're using iTunes on a desktop or playing music on an iPod or iPhone.

When you purchase music from iTunes, it comes completely organized. When you import music from a CD, iTunes automatically compares the CD to a list from Gracenote (www.gracenote.com) and tries to insert correct track information.

When it comes to iTunes organization, there are three challenges awaiting you: duplicate files, missing artwork, and missing and incorrect information, as discussed in the following sections.

Joining Tracks in iTunes Using Toast

When you import tracks into iTunes from a CD, it's possible to use the join tracks feature (choose Advanced → Join CD Tracks) to convert multiple tracks into one music file. This is great for importing audio books, or albums with multiple songs that blend together, such as classical music or dance tunes.

▶ You can set iTunes to remove the gaps between tracks by highlighting all tracks in an album and using the Gapless Album drop-down menu in the track info (⌘+I) window.

Unfortunately you can't join tracks into a single file after they have been imported into iTunes, at least not natively. However, if you own Toast (www.roxio.com), you can use its ability to create audio CDs to join up tracks in iTunes, as shown in Figure 16-3. Follow these steps:

1. **Open Toast.** Then choose Audio CD from the sidebar.

2. **Drag audio files to the main window.** Drag the tracks from iTunes to Finder (to copy them) and then drag the files into the main window.

3. **Reorder the files.** You might need to ensure that the tracks are in the correct order.

4. **Create a disc image.** Click Save As Disc Image, name the CD, and click OK. Now click Save and save it to the Finder (typically I just save it to the desktop).

5. **Mount the disc image using Toast.** Choose Utilities → Mount Disc Image from Toast to mount the disc image you've just saved onto Finder. (You can't mount this file using Disc Utility, incidentally).

6. **Open iTunes.** The audio CD should now appear in the iTunes sidebar, as if you'd inserted a physical disc. Highlight the tracks and choose Advanced → Join CD Tracks.

7. **Start the import.** Click Import CD to import the joined up tracks as a single track in iTunes. Don't forget to delete the original tracks unless you want both copies in iTunes.

Create an audio CD

Add tracks to this window

Save as Disc Image

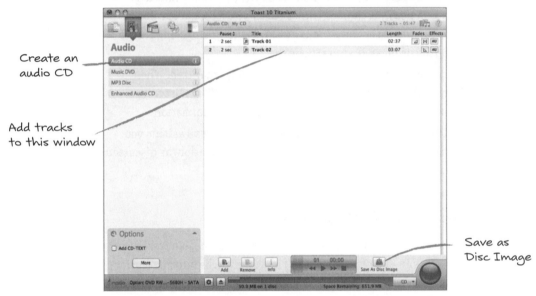

FIGURE 16-3: Toast can be used to mount audio disc files to the desktop, so you can re-import them in iTunes as single tracks.

Although it's a bit of a hassle using the two programs, it's an easy enough process once you get the hang of it. And it's a great means to join up disparate tracks that really should be one long piece of audio.

Removing Duplicate Files from iTunes

Every time you add a file to iTunes, it is referenced in the Library. Therefore, it's possible to end up with the same file multiple times. Having multiple files in the iTunes Library is a waste of space and can make the Library confusing to navigate.

You can delete duplicate files from iTunes by highlighting one of the unwanted files and choosing Edit → Delete. But trolling through a large iTunes Library and trying to spot individual duplicates can be time-consuming. This is where the iTunes Display Duplicates command comes to the rescue. When you choose File → Display Duplicates, the main window displays just files that are duplicated, as shown in Figure 16-4, which makes it easier to go through the Library and seek out duplicated files.

▶ iTunes recognizes the same file being added twice, but if the file has been modified and saved since it was last imported, iTunes references it as a new file.

FIGURE 16-4: The Display Duplicates command makes it easier to locate and delete duplicated files.

WARNING The Display Duplicates command searches for duplicated song titles, but be aware that the same song may exist in multiple albums. iTunes will
display these as duplicates, but you might want to keep both songs to keep both
albums intact. Keep an eye on the Album column to make sure they really are
duplicated files. Be aware that the duplicates algorithm is pretty clumsy and it
marks some with the same name, regardless of format (AAC, MP3, and so on)
as duplicates. Be careful when using it.

When you want to show all the files again, you click Show All at the bottom of the
iTunes Library (or choose File → Display All).

If you find it tedious to manually work though iTunes and remove duplicated files
one at a time, you can use a script called Dupin (http://dougscripts.com/itunes/
itinfo/dupin.php). You follow these steps to use Dupin:

1. Choose the Library or a Playlist from the Music drop-down menu in the
   sidebar.

2. Use the Criteria check boxes to select which iTunes data you want to search
   for. By default, Name, Track Number, Artist, and Album are selected.

3. Click Get Dupes in the menu bar.

4. Choose Select → Select All and click Filter to determine which tracks to use. Select an option and click Filter. This removes one set of duplicates (the ones that remain in the list are the ones you will remove). Options include when files were added, when files were modified, the bit rate or file type, and so on.

5. Choose Select → Select All Non Keepers. This highlights all the files that weren't filtered in the previous step.

6. Click Tools → Purge, choose Selected Dupin Tracks, and then click Remove. Finally, click Move to Trash to delete the files from iTunes.

> **NOTE** You can recover files from Trash if you delete them accidentally.

Dupin is a great add-on for making short work of unwanted tracks in iTunes. But it's wise to use Dupin carefully.

Downloading Artwork to Go with Tracks

▶ You can drag images directly from most websites (such as Google Images) to the Selected Item window.

When you purchase albums from iTunes, they come complete with album art. This art displays in the Selected Item window in iTunes, and it appears on the screens of portable devices such as iPods and iPhones. Unfortunately, tracks that you import from CDs or add manually do not always come with album art, and you may have to add the art manually.

Adding artwork for each track in iTunes is a chore. Although you can select multiple tracks and use the Info window (by choosing Edit → Get Info) to drag images to the Artwork pane, you'll save time by automating this process.

▶ You need to be signed in with an iTunes account in order to get artwork.

iTunes can download artwork from the iTunes store and add it to the files in the Library. To go this route, you highlight any tracks with artwork (or choose Edit → Select All for the entire Library) and choose Advanced → Get Artwork.

Adding artwork to your iTunes collection can be a laborious process, even using the download artwork feature (which doesn't always complete your collection). However, it's a task well worth doing as it makes iTunes much more visual, and music displays much better on iPods and iOS devices when album art is present.

Completing iTunes Info with TuneUp

If you have seriously messed up iTunes Library and don't want to go through each and every track to manually add info, you should investigate a program called TuneUp (www.tuneupmedia.com). TuneUp attaches itself as a new window to the right of iTunes, as shown in Figure 16-5.

TuneUp cleans up any missing track information

FIGURE 16-5: TuneUp searches online for complete track info for songs.

You follow these steps to use TuneUp with iTunes:

1. Click the Clean tab.
2. Drag a track that is missing information from the iTunes Library to TuneUp.
3. Check the track information. If it is correct, click the icon shaped like a floppy disk to save the track information to iTunes.

TuneUp uses the same Gracenote information that iTunes uses when you insert an audio CD. The difference is that TuneUp uses acoustic fingerprinting—it listens to a sample of a song and then matches it to the online database. This means that you don't need any track information at all for it to be able to recognize songs and correctly enter all information and album art.

MOVING THE ITUNES LIBRARY

At some point, you may decide to move your iTunes Library. Typically the Library sits on your hard drive, inside your user account's Music folder. But if the hefty iTunes folder it is taking up too much space on your internal hard drive, you might want to move it to an external drive. It might seem like the logical thing to do is to drag the iTunes folder in Finder to another drive; however, this is completely the wrong thing to do.

WARNING Don't drag the iTunes folder from one hard drive to another. If you move it from one part of Finder to another on the same drive (which I don't recommend), iTunes will continue to work. But if you move the iTunes folder to another hard drive, iTunes will lose all the information, the tracks will stop working, and you'll have to re-enter everything all over again.

▶ Usually it's advisable to create an iTunes Media folder in the destination before moving the files.

To move the iTunes Library from one place to another, follow these steps:

1. Tidy up iTunes by using the Consolidate Files option described earlier in the chapter. You should have all files in the iTunes Media folder prior to moving them.

2. Choose iTunes ➔ Preferences and click Advanced.

3. Click the Change button next to iTunes Media Folder Location. Now use the Choose dialog to locate the new location for the iTunes folder.

4. Click OK to close Preferences. A dialog appears, asking if you would like iTunes to move and rename the files. Click Yes.

5. Choose File ➔ Library ➔ Organize Library. Ensure that the Consolidate Files check box is selected and click OK.

The Consolidate Files option copies all the media files from their location in the original file to the location you selected. Your iTunes information (including all the track data and artwork) remains in the iTunes folder, preventing any problems from occurring.

NOTE You can move files around on the same volume, and iTunes will recognize them because Mac OS X keeps track of files on a volume. However, this won't work if you are moving files to another volume. It's generally better to use the Consolidate Files option.

The Consolidate Files command is particularly useful if you use an external drive to hold all your files. If you unplug the external drive (for example, when taking your notebook out and about) and import or purchase any new tracks, they will be placed in the usual location in the Music folder on your internal hard drive. When you again plug in the external hard drive, you can use the Consolidate Files command to transfer them to the external drive.

SUMMARY

iTunes is a great program for managing music and other audio and video content. But it's easy to end up with an iTunes Library that is a complete mess. Years of adding and removing audio tracks from Finder can result in an iTunes Library that's impossible to navigate. If you have a seriously scruffy iTunes library, you might want to consider using a program like TuneUp to automatically tidy up iTunes. Intense iTunes users will find this program invaluable. Also, you should pay particular attention to the way iTunes organizes its files with Finder, and you should use the Consolidate Files feature in iTunes along with the iTunes preferences to ensure that all files are located within the iTunes Media folder. If you decide to move the iTunes Library from one location to another, make sure you do it using iTunes, not Finder. You can combine the iTunes Media Folder Location and Consolidate Files commands to choose and move iTunes files. Following these steps will keep iTunes running smoothly.

CHAPTER 17

Working with Digital Photographs

Images are close to the hearts of modern computer users, especially Mac users. Designers and artists love good design and art, so it's no surprise that they typically use Macs. Because of this, there are some amazing image manipulation programs designed for Mac OS X. What's often lost among Mac users is just how good Mac OS X itself is at importing, managing, displaying, and manipulating images. In this chapter, we're going to look at some great tricks for working with images right inside Mac OS X. Once you learn these tricks, you'll never look at images the same way again.

ADJUSTING IMPORT OPTIONS

Before you can start using images in Mac OS X, you first need to get them into Mac OS X so you can start working with them. By far the most popular method of importing images is to get them from a digital camera. But you can also import images from a device, such as an iPhone, that has a camera. Or you can insert an SD card from a digital camera into a Mac that has an SD card port.

▶ *If your Mac doesn't have a SD card port, you can always use a USB card reader.*

One of three main things happens after you connect your camera to your Mac running Mac OS X:

- ▶ iPhoto opens, and you can import the images.

- ▶ Image Capture opens, and you can use it to copy images.

- ▶ Nothing happens, and you can either drag and drop images manually or open Image Capture or iPhoto manually and import the images.

▶ *Most people select Yes without thinking and find that iPhoto is forever associated with imports from digital cameras.*

The first option is the most likely to happen. The first time you launch iPhoto, it displays the Do You Want to Use iPhoto When You Connect Your Digital Camera? dialog, as shown in Figure 17-1. Clicking Yes ensures that iPhoto launches whenever your camera is connected.

You don't have to associate iPhoto with your camera

Do you want to use iPhoto when you connect your digital camera?

If you decide not to use iPhoto you may have to install other software to download photos from your digital camera.

[Decide Later]   [No]   [Yes]

FIGURE 17-1: The first time you launch iPhoto, it attempts to take over control of digital cameras, which can be annoying after a while.

In some ways, this is a great thing because iPhoto is a great program. But in other ways, it can be extremely annoying. I take a lot of pictures on my iPhone or digital camera that I don't particularly want in iPhoto. I may, for example, just want to use them in a document that I'm working on. The key is to tell Mac OS X that you don't want iPhoto to open whenever you attach the camera or insert an SD card. There are two ways to do this, as described in the following sections.

Changing Import Options in iPhoto

You can change the import options in iPhoto by using the iPhoto preferences pane, as shown in Figure 17-2.

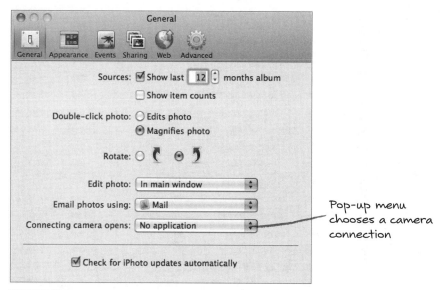

FIGURE 17-2: You can use the iPhoto preferences pane to determine what happens when you connect a camera or digital device.

You follow these steps to change the iTunes import preferences:

1. Connect the camera (or insert the memory card) and open iPhoto.
2. Choose the camera (or memory card) under the Devices list.
3. Open the iPhoto preferences pane (by choosing iPhoto → Preferences).
4. Click General and use the Connecting Camera Opens pop-up menu to set which application opens when you connect the camera.

Note that the option you choose here affects only that device. Image Capture is updated with the same options chosen in iPhoto.

Changing Import Options in Image Capture

You can use Image Capture to determine what happens when you connect a camera or digital device, as shown in Figure 17-3. This is handy if you don't have iPhoto installed, or want to use another program than iPhoto.

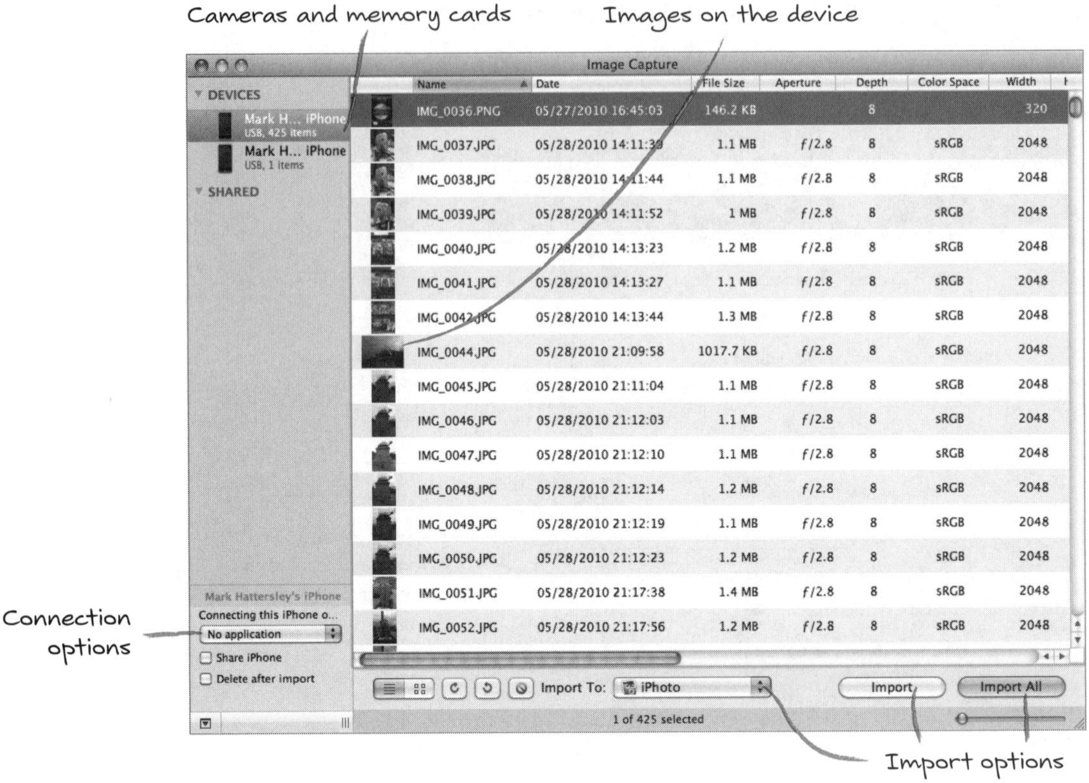

Cameras and memory cards   Images on the device

Connection options

Import options

FIGURE 17-3: You can use the pop-up menu in Image Capture to determine what happens when you connect a device.

You follow these steps to use Image Capture to change the import options:

1. Connect the camera (or insert the memory card) and open Image Capture.

2. Choose the camera (or memory card) from the Devices list.

3. Choose the application or device from the Connecting This Opens pop-up menu.

Note that the option you choose here is mirrored in iPhoto.

You can also share devices in Image Capture. To do so, you select the Share This Device check box in Image Capture, and the device appears in Image Capture on other Macs on the network.

USING IMAGE CAPTURE TO TRANSFER IMAGES

I advise anybody who spends a lot of time using images to investigate Image Capture as an alternative to iPhoto. Not only does Image Capture launch faster than iPhoto, but also it offers a greater selection of options for getting images from a device and into Mac OS X, as shown in Figure 17-4.

Choose from multiple devices   Indicates image already imported

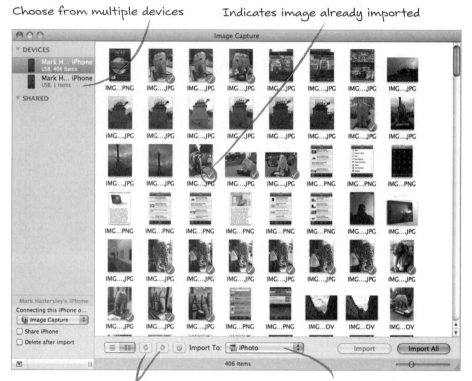

Rotate images before importing   Choose where to send imported images

FIGURE 17-4: You can use Image Capture to determine where to send images.

You follow these steps to import images with Image Capture:

1. Connect the camera (or insert the memory card) and select the camera (or memory card) from the Devices list in Image Capture.

2. Open Image Capture and highlight the images you want to import. (You don't need to highlight anything if you want import all the images.)

3. Use the Import To pop-up menu to choose where you want to send the images. You can send them to key areas within the Finder, or to specific applications such as iPhoto, Mail, Preview, and so on.

4. Click Import to import images selected in the Image Capture window or click Import All to import all images from the device.

With Image Capture, not only can you determine which application to use on the spot, but also you can create web pages, PDF documents, and e-mails straight from the contents of your camera.

▶ If you use the Build Web Page option, you can save the web page in Safari (by choosing File ➜ Save As) to quickly create an interactive file that you can e-mail to other people.

SCANNING PHOTOGRAPHS AND OTHER ARTWORK

A popular source of images is old photographs and other hard copies. So that you can use these types of images on your Mac, Image Capture works with compatible scanners, and the scanner appears in the Devices window. Many scanners also come with their own software, which you may need if the scanner is not compatible with Image Capture. Image capture uses QuickTime Image Capture technology, rather than the TWAIN software protocol that is used by many scanners and printers.

However, probably the most powerful tool for scanning software is a program called VueScan (www.hamrick.com). VueScan is continuously updated and supports just about every scanner on the market. It even adds some functionality to scanners that manufacturers don't include in their own software.

CAPTURING IMAGES FROM THE DESKTOP

A popular technique (especially among authors) is to capture images of the Mac OS X desktop. These are known as *screen shots, screen captures, snapshots, screen grabs,* or just *grabs*. A grab can be anything from a picture of the whole display to a selected partition or individual application windows.

You capture images from the desktop in several ways: either by using keyboard shortcut combinations, or by using a Mac OS X application such as Grab or a third party app such as Snapz Pro X (www.ambrosiasw.com).

Using Grab to Take Screen Shots

Grab is a great utility that enables you to capture snapshots and save images. It offers a number of advantages over using keyboard shortcuts because you can also include the cursor and take timed images that allow you to adjust the display before the grab is taken.

You follow these steps to use Grab, which comes with Mac OS X, to take an image of your display:

1. Arrange the desktop and open Grab. It's best to have everything in view so you can access what you want to capture.

2. Choose Capture from the menu bar. You can choose to capture a selected area only, an entire window, or the entire screen. You can also choose to grab the entire screen as it appears 10 seconds after you start the timer, as shown in Figure 17-5.

3. Take the grab. After you choose the menu option, a dialog appears, offering additional directions. Depending on the option you want, you either click the window to take the grab or click the area outside it. Note that the dialog itself isn't included in the capture.

4. Save the image. Grab displays the image in a window. Choose File → Save to save it to the desktop or somewhere in Finder.

▶ If you want to include the pointer in snapshots, choose Grab → Preferences and select a pointer.

Mac OSX window (captured)

Grab dialog window (not captured)

FIGURE 17-5: Grab enables you to take images of the desktop or individual windows.

Using Grab is great, but it can be a bit unwieldy if you have lots of different images to capture. In this case, you're better off learning the keyboard shortcuts.

Using Keyboard Shortcuts to Take Screen Shots

In addition to using Grab, another method of taking screen shots is to use keyboard shortcuts. In this way, you can quickly take a snapshot of the desktop or a part of the screen and save the file to the desktop. Table 17-1 lists the snapshot shortcuts.

Images are saved to the desktop using the PNG image format.

TABLE 17-1: Shortcuts to Capture Screen Shots

KEYBOARD COMMAND	RESULT
Shift+⌘+3	Captures the display
Shift+⌘+4 then drag a marquee	Captures the selection
Shift+⌘+4 then spacebar and then click a window	Captures the selected window

> **TIP** Hold down the Ctrl key when using a screen shot capture keyboard shortcut. Then, instead of saving the file to the desktop, you copy it to the Clipboard, and you can then paste it directly into an application.

GRABBING APPLICATION ICONS

A neat trick is to copy and paste application icons. To do this, you locate an application in Finder (usually in Applications or Utilities) and choose Edit → Copy. Then you open a program that can accept images, such as Preview, and choose Edit → Paste. The application icon is pasted in as a graphic.

You don't just capture images in Mac OS X. You can also work on images with a level of functionality that surprises many people.

WORKING WITH IMAGES IN PREVIEW

Preview is an incredibly powerful program, much more so than most people realize. Although it was originally designed just to display images and other documents, it has evolved into a powerful editing tool. Most people use it to look at image and PDF documents, though, and that's a real shame. Here are some of the cool things you can do with Preview:

▶ **Rotate and flip:** You can choose Tools ➜ Rotate Left or Tools ➜ Rotate Right (or press ⌘+L or ⌘+R) to spin images around. There are also Flip Horizontal and Flip Vertical commands.

▶ **Crop:** You can click the Select button in the toolbar and drag a marquee around a portion of the image. Then you choose Tools ➜ Crop (or press ⌘+K) to crop the image.

▶ **Size:** You can choose Tools ➜ Adjust Size to change the size of the image.

▶ **Convert:** By using the File ➜ Save As command, you can convert images from multiple file types.

▶ **File Size:** If you select JPG as the file type, you can use the Quality slider to adjust the size of the output file.

▶ **Annotate:** Click Annotate to bring up a selection of tools at the bottom of the Preview window. You can draw arrows or lines, add notes, and highlight objects in an image using these tools.

As you can see, it's possible to perform the kind of basic adjustments in Preview that many people do with more expensive programs, such as Adobe Photoshop.

Correcting Color and Other Image Elements

As well as performing basic edits, it is possible to perform quite powerful color correction from within Preview. You choose Tools ➜ Adjust Color to open the Adjust Color pane, as shown in Figure 17-6. Here you have granular control over the color and other controls.

Level sliders

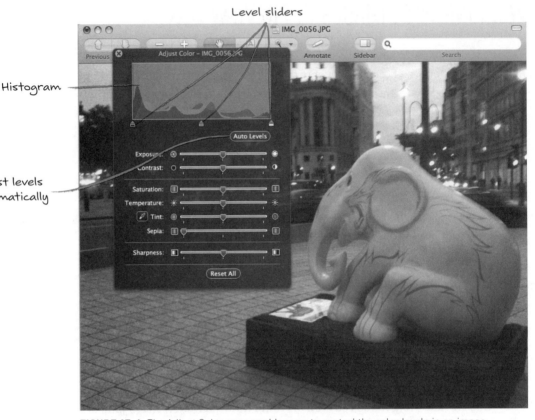

Histogram

Adjust levels automatically

FIGURE 17-6: The Adjust Color pane enables you to control the color levels in an image.

The following controls are of interest:

▶ This is a professional chart used to map out tones and contrasts.

- ▶ **Histogram:** At the top of the Adjust Color pane is a histogram. Below the histogram are three slider controls you can use to adjust the image.

- ▶ **Auto Levels:** Clicking this option enables Preview to automatically adjust the color levels.

- ▶ **Exposure:** You can drag this slider to the right to increase the exposure or to the left to decrease it.

- ▶ **Contrast:** You can drag this slider to the left to decrease contrast or to the right to increase it.

▶ Dragging the slider all the way to the left creates a black-and-white image.

- ▶ **Saturation:** You can drag the slider to the right to increase the amount of color or to the left to decrease it.

▶ **Temperature:** You can drag this slider to the right to boost warm colors, such as reds and yellows, and to the left to emphasize cool colors, such as blues and greens.

▶ **Tint.** This slider rotates through color tints, from green to magenta.

▶ **Color cast eye-dropper:** Next to the Tint slider is an eye-dropper icon. You can click this icon and then click on a color to remove that color.

▶ **Sepia:** You can drag this slider to the right to add a brown color effect reminiscent of older photographic images.

▶ **Sharpness:** You can drag the slider to the right to increase sharpness or to the left to make the image fuzzier.

▶ **Reset All:** You can click this button to cancel all adjustments.

> **TIP** If you want to know more about color management and histograms, check out *Color Management for Digital Photographers for Dummies*, by Ted Padova and Don Mason.

As you can see, you can make a lot of complex changes to an image from within the Mac OS X operating system.

Using Lasso Tools and Instant Alpha

Preview enables you to cut out parts of images you don't want. The Crop tool enables you to cut out rectangular or circular parts of the screen. Preview also features three powerful tools that enable you to select complex shapes: Lasso, Smart Lasso, and Instant Alpha.

▶ *The Rectangular Selection tool is selected by default, but you can click the Select icon to choose the Elliptical Selection tool to draw circles, for example.*

USING LASSO AND SMART LASSO

Lassos are, as the name suggests, circular lines that you draw around images to select irregular-shaped items.

There are two types of lasso:

▶ **Lasso Selection:** This tool draws a single-pixel-wide line as you drag the pointer around an image. The line joins to form a selection.

▶ **Smart Lasso:** This tool draws a thick red line as you drag the pointer around an image. The colors inside the line are compared to detect different objects.

▶ The selection line is sometimes referred to as the "marching ants" line because of the animated black-and-white dots.

There are upsides and downsides to both of these tools. The Lasso Selection tool enables you to precisely draw a selection line around an object, but it requires a keen eye and a steady hand; the Smart Lasso is easier to use, as shown in Figure 17-7, but its accuracy depends on the complexity of the image.

Smart Lasso tool

Secection with Smart lasso

FIGURE 17-7: The Smart Lasso tool enables you to select an object in an image by drawing a thick line around it.

> **TIP** Use View ➔ Invert to select the area outside the selection. This enables you to cut or copy the background rather than the selection.

The next step beyond using lassos is to investigate alphas. This is where you select shapes based on the content of the image rather than by drawing lines around them.

USING INSTANT ALPHA

By using the Instant Alpha tool, you can select part of an image, as you would with the Smart Lasso tool. However, instead of requiring you to draw around an image, Instant Alpha attempts to automatically detect the shape for you.

You follow these steps to use Instant Alpha:

1. Click Select in the toolbar and choose Instant Alpha.

2. Click inside the part of the image you're trying to select and hold down the mouse button. For example, to cut the flower out of a background, click in the middle of the flower.

3. Slowly move the pointer to the outside of the image. As you move the mouse, the selected area will be highlighted, as shown in Figure 17-8.

▶ Both Smart Lasso and Instant Alpha work best on images with clearly defined objects and contrasting colored backgrounds.

Instant Alpha tool

FIGURE 17-8: Preview can use the Instant Alpha tool to automatically detect objects within images.

4. Move the pointer back in toward the original part of the image to decrease the size of the selection.

5. Let go of the mouse button to create a selection line the size of the red high-lighted area.

As with the lasso tools, you can use the selection line with the Cut, Copy, and Crop tools to remove and paste parts of the image into other images.

Most people really never realize just how powerful Preview is, and if you get used to using it properly you may be able to get by without having to invest in a much more expensive program such Adobe Photoshop.

SUMMARY

Mac OS X is so good at managing and editing images that you may not need any other program. In this chapter, we looked at ways to import images using Image Capture, a great Mac OS X application that's faster and in some ways more versatile than iPhoto. You can use Image Capture to send images to any application or to automatically pull images into your Pictures folder. You should also take a good look at Preview—chances are you haven't realized just how powerful it is. Far from just showing off images, Preview enables you to cut, crop, resize, and even color-correct images to a professional level. You can even create lassos and use instant alpha channels to remove the back-grounds from photographs. The things you can do with images from inside Mac OS X are astounding; take time to play around and discover just what is possible.

CHAPTER 18

Watching, Editing, and Sharing Movies

IN THIS CHAPTER

▶ **Watching all kinds of video formats in Mac OS X**

▶ **Extending the video formats you can watch** with third-party software

▶ **Recording video and audio in Mac OS X** with internal and external capture devices

▶ **Converting video files to different** video formats

▶ **Using QuickTime to edit video**

▶ **Sharing your videos with QuickTime Player**

Macs are great machines for watching, editing, and sharing digital video. Not only do most Apple computers feature high-quality displays, Mac OS X comes with Apple's QuickTime software and a host of other digital video features. Versatile as it is, QuickTime isn't the only tool for working with video in Mac OS X. Plenty of Mac programs enable you to import video from DVDs, convert video files that you've downloaded, and share video files with other people. In this chapter, we're going to look at working with video in Mac OS X, so grab some popcorn, and let's go to the movies.

WATCHING VIDEO IN MAC OS X

▶ You can also open video files in iMovie or other video-editing playback software if you want to edit them.

Watching video files in Mac OS X is pretty simple, and you'll typically watch videos in one of these places:

▶ **QuickTime Player:** You can open files in QuickTime Player and play them directly in a window on the desktop.

▶ **VideoLAN VLC:** There are many independent applications that play videos, but VideoLAN VLC (www.videolan.org/vlc) is probably the most highly regarded and widely used.

▶ For the purposes of this discussion, Apple devices include iPods, iPhones, and iPads.

▶ **iTunes:** You can add video files to the iTunes Library, and you can then play them in iTunes and sync them with other Apple devices.

When you double-click a video file, it will open in either QuickTime Player or iTunes (unless you have associated the video file with a different program). You can associate video files with either QuickTime or iTunes on an ongoing basis in the Open With pop-up menu in the Info window (which you open by pressing ⌘+I). You can also use the Open With command or drag the file to either QuickTime or iTunes to play the file in that application if it's associated with another program.

Playing Video in QuickTime Player

In Mac OS X 10.6, Apple introduced a new version of QuickTime Player called *Quick-Time X*, which enables you to record, edit, and share video as well as watch it. In addition, QuickTime X has a fantastic interface that disappears when you click play, enabling you to focus on the video itself.

▶ You can drag the playback controls around the window by clicking anywhere except the buttons and then dragging to the desired location.

As you can see in Figure 18-1, QuickTime Player plays video in a window that is unlike any other application in Mac OS X. Instead of appearing on the usual gray window, the video appears on screen with a black translucent title bar that contains the *playback controls*. These controls disappear while a video is playing or as soon as you move the pointer outside the window.

> **TIP** If you hold down the Alt key while clicking the fast-forward and rewind shuttle playback controls, you increase the speed by 0.1 at a time instead of the usual 2x, 4x, and 8x speeds.

Title bar and controls fade during playback

Share your video with others

Full screen

Playback controls

FIGURE 18-1: The QuickTime Player interface has a title bar and playback controls that fade while a video is playing.

You can bring back the controls by moving the pointer inside the video window.

Prior to Apple releasing QuickTime X, the version of QuickTime Player was Quick-Time 7. QuickTime X was a radical update, and the earlier version had a more regular interface and slightly different options (such as trim bars and the ability to set in and out points when editing video). However, you must upgrade to a Pro version (at a charge of $29.99) to edit and export video clips. The great news is that QuickTime 7 is still included with Mac OS X and can be found on the installation disc under Optional Installs.

Moving Beyond QuickTime

QuickTime Player can play a wide range of video files (including MOV, AVI, MP4, and so on) using a wide array of codecs. Typically, QuickTime Player has little trouble playing any video you've recorded yourself or downloaded from iTunes. But if you start sourcing video that other people have created, you'll likely encounter a file type that QuickTime Player will struggle to play, either because the file type itself is incompatible or because you don't have the required codec installed.

▶ Codec stands for compressor/decompressor and is a technology used to decrease, or squeeze, file sizes.

To watch some video file types, you need to extend QuickTime. Take a look at some of the following options:

▶ **Apple website:** Apple (www.apple.com/quicktime/extending/components.html) hosts a number of links to codecs.

▶ **Perian:** (http://perian.org) is an absolutely fantastic plug-in. Referred to as the "Swiss Army Knife for QuickTime," Perian installs as a System Preference and enables QuickTime to play just about any video file type.

▶ **Flip4Mac:** Flip4Mac (www.telestream.net/flip4mac-wmv/overview.htm) is a program that enables you to play Windows media formats (WMA and WMV) inside QuickTime.

▶ **VLC Player:** If you find that QuickTime simply can't play a video file, you should investigate a free program called VLC (www.videolan.org/vlc), which is capable of playing just about any kind of video file available.

▶ In my experience, you should go this far only if you are creating video at a fairly professional level.

I recommend that you install Perian and Flip4Mac, which will enable QuickTime to play just about any file. If QuickTime then fails to play a file, you can install and use VLC. You can also install individual codecs and file types.

UNDERSTANDING CODECS

Video can be confusing in that there are two distinct parts. There's the file type (MOV, AVI, MP4, and so on), and there's the codec that the file uses. By default, video clips take up huge amounts of disk space; codecs enable file sizes to become smaller, and they can also affect the quality of the video. If a person uses a particular codec to compress a video file, you need to have that same codec installed in order to play the file.

Adjusting QuickTime in Terminal

It is possible to use Terminal to adjust QuickTime's features and functionality. For example, older versions of QuickTime had an option to play movies as soon as a file was opened. It is possible to regain this functionality in QuickTime X by entering code in Terminal.

▶ If YES is at the end of the command, you use NO to return to the default setting and vice versa.

To begin, you open Terminal and type the following command plus either YES or NO at the end:

```
Defaults write com.apple.QuickTimePlayerX MGPlayMovieOnOpen YES
```

To set QuickTime back to the default, type this:

```
Defaults write com.apple.QuickTimePlayerX MGPlayMovieOnOpen NO
```

The following commands are also available:

▶ Make the window corners square:

```
defaults write com.apple.QuickTimePlayerX
    MGCinematicWindowDebugForceNoRoundedCorners YES
```

▶ Hide the control bar once video is playing and the pointer has left the screen:

```
defaults write com.apple.QuickTimePlayerX
    MGUIVisibilityNeverAutoshow YES
```

▶ Never display the control bar:

```
defaults write com.apple.QuickTimePlayerX
    MGCinematicWindowDebugForceNoTitlebar YES
```

▶ Always display the control bar:

```
defaults write com.apple.QuickTimePlayerX
    MGUIVisibilityNeverAutohide YES
```

▶ Automatically display subtitles:

```
defaults write com.apple.QuickTimePlayerX
    MGEnableCCAndSubtitlesOnOpen YES
```

▶ Play video on the desktop while working in other applications:

```
defaults write com.apple.QuickTimePlayerX
    MGFullScreenExitOnAppSwitch NO
```

▶ Otherwise, the video remains in full screen mode when you switch to another application.

▶ Allow multiple simultaneous recordings:

```
defaults write com.apple.QuickTimePlayerX
    MGAllowMultipleSimultaneousRecordings YES
```

▶ Display video when trimming audio (by holding down the Alt key):

```
defaults write com.apple.QuickTimePlayerX
    MGTimelineDisableAudioTrackForVideoMovies NO
```

You can customize QuickTime by judiciously using these commands. Be careful with some of them, though, especially the ones that disable the onscreen controls, because they can make QuickTime more difficult to use.

RECORDING VIDEO AND AUDIO IN MAC OS X

QuickTime X isn't just good for playing video; you can also use it to record video. By using QuickTime X, you can perform three different types of recording:

▶ **Movie recording:** You can record video directly from a connected camera. On iMac and MacBook notebooks, you can use the built-in iSight webcam, or you can use a separate digital camcorder. Choose File → New Movie Recording to open a movie recording window and click the red Record button to begin recording; click this button again to stop recording.

▶ **Audio recording:** You record audio the same way you record movies, except you use a Mac's built-in microphone or a microphone attached to the machine through either the line-in port or USB port.

> **TIP** When you're recording a video, the volume slider is present but set to mute. This prevents audio feedback from looping from the speaker back into the microphone. However, if you attach earphones to the Mac, you can use the volume slider to listen to the audio being recorded.

▶ **Screen recording:** You can record a video of the desktop display, including the pointer and any mouse movements. This can be useful for recording step-by-step instructions or other demonstrations. To begin recording, you click the red Record button. The Record dialog is hidden during recording, so to stop recording the screen, you click Stop Recording in the menu bar (or press Ctrl+⌘+Esc).

After you have finished, the recording is automatically saved as a QuickTime file with the .mov extension in the Movies folder.

▶ Audio files are recorded as QuickTime Movie files, even though they have just the audio track.

Recording External Video

You can use QuickTime to record video from an external source (such as a video recorder or home videogame console), called an *external capture device*. External capture devices typically connect to a Mac via a USB port and enable you to connect the S-Video or composite RCA cables. You can then select the device in QuickTime and output video from the device (by pressing Play on a VHS player, for example).

If you're interested in recording video from a VHS player, DVD player, or game console, I recommend two external devices: the Elgato Video Capture (www.elgato.com) or Pinnacle Video Capture for Mac (www.pinnaclesys.com).

Internal capture cards, such as those shown in Figure 18-2, are designed to fit inside a Mac Pro, attached to a spare PCI express slot, and they typically enable faster performance and also a wider range of formats, such as high-definition, including HDMI and high-end video formats such as 2K.

FIGURE 18-2: Capture cards enable you to connect video devices to a Mac and record the video.

If you're interested in recording on a Mac Pro, take a look at an AJA Kona (www.aja.com/products/kona) or BlackMagic Intensity (www.blackmagic-design .com/products/intensity). These companies sell internal PCI Express cards that enable you to capture high-definition video.

CROSS-REF Chapter 10 has more information on upgrading a Mac and inserting graphics cards into a Mac Pro.

Recording Television

It is possible to record live television directly in Mac OS X. While it is possible to do this using a video capture card and a television output device (such as a cable box), by far the most common means of recording television on a Mac is to use an Elgato device, such as the Elgato Hybrid for over-the-air broadcasts, or Elgato HD for satellite or cable television.

The advantage of using an Elgato device is that it comes with Elgato's EyeTV software, which is custom built to enable you to schedule and record television programs. You can then either play these programs directly or convert them to work within iTunes and then share them with other Apple devices.

CONVERTING VIDEO FILES FROM ONE FORMAT TO ANOTHER

▶ In QuickTime X, you can only convert file types into MPEG-4 (with an .m4v extension).

Occasionally, such as when editing video or creating DVDs, you might want to convert your video files from one file format to another. There are lots of different programs out there that enable you to convert video file types; it's even possible to convert files inside QuickTime Player using the Share function.

Converting Video into iTunes Format

▶ It's best to use the Apple TV setting if you are converting video to watch on an iPad.

To convert a video file into an iTunes format, you choose File ➔ Share. QuickTime displays three options, as shown in Figure 18-3: iPhone & iPod, Apple TV, and Computer.

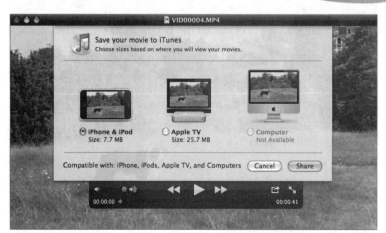

FIGURE 18-3: You can convert files to iTunes-compatible MPEG-4 files by using QuickTime.

The resolution of the files and the data size of the files increase with each option. Below each option, you see the size of the file that the format will produce. Clicking Share begins the conversion process. The file is added to iTunes when it has finished converting.

INSTALLING QUICKTIME PRO

Apple provides a version of QuickTime called QuickTime 7 Pro that enables you to convert just about any video file type from one kind to another. If you're serious about digital video, you should grab a copy of QuickTime 7 Pro (www.apple .com/quicktime/extending). At this writing, QuickTime Pro is available only in the older version 7, which lacks the swish interface of QuickTime X. However, its ability to import and export just about any video file type makes it a must-have tool for any serious videographer.

Using Third-Party Programs to Convert Video

In addition to QuickTime Pro, these other programs are of interest to Mac users looking to convert video:

▶ **Turbo H264:** This Elgato (www.elgato.com) product combines a small hardware USB device with Elgato's Turbo 264 software to convert video into files that can be played in iTunes. Because the conversion takes place in hardware, it's much faster than using a software-only solution.

▶ **iSquint:** iSquint is a fast conversion program, especially on a reasonably powerful Mac. Although this program is no longer being developed, you can download it from http://isquint.en.softonic.com/mac.

▶ **ffmpegX:** This free program enables you to convert just about any video clip from one format to another. See http://www.ffmpegx.com.

▶ **MPEG Streamclip:** This program offers a wider range of functions (including, in the latest version of MPEG Streamclip, the ability to convert YouTube video clips). It also has great image quality. See http://www.squared5.com.

▶ **Handbrake:** This program enables you to convert movie DVDs into video files that can be imported into iTunes and played directly on Apple devices, such as the iPad. It's an absolute must-have utility for people looking to convert a DVD collection into digital movie files. See http://handbrake.fr.

How much time you want to spend converting file types is up to you. Using a plug-in such as Perian or a well-rounded player such as VLC can enable you to play most videos without converting them first. However, if you want to play videos in iTunes or transfer them to another Apple device, you'll need to convert them into a compatible file format.

EDITING AND ADJUSTING VIDEOS WITH QUICKTIME

QuickTime X doesn't just play video; it also enables you to edit video (albeit at a fairly basic level). For example, you can remove the start and end of a video by using the Trim command. To do so, you complete the following steps:

1. Choose Edit → Trim. The Control Panel expands to display the Trim controls, as shown in Figure 18-4.

2. Click on the yellow trim handles at the left and right sides of the Trim controls and drag them inward. The area inside the yellow area will be the video that remains. You can also click and drag the red line (known as the *scrubber*) to move through the video.

FIGURE 18-4: The Trim controls in QuickTime X.

3. Check the audio. It's possible to view an audio waveform instead of the video by holding down the Option key. This enables you to search for the parts of a video where no audio is present.

4. Click the Trim button to shorten the video clip. Note that the original file isn't changed at this point.

5. Choose File ➜ Save As to save a copy of the shortened video.

Although it's possible to shorten video clips in QuickTime X, you can't combine multiple clips. For more advanced editing such as this, you should investigate a more comprehensive program such as iMovie or Adobe Premiere Elements 8.

SHARING VIDEO CLIPS WITH QUICKTIME PLAYER

As well as watching and editing video in QuickTime Player, it is possible to share video as well. You can access options to share a video using the Share menu or by clicking the Share icon (shaped like an arrow coming from a square) in the playback controls.

Three sharing options are available:

▶ **iTunes:** Selecting this option converts the video into iTunes format and places it into iTunes, as outlined earlier in the chapter.

▶ **MobileMe:** Choosing this option compresses the video and uploads it to the iDisk space on MobileMe. Be sure to select the Compatibility check box if you wish to ensure it can be viewed on an iPhone or iPod touch device.

▶ **YouTube:** Choosing this option compresses the video and uploads it to a You-Tube account. You will be required to enter your YouTube name and password.

These are great options for uploading to these specific services, although you may want to upload to other online sites, like the superb Vimeo (www.vimeo.com). In this case, you should use the Save As function to save the video as a file, and then use this to upload directly to the web site.

However, for quick-and-dirty sharing to sites such as YouTube, it's hard to beat the simplicity on offer with QuickTime Player. Set up an account, and you'll find yourself sharing video much more than ever before.

▶ If you want to share video via custom web services, you might want to investigate QuickTime 7 Pro, which enables you to control size and aspect ratios more accurately.

SUMMARY

Mac OS X ships with an incredibly slick video program called QuickTime Player, which has a beautiful interface that fades away to enable you to concentrate on the moving images. QuickTime Player is pretty versatile, but you'll likely find files it can't play. In such cases, it's worthwhile to take a look at a plug-in called Perian, or if that doesn't work, a player called VLC. And did you know that you can do a lot more with Quick-Time than just watch videos? With a little exploration, it's possible to get an incredible amount out of QuickTime Player and digital video. You can use the program to record audio and video, for example. With the right hardware attachment, it's also possible to record from a hardware source such as a VCR, a game console, or even directly from a live television broadcast. You can also use QuickTime to trim video clips and to export them into a format that can be played in iTunes. When you're finished editing, be sure to share your videos. QuickTime offers video sharing through iTunes, MobileMe, and YouTube.

CHAPTER 19

Getting More Out of Mac OS X with an iPad, iPhone, or iPod touch

In 2007 Apple changed its name from Apple Computer Inc. to just Apple Inc. The reason? It wanted the name to better reflect the range of devices it makes, most notably the iPod and the iPhone, which have since been joined by the iPad. There's no official collective term for all these different gadgets, although some people refer to them as *iDevices*. One thing is clear, though: All iOS devices are stunningly beautiful to look at and amazing to use. What you might not know is just how great the iOS-based devices are for Mac owners. Not only are they easy to set up and sync, but also they offer a range of functions that work great with Mac OS X. This chapter is all about bringing together iOS with Mac OS X and all the great things you can do with Mac computers and Apple devices to create a seamless, portable, and magical computing experience.

TRANSFERRING FILES FROM AN
iOS DEVICE TO ITUNES

▶ Technically, the iPhone, iPod touch, and iPad are all iOS devices because they run the iOS operating system, instead of running Mac OS X.

Managing media on an iOS device is pretty straightforward: You simply connect the device to your computer, select it under Devices in the iTunes sidebar, as shown in Figure 19-1, and use the selections at the top of the iTunes window to determine what content you want. Then you click Sync to copy the content from iTunes to the device.

Determine the content you want to transfer

Attached devices display here

Click to sync your files

FIGURE 19-1: You use iTunes to manage iOS devices such as iPods, iPads, and iPhones.

▶ Some older iPods and the original Apple TV all run custom operating systems (usually based on stripped-down versions of Mac OS X).

If you've used an iOS device to purchase any content from the iTunes Store, you can transfer it into iTunes by using the Transfer Purchases feature. Choose File ➜ Transfer Purchases From to copy the files from the device to iTunes.

Although Transfer Purchases is a great command to know, the downside is that it works only with content you've purchased from iTunes. Audio and video you've gotten from other online stores or sources won't be transferred. iTunes is designed to transfer content in one direction only, from iTunes to an iPod, iPhone, or iPad. This can be a problem if you have audio and video from another source on your device but want to move it into iTunes.

While iTunes doesn't support the capability to move non-iTunes purchases into iTunes, there are a few applications out there that can help you. The best of these is an app called Senuti (www.fadingred.com/senuti).

▶ Senuti is iTunes spelled backwards.

To use Senuti, you attach your iOS device to the Mac and open the application. All the media contained in the device is listed in the main window, with the playlists in the sidebar to the left, as shown in Figure 19-2. To transfer files, you highlight the ones you want (or choose Edit ➜ Select All to highlight all the files) and click Transfer. A dialog appears, asking if you want to transfer to iTunes or copy files.

ENABLING DISK MODE

In order to use Senuti on an iPod, you need to enable disk mode. To do this, you plug in the iPod while holding ⌘+Option to prevent automatic syncing (or select Prevent iPods, iPhones and iPads from Syncing Automatically from the iTunes Devices preferences pane). Then choose the iPod from Devices in the sidebar and select Enable Disk Mode.

▶ You can choose a different folder for copying files in Senuti preferences.

If you choose Transfer to iTunes, files are copied to the iTunes folder and appear in the iTunes Library. If you choose Copy Files, they are transferred to the iTunes Media folder.

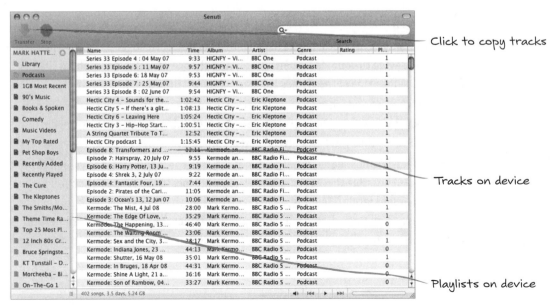

FIGURE 19-2: Senuti displays all the media contained in an iPod, iPad, or iPhone and enables you to transfer files to iTunes.

> **TIP** You can compare the files on a device with those in your iTunes library to see which ones you need to copy and which ones are already present. Choose View → Hide Songs → In iTunes to make songs you already have disappear from Senuti's main window.

Once your tracks are back in iTunes, you can then use it to sync and copy them to a device you want to use. Of course, iTunes is about much more than just media management. It's also used to control and manage the iOS operating system itself, which we'll look at next.

USING ITUNES TO UPDATE AND RESTORE THE OPERATING SYSTEM

▶ It's puzzling because the iPad makes a great portable computer, but you need a computer to set it up.

One slightly puzzling thing about Apple's iOS devices is that they don't work completely as stand-alone devices. Instead, iOS devices hook up with iTunes in Mac OS X (or Windows) for setup, software upgrades, and management of media (audio, video, photos, and so on). You also use iTunes for setting up, updating, backing up, and generally managing the operating system on an iOS device.

Updating a Device

The easiest way to update a device to the latest version of the operating system is to attach the device to your Mac, open iTunes, and choose your iPhone, iPod, or iPad from the Devices area of the iTunes sidebar, as shown in Figure 19-3.

▶ Updating an iOS device normally doesn't affect any of the content on your iPod, iPhone, or iPad. But you should back up your files first just in case.

To get iTunes to go online and see if there is a newer version of the software, you click Check for Update in the main window. Any available updates begin downloading, and iTunes takes you through the update process.

By default, iTunes searches online for updates to the iOS operating system. However, it is also possible to install updates from a file located in Finder (that you have downloaded separately). To do so, hold down Option when clicking Check for Update and iTunes and an Open dialog will enable you to select the update file. Members of the Apple Developer Connection (http://developer.apple.com) sometimes download upcoming versions of the iOS software to test, and this enables them to update the iOS software separately.

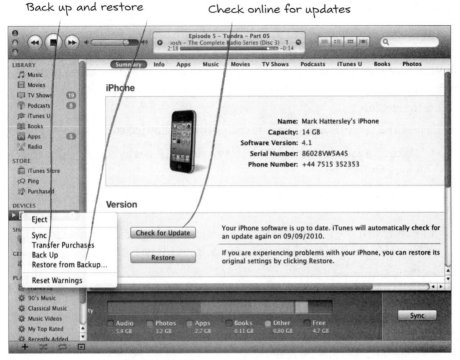

FIGURE 19-3: You use iTunes to update and restore iOS devices.

Backing Up a Device in iTunes

Every time you sync an iOS device with iTunes (as well as whenever you update or restore the device), you also perform a backup of the device. This backup contains most of the settings and apps contained on the device, but it doesn't include the audio, video, and photos.

It is possible to manually perform a backup. To do this, you Ctrl+click the device in the iTunes sidebar and choose Back Up from the contextual menu.

► You can sync these from iTunes to a device after you've restored the device.

TIP Another interesting menu item in the device's contextual menu in iTunes is Reset Warning. You can choose this command to reset all warnings associated with the device.

Restoring a Device in iTunes

▶ Restoring a device installs the latest version of iOS rather than the one the device originally came with.

It is possible to restore a device by using iTunes from a backup. You typically do this as a troubleshooting function when you are experiencing problems with the device. Restoring a device deletes all the data and restores the device to its factory settings before restoring the data from a backup. You then sync the device with iTunes to copy across the media.

To restore a device from iTunes, you complete the following steps:

1. Make sure you are running the latest version of iTunes by choosing iTunes → Check for Updates.

2. Connect the device to your Mac. In the iTunes sidebar, under Devices, select the device.

3. Ensure that the Summary tab is selected and click Restore (or Ctrl+click the device in the iTunes sidebar and choose Restore from Backup).

4. Click Restore.

▶ When you perform a backup, iTunes places the backup files in the ~/Library/ Application Support/ MobileSync/Backup folder.

5. A dialog asks if you want to back up the device before the restoration process. Click Back Up.

6. Click Restore again and click OK when the dialog indicates that the device has been restored to factory settings.

7. In the Set Up window in iTunes, choose a backup from the Restore from the Backup contextual menu and click Continue.

You can also restore an iPhone to factory settings (as if it were a new device) by choosing Set Up as a New iPhone (or iPod, iPad, and so on) in the final step.

Jailbreaking an iPhone

▶ It might be something you don't want it to do, either, such as harvest all your contacts for a spam list. Be careful when installing software that you obtain from outside the App Store.

Apple keeps tight control on the operating system used by iPhone, iPod touch, and iPad devices; it only allows you to install software from the iTunes Store, for example, and only software that it has approved. A process called *jailbreaking* enables you to adjust the iOS software to enable functionality beyond that allowed by Apple. When you jailbreak a device, you can install on it software from a wide range of non-Apple sources. This software can sometimes do things that Apple doesn't want it to do, such as change the visual style of the interface or run programs that Apple considers inappropriate or unsuitable (Apple won't allow pornography in the App Store, for example).

You can learn more about jailbreaking from the following websites:

▶ Redsn0w (http://redsn0w.com)

▶ Pwnage Tool (http://blog.iphone-dev.org)

▶ JailbreakMe (www.jailbreakme.com/faq.html)

> **WARNING** Jailbreaking an iOS device invalidates its warranty!

Apple consistently changes the security of iOS to prevent jailbreaking, so the means and methods of performing a jailbreak change over time.

SHARING FILES BETWEEN MAC OS X AND iOS

As iOS devices become more complex and competent, they become better at creating, editing, and working with files (documents, PDF files, and so on). iTunes manages some of these files—audio, video, epub and PDF files, and photos—through the sync process. However, this is somewhat limiting because it enables you to share only specific file types with specific iOS applications. However, it is possible to share files between Mac OS X and many iOS apps by using a variety of different methods, as described in the following sections.

Sharing Files with iTunes File Sharing

It's possible to share files directly between apps in iTunes and Mac OS X by using the File Sharing function in iTunes, as shown in Figure 19-4.

To share files, just follow these steps:

1. Connect the iOS device to your Mac and open iTunes.

2. In the iTunes sidebar, under Devices, select the device. Click Apps to open the Apps tab.

3. Scroll down below the Sync Apps list to locate the File Sharing section. Apps that support file sharing are displayed in the Apps list.

4. Choose an app for transferring files to and from iTunes.

Documents for selected app

Apps that support file sharing

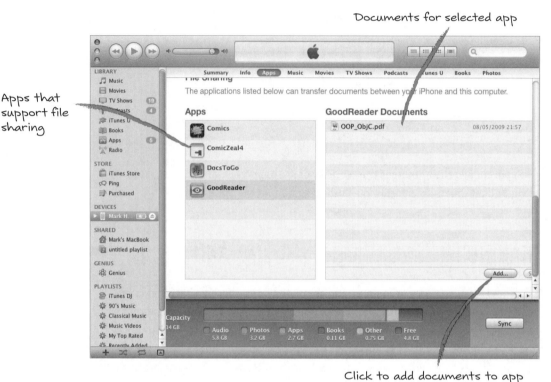

Click to add documents to app

FIGURE 19-4: The File Sharing part of iTunes enables you to transfer files between iOS apps and Mac OS X.

5. To add a file from Mac OS X, click the Add button and use the Choose dialog to locate the desired file. Click Choose to copy it from Finder to the app.

6. To transfer a file from an app to Mac OS X, highlight the file in the Documents list in iTunes and click Save. Then choose a location from the Choose dialog and click Choose.

> **TIP** You can drag and drop files directly from the Finder to the Documents list in iTunes.

Transferring files using the File Sharing feature is the fastest and most straightforward way to transfer documents to and from apps.

E-mailing Files to an iOS Device

In addition to using File Sharing, another way to get a file to an iOS device from Mac OS X is to attach a file to an e-mail message and open it on the iOS device. To do this, you follow these steps:

1. Attach the file to an e-mail message and send it to an e-mail account that is accessible on your iOS device.

2. Open Mail on the iOS device and open the e-mail message with the attached file.

3. Click and hold the attached file icon to bring up a series of selections, as shown in Figure 19-5. iOS chooses the app most likely to be used for this kind of file.

4. Tap Open In *"name of app"* to use this app. Alternatively, tap Open In to bring up a selection of supporting apps.

This process sends the file from the e-mail message to the selected app. The file then appears in that app in the same way it would if you used File Sharing in iTunes.

▶ You can also use File Sharing to transfer files opened using e-mail back into Mac OS X.

Attached file

Use Quick Look to read the file in Mail

Open the default app

Choose an app to open file in

FIGURE 19-5: You can open files in the Mail app in iOS by using different applications.

Transferring Files with MobileMe

If you have an active MobileMe account, you can use the iDisk function to transfer files from Mac OS X to an iOS device. To do this, you need to install the iDisk app from the App Store on your iOS device.

▶ Open the iTunes Store and search for iDisk. Or use Safari to visit http://itunes.apple.com/us/app/mobileme-idisk.

> **TIP** Unlike with the e-mail method, with iDisk, you can only send files that can be opened in iDisk preview. For example, you cannot transfer epub documents because the default iPhone Quick Look preview can't read them (even though iBooks and other apps can). However, you can use iDisk to e-mail a link to the file by using the Share icon. Then you open the file in Mail as outlined earlier and transfer it to a supporting app.

To transfer a file from iDisk to an app on your iOS device that supports the file, you follow these steps:

1. Transfer the file to a location in iDisk.

2. Open the iDisk app on the iOS device.

3. Locate and open the document in the iDisk app. This will open a preview of the file.

4. Tap the screen to bring up the menu icons and tap the Share icon. This brings up a list of supporting apps.

5. Select an app. The file is transferred from iDisk to the app.

This technique enables you to store files on iDisk and transfer them to an iOS device as you need them, saving on vital storage space within the device.

> **CROSSREF** Chapter 20 has more information on using iDisk and MobileMe.

STREAMING MEDIA FROM MAC OS X TO AN iOS DEVICE

It is possible to use Apple iDisk and other services to stream media remotely to an iOS device. This is great because most iOS devices have fairly limited storage space.

> **WARNING** When streaming data remotely to an iOS device, be sure that you
> are not exceeding your data limit with your data provider. Many cell phone con-
> tracts come with a stringent data allowance, and exceeding that limit can be
> costly. If you plan on streaming large files (especially video), you should stick
> to streaming over a Wi-Fi connection unless you are confident of your data al-
> lowance. You can check how much data you have used by selecting Settings ➜
> General ➜ Usage. You should choose Reset Statistics at the start of a billing
> period and check your data usage as you go.

Streaming video from iDisk is pretty straightforward. You simply open the iDisk app on an iOS 4 device and click on the file to open it. Media files open in the Quick-Time app; other files (such as PDF documents) open in the iDisk Quick Look preview window.

Discovering Alternatives to iDisk

You don't have to use Apple's iDisk to transfer files to an iOS device. Two of the most popular alternatives are SugarSync (www.sugarsync.com) and DropBox (www.dropbox .com). Both of these file-syncing services are outlined in Chapter 7, and both have iOS apps available. With these services, you can access synced files directly on the iOS device in much the same was as with iDisk.

You can also access documents from your Mac, either on a local network or remotely using apps. These typically work in conjunction with an application you install in Mac OS X (known as server software) and enable you to browse the Finder and open documents directly.

> ▶ You can't open digital rights management (DRM)-protected files—such as those purchased from the iTunes Store—in iDisk or stream them to an iOS device due to licensing restrictions.

Some apps are worth investigating here:

▶ **Here, File File** (http://herefilefile.com) is an iPhone and iPod touch app that enables you to use your device to browse and open files on a Mac. You need to install a companion server application in Mac OS X. You can create a password in this software that enables you to log in to Mac OS X remotely.

▶ **AirSharing Pro** (http://avatron.com/apps) is dedicated to movies and works in a similar way to Here, File File. You install a program called AirServer in Mac OS X and use it to determine which files and folders to share with the remote app installed on iOS devices.

▶ **FileBrowser** (www.stratospherix.com) is an iPad-only app that enables you to browse local network drives. However, it lacks the supporting desktop-side software, so to get it to work, you must enter the IP address and login details manually. The setup is slightly more complex for this app than for the others mentioned here, but it's a free app.

I am a keen user of Here, File File to access files remotely on my Mac, although for audio and video access there are other, more specific, apps that you should investigate.

Streaming Files from a Local Mac

▶ The network could be your local Wi-Fi network or, with a little legwork, the wider Internet.

A great trick is to set up your iOS device to access the files on your Mac or network attached storage (NAS) drive so you can play the media files over the network. These programs typically work in a similar fashion to apps mentioned as alternatives to iDisk (in that they require software to be installed in Mac OS X, and an app installed on the iOS device), but they focus on locating and playing media files (such as audio and video).

Some programs to investigate here include the following:

- **AirVideo (www.inmethod.com):** This superb program enables you to stream video from a Mac directly to an iPad or iPhone. What's great about AirVideo is that it can convert video files before streaming them, so it can play just about any video file. It can also be used to convert and add video clips to iTunes. By entering a PIN into the iPhone app (provided by the Mac OS X software), you can even stream video over the Internet.

▶ Both AirVideo and StreamToMe work happily together on Mac OS X, and I have both installed. I use AirVideo to watch video clips remotely, and StreamToMe for audio.

- **StreamToMe (http://projectswithlove.com):** This works like AirVideo, and also converts files into iOS friendly formats. However, it also streams audio as well as video, making it a good option for listening to music, audiobooks, and podcasts remotely.

- **EyeTV (www.elgato.com):** This app enables you to watch live television streamed directly from Mac OS X, as well as record and watch television remotely. You will need a compatible Elgato eyeTV hardware product attached to your computer.

- **SlingBox (www.slingmedia.com):** This is a slightly unusual product that sits between your digital set top box (such as cable or satellite receiver) and your television; it then pushes the live TV signal over the network and you can access it using the SlingBox app (or via a web-based viewer). It's a good solution for watching live television remotely, if somewhat tricky to set up correctly.

These programs enable you to play media files remotely (as well as access all your other files). This can save you countless amounts of storage space on an iOS device and make your media experience much more lively.

CONTROLLING MAC OS X REMOTELY WITH AN IOS DEVICE

One final trick that I want to share here is the ability not just to share files but also to remotely control Mac OS X via the small screen of an iPhone, iPad, or iPod touch. A couple of applications enable you to do this, and my favorite is LogMeIn Ignition (www.logmein.com), which enables you to access your Mac OS X desktop via an iOS device (iPhone, iPod touch, or iPad), as shown in Figure 19-6.

Controlling Mac OS X remotely

FIGURE 19-6: LogMeIn Ignition enables this iPad to access and control a Mac OS X computer.

Like many other apps that enable you to access your Mac, LogMeIn comes in two parts: the server software that you install in Mac OS X and the LogMeIn Ignition app that you install on the iOS device.

The LogMeIn Ignition interface interacts slightly differently on the small-screen iPhone and iPod touch than it does on the iPad. On the iPhone and iPod touch, the pointer remains in the center of the display, and the desktop moves around it. You drag your finger to move the desktop, and you pinch to zoom in and out. Tapping the display sends a mouse press to the computer, and a variety of double-taps, and tap-and-holds enable you to drag and drop windows and perform all other tasks.

The iPad's slightly larger display enables the app to act in a slightly more computer-like manner. The pointer moves around the display as you drag your finger, and tapping anywhere on the screen acts as a mouse press.

▶ It's possible to set the iPad app control to resemble the iPhone app or to act as direct input, with the pointer clicking exactly where you tap the screen.

USING AN IOS DEVICE AS A SECOND SCREEN

A neat trick to perform with an iPad, iPhone, or iPod touch is to use the device as a second screen. By using an app called Air Display (`http://avatron.com/apps/air-display`), you can extend the display of your Mac onto your iPad or another iOS device. You can also control the windows on the display by using the touch-screen interface.

The great thing about LogMeIn is that you can use it to access a Mac with the server software installed on any other computer via a web browser, and the software works pretty well even over a data connection. It's saved my bacon a couple of times!

SUMMARY

This chapter is all about using Apple's incredible iOS devices (the iPad, iPhone, and iPod touch) with a Mac OS X computer. Because Apple designs both the iOS devices and Mac OS X, they all work seamlessly together. With a few tricks, you can transfer files between iOS and Mac OS X in a variety of ways. You can tether your iOS device to Mac OS X and use the iTunes File Sharing service, or you can bounce the files using a variety of wireless methods. It's also possible to hook up your iOS device to Mac OS X and store media on the Mac's spacious hard drive; then you can stream it directly to an iPhone, iPod, or iPad. Combine this with online storage services, and you can access all your computer files from anywhere you have a data connection. For the ultimate in remote control, it's possible to completely take over Mac OS X from an iPhone, performing all the big tasks that Mac OS X can execute. In addition, programs such as LogMeIn demonstrate just how powerful Apple's small iOS devices really are.

PART IV

TRAINING UP AS A MAC GENIUS

CHAPTER 20

Getting Your Head in the Clouds with MobileMe

IN THIS CHAPTER

▶ Syncing the information on your Macs with a MobileMe account

▶ Using iDisk to store files so that you can access them from anywhere

▶ Accessing the files on your Mac remotely by using Back to My Mac

▶ Locating a lost or stolen iPhone, iPad, or iPod

▶ Using web apps on the MobileMe website

You might have heard the term "cloud computing" thrown around over the past few years. Cloud computing is something of a buzzword, with many tech watchers thinking it represents the way we'll all work in the future. In essence, with cloud computing, your data, computer applications, and even the computer processing power are all provided by an online server and streamed to your computer. Apple offers a wide range of cloud functions as part of MobileMe (www.me.com). Like many other cloud services, you can use MobileMe online through the Safari web browser, but some of its services integrate closely with Mac OS X. MobileMe also offers Mac OS X users some features that you can't find anywhere else. This chapter is all about using MobileMe with Mac OS X to perform that unique form of computing in the clouds.

USING MOBILEME TO SYNC YOUR MACS

To take advantage of the MobileMe services, you need to sign up to MobileMe for a 12-month period (currently $99 per year). MobileMe is available as a single-user service with 20GB of e-mail and file storage space, or as a family pack. The family pack enables an additional four users to each have an e-mail address and 5GB of storage. If you get the family pack, you get a Shared folder in iDisk, and all members using the same family pack account can share files by simply dropping them into this folder.

> **TIP** For some reason, it's always cheaper to buy a boxed copy of MobileMe from Amazon.com (and enter the supplied code to get another 12 months of service) than it is to buy it from Apple. Check what deals Amazon and other online resellers are offering before signing up for MobileMe.

One of MobileMe's most popular services (in addition to providing you with a me.com e-mail address) is its ability to sync up data between multiple Mac computers and iOS devices, such as your iPhone, iPad, or iPod touch.

If you haven't done so already, you'll want to sign up and sign in to the service, using your username and password. Once you've signed in to MobileMe, you can sync information using the Sync tab in the MobileMe preferences pane.

Adjusting the Sync Settings

In the MobileMe preferences pane, you click the Sync tab and then the Advanced button to display a list of all the different computers that are being synced with your MobileMe account, as shown in Figure 20-1. To stop a machine from syncing with MobileMe, you choose the computer from the list and click Stop Syncing Computer.

Another neat trick to know is Reset Sync Data, which you can find by clicking the Advanced button on the Sync tab. This function enables you to replace data on your Mac with the data on MobileMe, or you can replace MobileMe data with the data on your Mac, as shown in Figure 20-2. This can be useful if you have a discrepancy between the data in either place and decide to replace the incorrect data with the set that you know is correct.

▶ MobileMe's e-mail service uses push technology, which means e-mails are sent straight to your iOS device as soon as they are received at Apple's server.

▶ You can also use MobileMe to sync information on a Windows PC, but iOS devices such as the iPhone and iPad don't appear in the list of computers, even if they are syncing information.

▶ If your data becomes messed up on MobileMe, you can use Time Machine to replace the data on one machine and use Reset Sync Data to replace it on MobileMe and all the other machines.

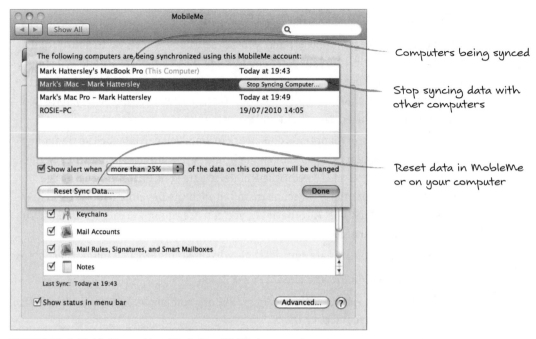

Computers being synced

Stop syncing data with other computers

Reset data in MobileMe or on your computer

FIGURE 20-1: MobileMe enables data in Mac OS X to be synced across multiple Macs.

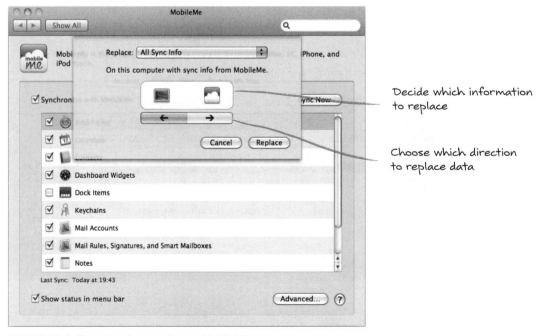

Decide which information to replace

Choose which direction to replace data

FIGURE 20-2: Resetting the sync data on MobileMe.

Changing MobileMe Sync Intervals

▶ For a complete outline of syncing schedules for MobileMe, see http://support .apple.com/kb /TS1155.

Using the MobileMe preferences pane, you can set the sync interval to hourly, daily, weekly, or automatic intervals. Most people stick with automatically and sync important information (contacts, calendars, bookmarks, and so on) within a minute of the information being changed. Less important information, such as the Keychain and preferences, are synced every hour and every four hours, respectively.

If the default interval options don't work for you, you can change the frequency of syncing to a regular interval—for example, every five minutes—that suits your needs. To do this, you need to edit the MobileMe data sync Plist file by using the Property List Editor utility, which is installed with the Developer Tools from the Mac OS X optional installs. Alternatively, you can use a program called PlistEdit Pro (www.fatcatsoftware.com).

▶ Plist files (or property list files) are files contained in the Library that contain settings for a program. Plist editors enable you to manually change the settings of Plist files.

To edit the MobileMe data sync Plist file with PlistEdit Pro, you follow these steps:

1. Open PlistEdit Pro and choose File ➔ Open.

2. Navigate to ~/Library/Preferences/ByHost/com.apple.DotMacSync.[*your Mac address*].plist and click Open.

3. Locate the AutoSyncInterval setting and change the number in the Value column to the number of minutes you want, as shown in Figure 20-3. (If the preference is set to Automatically, the Value column will show 60.)

4. Choose File ➔ Save.

The new schedule will remain in place until you open the MobileMe preferences pane and choose a different sync schedule.

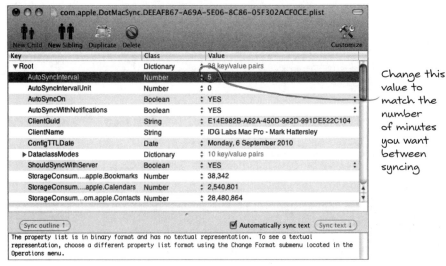

FIGURE 20-3: You can use PlistEdit Pro to adjust your syncing preferences.

USING IDISK FOR CLOUD STORAGE

An excellent feature that MobileMe offers subscribers is an online storage space called *iDisk*. The really neat part about iDisk is that—unlike most other online storage services—it integrates completely with Mac OS X, enabling you to drag and drop files from within Finder, as if it were a hard drive attached to your computer.

The iDisk appears under Devices in the Finder window's sidebar. By default, it comes with a selection of empty folders—Documents, Movies, Music, Pictures, and so on—and you are free to add your own folders.

▶ iDisk can run substantially more slowly than a regular hard drive, however, depending on the speed of your Internet connection.

> **CROSS-REF** The Software folder is designed to enable Apple to deliver programs to you, although it has only contained the Backup application for a long time now. Chapter 7 has more information on backing up data.

Setting Up iDisk Sync

By default, Mac OS X sends and receives data to and from iDisk as it's required. However, it is possible to set up Mac OS X to create a complete copy of the iDisk folder in Mac OS X. All the files are kept locally, and only changes to the local files are sent to the remote server. This has two major advantages. First, you can access the files from iDisk even when you're not connected to the Internet. Second, it ensures that files can be opened, copied, and worked on much faster (after they have been copied to the local disk).

The downside is that you lose a portion of hard drive space, although with the default iDisk typically taking up 20GB of space, it's bound to fit on your hard drive. To copy the iDisk contents to the local hard drive, you click Start in the iDisk tab of the MobileMe preferences pane.

PREVENTING CONFLICTS

One problem with iDisk syncing is that conflicts can occur between files that have been changed in two different areas before the sync has taken place. You can help prevent these conflicts by selecting the option Always Keep the Most Recent Version of a File. However, with this option selected, you run the risk of deleting data on the older file. For this reason, I don't use iDisk syncing.

Sharing Files with iDisk

As well as providing you with a place to store your files online, iDisk is really great for sharing files: both enabling you to send files to other people and allowing them to send files to you. Your iDisk contains a Public folder that you can use to share files with other Mac users.

When you add files to your Public folder, another user can download it online by using the URL http://public.me.com/[yourname]. As well as using the web interface, a Mac OS X user can choose Go ➜ iDisk ➜ Other Users Public Folder from the Finder menu and enter his or her MobileMe name to open the iDisk in Mac OS X.

If you select the Allow Others to Write Files in Your Public Folder check box in the MobileMe preferences pane, as shown in Figure 20-4, other users can use the same URL and Finder functionality to add files, and they can download files as well.

▶ It may be a good idea to password protect your Public folder. Select the Password Protect Your Public Folder check box and click Set Password.

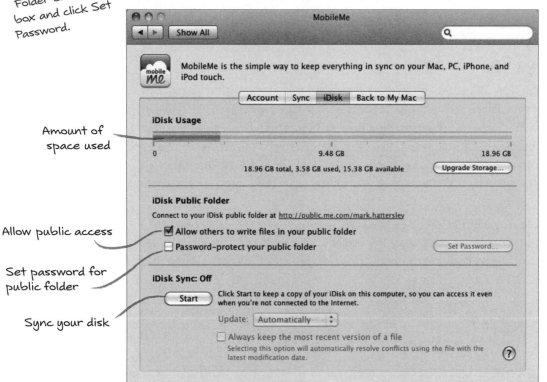

Amount of space used

Allow public access

Set password for public folder

Sync your disk

FIGURE 20-4: iDisk contains a Public folder that you can use to share files with other users.

SHARING IDISK FILES WITH ME.COM

It's possible to share a file in iDisk by sending an e-mail link to the file. You can do this only when using the iDisk web app, though, and not through iDisk in Finder. To do so, you follow these steps:

1. Copy a file to a location on iDisk. The file must be smaller than 1GB, or me.com will refuse to send the file.

2. Open a web browser and go to **www.me.com/idisk**. Enter your login and password.

3. Use the web interface to navigate to the file and click Share File.

4. Enter the e-mail address you want to send the file to and click Share. You can also add a message to go with the e-mail message.

The person at the receiving end gets an e-mail message containing the link and your message. Clicking the link downloads the file. This is a great way of sharing files larger than the 10MB to 20MB allowed by most e-mail servers.

As you can see, iDisk is not just great for storing files; it's great for sharing files as well.

ACCESSING YOUR MAC REMOTELY WITH BACK TO MY MAC

MobileMe provides users with a neat feature called Back to My Mac. This feature not only enables you to access the files on a Mac remotely via the Internet, it also enables you to control the Desktop of a Mac remotely, using Mac OS X's Screen Sharing technology.

You have to enable Back to My Mac on each of the computers that you want to access remotely. To do so, you open the Back to My Mac tab in the Mobile preferences pane and click Start. You also need to enable Screen Sharing and File Sharing in the Sharing preferences pane to access those features.

▶ There's also a good service called LogMeIn (www.logmein.com) that provides similar functionality and has iPhone and iPad apps. See Chapter 19 for more info.

> **WARNING** In order for Back to My Mac to work, your router needs to support NAT port forwarding. An Apple base station typically provides decent support, but you might need to access your router's settings and ensure that NAT port forwarding is switched on. If you are using a firewall, you might also need to ensure that Back to My Mac can get through the firewall.

Accessing computers remotely using Back to My Mac is exactly the same as if both Macs were on the local network and using Sharing services. All Macs running Back to My Mac will appear in the Shared area of the Finder's sidebar. You can choose Connect As to log on and share files or Share Screen to control the Mac remotely.

LOCATING YOUR IOS DEVICE REMOTELY

A great feature of MobileMe is called Find My iPhone, and you can also use it to find iPod touch and iPad devices. This feature is handy if you've lost an iPhone because it enables you to locate the device and lock it or wipe its data.

▶ iOS devices use a combination of Wi-Fi network triangulation and GPS to provide location information.

Find My iPhone uses the Location Services capability provided within iOS devices and sends the information to MobileMe. MobileMe then uses the information to provide the location of the device using Google Maps, as shown in Figure 20-5.

Click to access additional commands

Devices sending their location to Find My iPhone

Location of selected device

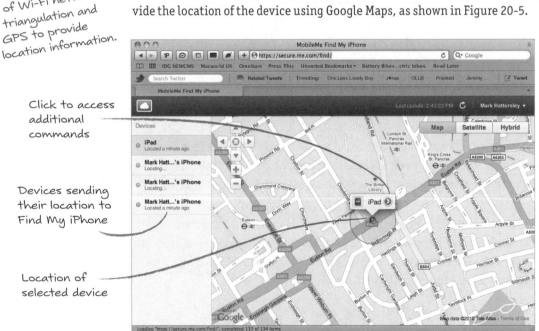

FIGURE 20-5: MobileMe can display the location of iOS devices.

To use Find My iPhone, you first need to set up an iOS device with a MobileMe account and turn on Find My iPhone. To do so, you choose Settings → Mail, Contacts, Calendars → MobileMe and then select On for Find My iPhone. With Find My iPhone switched on in the iOS device, you can use the MobileMe website to locate the device. Head to www.me.com/find and enter your login and password details. The Devices sidebar lists all the different iOS devices you have registered with MobileMe, and clicking one brings up its location on a map in the main window.

In addition to using it to locate a device remotely, you can use Find My iPhone to send commands to the remote device, as shown in Figure 20-6. To access these commands, you click the arrow icon next to the device shown on the map and choose one of the following commands:

▶ **Display Message or Play Sound:** This command sends a message to the device and plays an optional sound. It's handy if you've lost the device and want to send a message to let the finder know how to get hold of you.

▶ **Lock:** This command enables you to send a four-digit passcode to lock the device remotely. The person who has the device will need to enter the four-digit code to use any of its functions.

▶ **Wipe:** This command enables you to remove all data from the device and return it to a factory condition.

▶ Even if you lock your iPhone, the person who has it can still wipe the device and begin using it.

Message typed in web browser   Message appears on the device

FIGURE 20-6: You can use Find My iPhone to send messages remotely to an iOS device.

These features can be used to find a lost device, lock it, and send messages to it. Hopefully, your missing iOS device will be found by someone honest enough to respond to your messages and return it. If that fails and you need to remove sensitive information, you can always lock the device or wipe it.

> **WARNING** If you use the Wipe command, you'll no longer be able to use the Find My iPhone feature to locate, lock, or send messages to the device. I recommend that you lock the phone and try to use the messaging service to communicate with a person who has found it, before using the wipe function— unless, of course, you have extremely sensitive data on the device and need to wipe it as a precaution.

USING THE MOBILEME WEBSITE

In addition to providing services that hook up to Mac OS X, MobileMe features an incredibly rich website that enables you to access Mail, Contacts, Calendar, Gallery, iDisk, and Find My iPhone. You can log on to the MobileMe website by using the URL www.me.com, where you enter your user name and password. The main window displays programs in the web browser window.

▶ The only type of menu that is missing is the contextual menu (the one you access in Mac OS X by Ctrl+clicking or right-clicking).

The MobileMe web programs are more advanced than those in many other online services: You can click and drag items, resize window panes, and access interactive menus that offer a wide array of options.

There are currently six different applications available in MobileMe's web applications, as shown in Figure 20-7, and you move among them by using the App Switcher. You can click the cloud icon in the top left of the interface to access the App Switcher and then click the application that you want to open.

▶ This is similar to the App Switcher in Mac OS X, which you access by pressing ⌘+Tab.

Given all the advantages of using MobileMe, it's a good idea to sign up for an account (a free trial is available) if you haven't already done so.

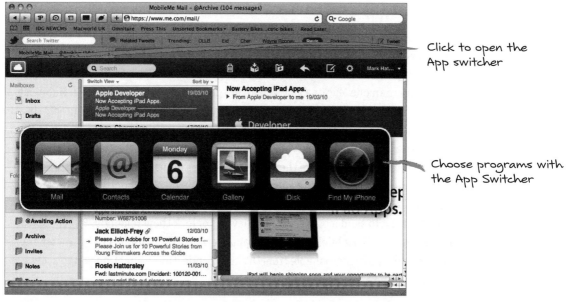

Click to open the
App switcher

Choose programs with
the App Switcher

FIGURE 20-7: The MobileMe web interface acts almost like an online operating system with complex web applications.

CREATING E-MAIL ALIASES

There's a neat trick you can perform in the MobileMe Mail web app that you can't do in the desktop app: You can create aliases.

With each MobileMe account, you are allowed up to five aliases. You follow these steps to set up an e-mail alias:

1. Go to **www.me.com**, enter your login and password details, and go to the Mail app.

2. Click the Actions icon and choose Preferences.

3. Click the Addresses tab.

4. Click the Add (+) icon next to Addresses, choose Mail Alias, and click Next.

5. Choose Mail Alias and click Next. Enter a name in the Alias text field and click Next.

6. If the alias is available, click Done to finish setting it up.

The alias works like a completely different e-mail account, and you can send and receive e-mail to the account from within the web-based Mail app and the Mac OS X-based Mail app.

SUMMARY

In this chapter you learned about cloud services and Apple's MobileMe offering. Although you have to sign up and pay for a yearly contract to use MobileMe, if you have more than one Mac or a Mac and an iOS device, it's worth the money. MobileMe provides you with push e-mail, plus instant syncing of calendars and contacts. It also syncs a lot of other Mac OS X information, which makes managing multiple Macs easier. There's also a great service called iDisk included with MobileMe where you can store files remotely and share them with others. In addition, Back to My Mac enables you to access files and control a Desktop remotely. Find My iPhone is another impressive MobileMe feature; it enables you to locate an iOS device remotely on a map, and you can use it to send messages to lost devices or lock them remotely. But the most impressive part of MobileMe is the web applications. They run in a web browser and are virtually indistinguishable from Desktop applications, enabling you to access your work from any computer.

CHAPTER 21

Troubleshooting Tricks and Recovery Tips

Mac OS X is a sturdy, stable, and simple operating system. Chances are you'll use it for many trouble-free months without any problems. That's not to say it's bulletproof, however. The more you use a computer—and the more complicated hoops you get it to jump through—the more you run the risk of something going wrong. In fact, sooner or later, you're bound to screw things up in some way or another, either because you don't know what you're doing or because you've tinkered to the point of destruction. But that's how a lot of computing is learned—by messing around, messing up, and then cleaning up the problem. Then you learn not just how the problem is caused but how to fix it. This is also a good way to learn more about the operating system. In this chapter you'll learn just what to do with your Mac when things go awry.

SPOTTING PROBLEMS AND SEARCHING FOR SOLUTIONS

Typically you'll know when you have a problem with a Mac because you'll spot some behavior pattern that you're unhappy with. While there are thousands of potential problems in hundreds of categories, most problems you'll encounter fall into one of these categories:

▶ **System failure:** This can be either a power failure or a failure to start up the Mac OS X operating system.

▶ **Network failure:** This occurs when the system itself works but the network the Mac is attempting to connect to doesn't. Symptoms include lack of Internet access, e-mail failure, and inability to connect to shared volumes.

▶ **Program crash:** With this problem, a program typically fails to start, quits unexpectedly, or hangs (that is, refuses to respond to user input).

▶ **Weird behavior:** A program or the operating system may generally behave oddly. Indications include error messages and unwanted dialogs. Other problems include features not working or the program not performing requested tasks.

> **NOTE** You might have heard the saying "don't fix something that isn't broken." It's not bad advice, because you can fix something to the point of breaking it completely. However, most Mac gurus learned their craft by tinkering, breaking, and fixing. If this sounds like you, then consider getting a spare system, known as a "dirty Mac," which you use for playing around with. Use another Mac sensibly for important work.

▶ When you are troubleshooting your machine, the first thing you should ask yourself is what you were doing or changing just prior to the problem occurring. The answer will help you find a solution.

Problems rarely occur for no reason, and they almost always result from some change in the hardware or software. Have you installed any new software, made any significant changes to Mac OS X, or installed any new hardware (new RAM, hard drive, graphics card, and so on)? Understanding what has changed can help you solve the problem. In extreme cases, you may need to take the computer back to an older state by removing the new hardware, uninstalling the software, setting System Preferences settings back to their default settings, and so on.

> **TIP** "Turn it off and back on again" is an adage that's been trotted out so many times that it's become almost a joke. But it very often works. So before looking for solutions or heading into System Preferences to change settings, try restarting your computer, base station, and any associated hardware and see if your problem goes away.

One of the best things you can do when fixing a computer is to go online and see if somebody else has encountered the problem. The following reputable sites can help you troubleshoot and solve all sorts of common and unusual problems:

- ▶ **www.google.com:** If you encounter an error message, don't just click OK or Cancel to get rid of it. Instead, copy and paste the message into a search site, such as Google. Chances are somebody has written about the message, its causes, and solutions.

- ▶ **www.apple.com/support/quickassist:** Apple's online support site can help you with common errors.

- ▶ **http://support.apple.com:** Apple's more in-depth support site is full of information on just about every type of service.

- ▶ **http://discussions.apple.com:** Apple's incredibly deep forum provides information on just about every Apple product, program, and service.

- ▶ **http://forums.macworld.com:** The Macworld forums offer a wide range of information, and you can use them to request advice from other knowledgeable Mac fans.

Heading online should always be your first port of call with any problem you don't already know how to fix.

FIXING SYSTEM FAILURES

A system failure is the most terrifying kind of fault because it affects the entire system, which is now stubbornly refusing to do anything.

One cause of system failure is a power problem. Power problems can be relatively easy to fix, or they can require you to return the computer or take the Mac in for service. Before packing up your Mac and taking it in for testing, be sure to go through these tests:

▶ **Check the light.** Make sure there truly is no power going to the machine by checking the power light. This light should be a solid white if the computer is operating or pulsating if the Mac is in sleep mode.

▶ **Check the plug.** Ensure that the Mac and, if appropriate, the monitor, are both plugged in correctly.

▶ **Switch the power cable.** Get access to a different power cable (or in the case of a Mac notebook, a different power unit). Try replacing just the power cable on the power supply, as well as using a completely different power supply. Replacing the cable and even the power unit costs less than sending a Mac in for repair.

▶ **Test the power outlet.** It may not be the Mac but the power outlet that is at fault. By connecting a different electronic device to the outlet and ensuring that power flows to it, you can determine that it's the Mac at fault and not the power outlet.

If none of the preceding tips helps to fix your problem, then the problem is probably the result of an internal fault, with either the internal power supply unit or the internal components. In this case, you need to take the Mac in for repair.

Fixing Mac OS X Startup Problems

▶ I usually try Single User Mode first because it's faster, but the installation disc is a bit more user friendly.

Another kind of system failure occurs when you have power flowing to the Mac, but Mac OS X itself fails to start up. Many problems on the Mac result from Mac OS X not knowing where files are or have to do with the files themselves becoming corrupted. This can be annoying when the operating system is running, but if those files are vital to the startup process, it can bring your Mac to its knees. To fix your Mac, you have two options: You can use Single User Mode or try your installation disc.

To boot Mac OS X into Single User Mode and use text commands to perform a fix, you follow these steps:

▶ Single User Mode enables you to access the computer with a single superuser account that has root access.

1. With the Mac turned off, hold down ⌘+S and then start up Mac OS X. This boots the Mac into Single User Mode, which is a command-line interface where you have superuser privileges.

2. Type **/sbin/fsck -fy** to run File System Check and check the file system.

3. Check and check again. The display will return messages related to the checking and repairing of system problems. If Mac OS X has found problems (and it typically does), it reports "*****FILE SYSTEM WAS MODIFIED*****" at the end of the check.

4. Run File System Check until the problem is fixed. Type /sbin/fsck -fy again (and again) until the Mac reports "THE VOLUME MACINTOSH HD APPEARS TO BE OK."

5. Type **exit** to quit Single User Mode. Your Mac should now boot into Mac OS X.

To use the Mac OS X installation disc that came with your Mac (or the most recent version if you've bought an upgrade) to perform maintenance and repairs, you follow these steps:

1. Insert the Mac OS X disc into the optical drive and restart the Mac.

2. Hold down C during startup to run Mac OS X setup from the disc.

3. Choose a language when prompted to do so.

4. Ignore the Install Mac OS X window and choose Utilities ➜ Disk Utility from the menu bar to run Disk Utility.

5. Click Repair Disk to verify and correct any problems with the Mac OS X file structure.

6. Click Repair Permissions to check and fix any problems with the permissions related to system files.

7. Choose Disk Utility ➜ Quit Disk Utility to quit Disk Utility.

8. Choose Mac OS X Installer ➜ Quit Mac OS X Installer and click Restart to restart the Mac. It should now start up into Mac OS X.

Repairing the disk and verifying disk permissions is a good step toward fixing a wayward Mac OS X installation.

SHOULD YOU USE FSCK OR DISK UTILITY?

Apple notes that most users should use Disk Utility instead of the fsck utility in Single User Mode, although both techniques are worth knowing. Personally, I like the information provided by fsck, and it's a faster technique once you get the hang of it. Apple has more information on both of these techniques at its support website: http://support.apple.com/kb/ts1417.

Fixing a Gray Screen During Startup

A rare but documented problem is Mac OS X displaying just a gray screen during startup. Getting a completely blank screen during startup is somewhat scary, but it's not always fatal. If this occurs, you can follow these steps to identify and solve the problem:

1. Hold down the power button to force the Mac to turn off.

2. Disconnect all devices and network cables. Remove everything from the Mac except for the power cable, keyboard, and mouse, as well as the display cable if you're using a desktop Mac with an attached monitor.

3. Start up the Mac and see if it works. If not, skip to step 5.

4. Connect devices one by one to find out which device is causing the problem. You can try updating the firmware on the wayward device or connect via a different method (USB, FireWire, and so on), if possible.

5. Hold down the Shift key during startup to boot into Safe Mode. Mac OS X loads with a minimal set of preferences and drivers. If this works, then try removing preferences and drivers to isolate the problem.

> **TIP** You can see the progress of a Safe Mode boot during startup by holding down Shift+⌘+V to boot in Verbose Mode, which displays information during startup.

6. If booting into Safe Mode doesn't work, try starting the Mac while holding down Option+⌘+P+R to reset the PRAM. The PRAMparameter RAM (PRAM) holds information on port configurations, fonts, the startup disk, virtual memory, the clock, and so on. Resetting this information can help with startup problems but may also reset information on the Mac. For more information on resetting the PRAM, see `http://support.apple.com/kb/HT1379`.

7. Finally, you can try to start up from the Mac OS X disc. You can use the Disk Utility to fix problems as outlined earlier in this chapter. You can also use the installation disc to reinstall Mac OS X, if necessary.

▶ If Mac OS X still refuses to start, you can retrieve the installation disc by restarting and holding down the mouse or trackpad to eject the disc during startup.

Hopefully, following these steps will enable you to at least start up, or restore your Mac. If none of these options work, then it's likely a hardware error and you'll need to take your Mac in for repair. A program called AppleJack might be able to help, but only if you installed it before the problem occurred.

USING APPLEJACK TO TROUBLESHOOT MACS

AppleJack is a troubleshooting assistant for Mac OS X, and it's a key tool in any Mac guru's arsenal. It even enables you to troubleshoot a Mac when you can't load up the Mac OS X interface.

Like fsck, AppleJack works in Single User Mode; you access it by holding down ⌘+S during the startup process. AppleJack then provides a list of options for repairing disks, permissions, cache files, preference files, and virtual memory. Best of all is an Auto Pilot mode that performs all the necessary fixes for you.

You can download AppleJack from http://sourceforge.net/projects/applejack. During installation, AppleJack adds commands that you can access in Single User Mode.

Once you have AppleJack installed, you run it by following these steps:

1. Restart Mac OS X and hold down ⌘+S to open the text-based Single User Mode interface.

2. Type **applejack** and press Return to run AppleJack. The AppleJack menu options appear.

3. Type **a** and press Return to run all the repair tools for AppleJack. (Alternatively, enter the numbers 1 to 5 to run the individual tasks, as listed in the AppleJack menu.) AppleJack runs through each task. Each time it runs a task, it offers you the option to skip it or quit, by pressing s or q, respectively.

4. Wait 10 seconds for the tasks to run automatically.

5. When AppleJack has finished running all its tasks, restart it by entering **r**.

AppleJack is an absolute must for serious Mac users. The only downside is that you need to install it before any problems occur, so it's worth downloading a copy and installing it right away. It'll be there waiting for you when need it.

REPAIRING AND REINSTALLING

If AppleJack doesn't fix your problem, then you may have to reinstall Mac OS X from scratch. You can use Disk Utility from the Mac OS X installation disc to format your main hard drive and reinstall Mac OS X, if necessary, as outlined in Chapter 2. It's a good thing you performed a full backup, as outlined in Chapter 7, isn't it?

REPAIRING A NETWORK FAILURE

A network failure can be exceedingly frustrating. So much work is performed via the Internet or on a local server that an otherwise fully functioning computer without network access can be more frustrating than one that doesn't function at all. The following sections help you to repair problems with both wired and wireless networks.

Fixing a Wired Connection

Here are some steps to take if a traditional wired network is not behaving correctly:

1. If you connect to a network via an Ethernet cable, check that the cables are connected properly to both the Mac and the wall jack. The Ethernet cable will have clear plastic covers, and you should inspect the wires inside to ensure that they look correctly placed. If there are multiple Ethernet sockets available, try a different one.

2. Turn off your modem and leave it off for 10 to 30 seconds so that all the power completely leaves it. Then turn it back on.

3. Make sure the ISP is working. Network connections often go down. Rather than having a local problem, you might be having trouble with your Internet service provider (ISP). It's a good idea to check with your ISP to ensure that it's not struggling before starting to tear down and rebuild your network setup.

4. Open the Network preferences pane and check the status of the network in the sidebar. When it's working correctly, there is a green light and the word *Connected*; a red or amber light indicates a problem. You can click an item in the sidebar, and the Status portion of the main window should give some indication of the current status, as shown in Figure 21-1.

5. Check that the Configure IPv4 pop-up menu is set to Using DHCP. You should also check that the router or server you are connecting to is set up to use DHCP. Alternatively, you may have to input an IP address manually; choose Manually from the Configure IPv4 pop-up menu and get the address information from whoever set up the network.

6. You can manually reset and request a new DHCP address from the router, which can help in some circumstances. Click Advanced in the Network preferences pane, choose the TCP/IP tab, and click Renew DHCP Lease.

7. Click Assist Me from the Network preferences pane to launch Network Setup Assistant. Its dialog helps you to set up a network connection and can be useful in creating a new connection.

▶ Dynamic Host Control Protocol (DHCP) is technology that enables devices such as your computer to automatically connect to a network. Most networks use DHCP to assign Internet Protocol (IP) addresses to computers.

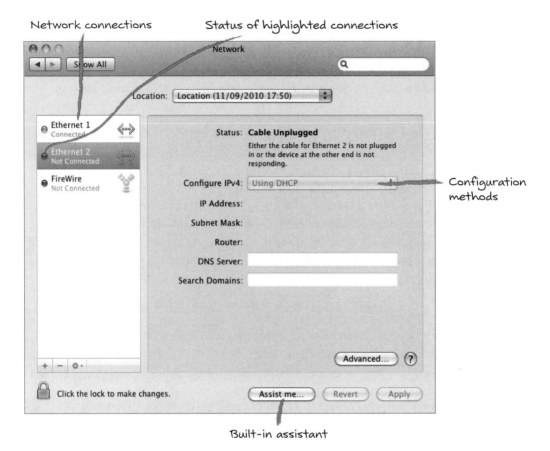

Network connections

Status of highlighted connections

Configuration methods

Built-in assistant

FIGURE 21-1: The Network preferences pane gives some indication about the current state of a network.

Working through these steps should help you with a failing network connection. I advise you to pay particular attention to step 3. I've spent hours rebuilding networks only to find that they suddenly start working again when the ISP fixes a problem on its back end.

> **TIP** Apple has more detailed network advice online at `http://support.apple .com/kb/HT1144`. One of the real problems with network connections is, of course, that looking for help online is a challenge when your network isn't working. Using an iPhone or iPad with a 3G Internet connection is a good way to search for help, and having one of these devices proves invaluable for frequent network troubleshooting.

Fixing a Wireless Connection

Fixing a wireless connection can be a pain, and much of the preceding advice for a wired connection applies here, too, although you need to check the wireless connection rather than the cables.

If you are fixing a problem with a wireless connection, also try the following steps:

1. Choose the AirPort icon in the menu bar and ensure that AirPort is set to On. (Alternatively, check in the Network preferences pane.)

2. The strength of a wireless network diminishes over distance (and when blocked by objects and walls). You might find an Internet connection to be intermittent at the edge of the router's range. Try moving closer to the router or moving the router closer to you or to an area with more space around it.

3. Microwave ovens, cordless telephones, and other electronic devices can interfere with a wireless network. Check nearby devices and turn them off to see if that helps.

4. Turn off the base station, wait 30 seconds, and turn it back on again.

As with a wired connection, it's a good idea to find out whether the ISP is having problems before taking apart the network.

TROUBLESHOOTING WAYWARD PROGRAMS

Sometimes your installation of Mac OS X is working fine and the network is just dandy, but you're having a problem with an individual program. All computer programs are complex, and problems can range from program to program. A program may not open, may open but freeze up, or may fail to quit correctly; or it may just act in a strange manner.

Whatever the program and problem, here are a few things you can try:

▶ **Clear the preferences.** Open the ~/Library/Preferences/ folder (as shown in Figure 21-2), look for files that relate to the program, and drag these files to the Trash. This will reset all the preferences for the program.

▶ **Remove and reinstall.** You can delete the program and reinstall it. Completely removing a program is easiest using a program like AppZapper (www.appzapper.com). Chapter 4 has more information on removing and installing software.

▶ Don't worry. These files are re-created when you restart the program.

Delete preferences files related to the poorly performing program

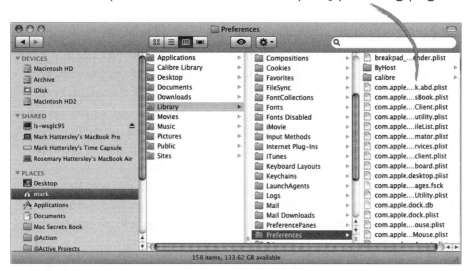

FIGURE 21-2: Deleting items in the Preferences folder can help Mac OS X applications run correctly.

- ▶ **Check system requirements.** Make sure your system and the program are compatible. Sometimes, for example, older programs that have not been updated may not run correctly on the latest version of Mac OS X.

- ▶ **Check online.** As with most other problems, you can usually find a solution online. Be sure to check the developer's website (usually a link to it can be found under the Help menu) and don't be afraid to e-mail the developer and ask questions. Most developers, especially those on small teams, are happy to have feedback from customers and will happily help you get the program running.

Most software problems can be fixed by deleting the preferences or reinstalling the program; if that doesn't work, then typically there is a more fundamental problem between the program and the specific Mac OS X version, and you may have to wait for the developer to fix the problem. Sometimes there may also be a conflict between the program and a non-Apple system extension or system preference.

▶ Checking the developer's website may give you some clue about the status of the program and when an update will be available.

SUMMARY

Macs are great fun when they work, but as with all other computers, things can go wrong, and that's when the fun stops (unless, of course, you like breaking and fixing things). All computers are complicated machines, and the problems you encounter will be vast and varied, but the Internet is your friend. Get into the habit of typing concise problem descriptions into search engines to find out whether other people have had trouble before you. If you can't find help from websites, try posting your problem on the Apple or Macworld forums. Of course, looking online for help works only if you can start up your Mac and get online, so in this chapter we've looked at some of the serious trouble spots you can encounter. Don't worry if your Mac doesn't start up; you can often get it up and running again. If there's one piece of advice to take away from this chapter, it's to install AppleJack on your Mac before trouble starts. It's a lifesaver.

Getting Under the Hood

You may think you're pretty good with a Mac, but among real Macheads, if you don't know what's going on under the hood, you don't know a thing. Mac OS X is a UNIX-certified operating system with a custom Aqua graphical user interface (GUI). If you want to be a real Mac professional, then learning how to use UNIX is a must. It's also rewarding, because UNIX gives you a much more direct means of interacting with Mac OS X. So if you've ever wanted to back out of the graphical richness that is Mac OS X and into the text-based world that lies beneath, this chapter is for you. A wonderful feature in Mac OS X called *X11* opens a whole new world of windowed applications. These applications offer a wide range of functions, and most are open-source programs. By the end of the chapter, all will be clear, and you'll be a better Mac user by far.

DISCOVERING UNIX ON A MAC

UNIX is the operating system that lies beneath Mac OS X, and you can get direct access to by using Terminal, as shown in Figure 22-1. Terminal is—in some ways—a text-based equivalent to the Finder, in that it enables you to view files and folders, move and edit items, open documents, and launch programs.

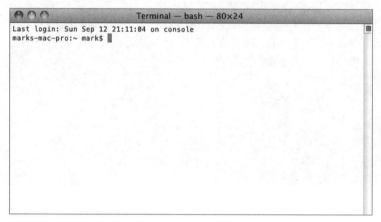

FIGURE 22-1: Terminal enables you to type UNIX commands directly into Mac OS X.

In some ways you might wonder why you'd ever use UNIX to work with files and folders, when the Finder is much easier. While UNIX is trickier to understand than the Finder, it's also much more powerful. And if you want to use UNIX commands, you really need to know how to navigate your way around the directory structure in Terminal. So stick with it.

When you open Terminal, a window appears, displaying some text like this:

```
Last login: Sun Sep 12 21:11:04 on console
marks-mac-pro:~ mark$
```

▶ The string of text before the command entry depends on which UNIX shell you are using. You can also edit the default text using the Terminal preferences.

The first line is a reference to when you last logged in to Terminal and from where (it may say Console or TTYS and a number). TTYS stands for teletypewriter and is a throwback to the old days when computers were often dumb terminals (or electronic typewriters with screens) connected to a server. Terminal emulates those computers.

The second line consists of the name of your computer and the account you are logged in to, with a tilde (~) before it and a dollar sign ($) after. This second line is the command line, and you enter commands after the dollar symbol ($).

▶ The tilde (~) symbol in UNIX stands for your home directory.

Try entering the following command:

```
ls
```

The ls command stands for *list* and displays all the files and folders in the directory, as shown in Figure 22-2. By default, you will be in your home directory, so it should list Applications, Documents, Movies, and so on.

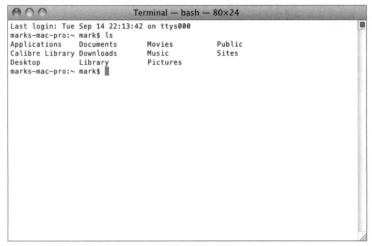

FIGURE 22-2: Files and folders are listed in columns using the **ls** command.

Now that you've discovered the command line interface, it's time to learn how to work your way around the directory structure in Terminal.

NAVIGATING FILES AND DIRECTORIES

Because Terminal is a command-line interface, rather than a GUI, you need to get used to navigating through folders by using text commands rather than by using the rich graphical interface of Finder.

To navigate through directories, you use the cd (change directory) command followed by the folder name. For example, to move to the Documents directory, you can type:

```
cd Documents
```

Now, if you use the ls command, you'll see the contents of your Documents directory rather than your home directory.

If you want to move to a directory that has a space in its name, such as Web Receipts, you can enclose the name in double quotation marks, like this:

```
cd "Web Receipts"
```

▶ In UNIX, folders are typically referred to as directories. These two terms mean the same thing. If you create a directory in UNIX, it appears as a folder in Finder.

Or you can close up the gap by using the backslash character, like this:

`cd Web\ Receipts`

The directory that contains the current folder (that is, the folder above the current folder) is known as the *parent*. To move back up to the parent directory, you type cd and two periods (..), like this:

`cd ..`

> ▶ In UNIX, a single period (.) means the current directory, and two periods (..) means the parent directory.

To navigate multiple directories at once, you use the slash (/) character. If you are in the home folder, you can change directly to the iTunes folder, for example, by using the following command:

`cd Music/iTunes`

It's also possible to navigate up multiple directories by combining double periods with a slash. For example, you use this command to move up two directories:

`cd ../..`

> **TIP** You can use just **CD** to quickly move back to your home folder. You can also move to the root of the hard drive by using the **cd** / command.

Finally, bear in mind that you can use `ls` to view the contents of folders other than the one you are looking at. If you are in the home folder, for example, you can enter the following to look inside the Movies folder:

`ls Movies`

When you use the `ls` command to view other folders, you remain in the folder you are currently working in. Fortunately, the `pwd` (print working directory) command can tell you which folder this is.

After you've entered commands, you can also enter a modifier to adjust the command. Here's an example:

`ls -a`

This command lists all the files in a directory, including hidden files, which are files that begin with a single period (.).

You can also get more information on the contents of a directory with this command:

`ls -l`

ABSOLUTE VERSUS RELATIVE PATHS

When using the **cd** and **ls** commands, it's important to know the difference between absolute and relative paths in Terminal.

An absolute path begins with / or ~. The path from the root folder starts with /, and the path from the home folder starts with ~. For example, the following two commands both use absolute paths to display the contents of my iTunes folder:

```
ls /Users/mark/Music/iTunes
ls ~/Music/iTunes
```

The first is an absolute path from the root of the hard drive, and the second an absolute path from the home folder. Both of these work no matter what directory you're currently in.

Relative paths, on the other hand, do not begin with / or ~ and are therefore evaluated in relation to the current folder.

For example, consider this command:

```
ls Music/iTunes
```

This command lacks the ~ or / at the front, so it will work only if you are currently in the directory containing the **Music** folder (in this case, the home folder). So if you have used the **cd** command to look at a different folder, such as the **Movies** folder, Terminal returns the message **ls: Movies: No such file or directory**.

The -1 modifier command stands for *long* and lists extended information on the contents of the list, as shown in Figure 22-3.

The permissions listing consists of 10 symbols. The first character indicates whether the item is a file (-) or a directory (d); the next three symbols are the read (r), write (w), and execute (x) permissions for the user; the next three are the read, write, and execute permissions for the group; and the final three are the read, write, and execute permissions for other users. If the permission is not set, a dash (-) appears in its place.

▶ You can use the Tab key to auto-complete items when typing. For example, you can type ls Mo and press Tab in the home folder to automatically enter ls Movies/. Autocomplete adds the slash character; you do not need to enter it manually.

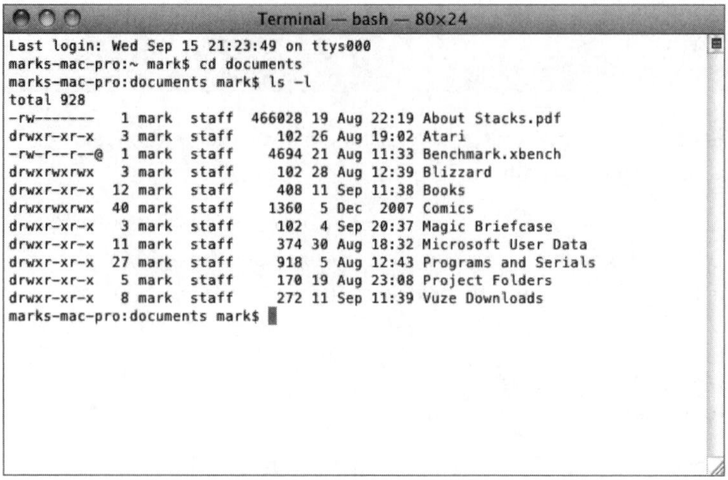

FIGURE 22-3: The `ls -l` command can display long information, offering more details on the contents.

Now that you know how to navigate files and folders, it's time to learn how to create and remove them.

Creating Files and Folders

You can create files and folders by using the `mkdir` (make directory) command. You need to enter the name of the directory after it, like this:

```
mkdir MyFiles
```

This code creates a folder in the current directory called `MyFiles`.

You can also create a text file by using the `touch` command:

```
touch letter
```

This creates a new file called `letter` in the current folder.

Now that we've created a file, let's learn how to move it.

Moving Files and Folders

A powerful use of UNIX is to move files and folders. You move items in UNIX by using the `mv` (move) command and specifying the file and the new location. (The location can be absolute or relative, as outlined earlier in the chapter.) For example, to move a file called `letter` from the home directory (assuming that you're in the home directory) to the `Documents` folder, you'd use the following:

```
mv letter Documents
```

▶ All documents created using touch are essentially strings of bytes, although you would most notably open them as text documents. You can open a document by using the open command; for example, you can use open letter to open the letter file in TextEdit.

To move the `letter` file from the current folder to the parent directory, you'd use the following:

```
mv letter ..
```

You can also use relative filenames. For example, you can use the following command to move the `letter` file from the home folder to a folder called `MyWork`, which is inside a folder called `MyFiles` on the root of the hard drive.

```
mv ~/letter/MyWork/MyFiles
```

You can also use `mv` to rename files and folders. For example, you can rename the `MyFiles` folder to `MyDocs` by using the following command:

```
mv MyFiles MyDocs
```

Now that we've moved and renamed a file, let's learn how to remove it.

Removing Files and Folders

You delete files by using the `rm` (remove) command. For example, the following command removes your `Letter` file:

```
rm Letter
```

It's also possible to remove multiple files by using `rm`:

```
rm Letter Letter2 Letter3
```

This removes files called `Letter`, `Letter2`, and `Letter3` inside the current directory.

To delete a directory, you use the `rmdir` (remove directory) command:

```
rmdir MyFiles
```

You can use the `rmdir` command only if the directory is empty. Otherwise, Terminal will throw a `Directory not empty` error.

To remove the folder with files inside, you need to include the `-r` (recursive) option with the `rm` (remove) command:

```
rm -r MyFiles
```

Because the `-r` option is quite powerful, it's best to get into the habit of using it with the `-i` (interactive) option. This provides a yes/no option to examine each file before deletion. You combine options by using both letters together, like this:

```
rm -ri MyFiles
```

▶ UNIX can look daunting to the uninitiated, but once you start using UNIX, you quickly get the hang of how it works.

▶ The `mv` command doesn't actually move the file. It creates a duplicate and then deletes the original.

▶ If one of the files listed with `rm` doesn't exist, you get an error message, but the correctly named files will still be deleted.

> **WARNING**   UNIX doesn't move files to the Trash. When you use the **rm** command to remove files or directories, they're removed from your filesystem. Although the data remains on the drive until overwritten, it may be difficult to recover.

Now that we've learned how work with files, let's make the most of using UNIX commands.

Repeating Commands

One of the frustrations of a command-line interface is having to type out long commands repeatedly. However, there are some shortcuts you can use to repeat commands. For example, the ↑ and ↓ keys enable you to scroll through previous commands.

You can also see a full list of all your previous commands by typing history. This lists all the previous commands in a numbered list. To repeat a command from your history, you type an exclamation point (!) and its corresponding number, like this:

```
history
!103
```

This sequence lists all the commands that you've typed and then re-enters the 103rd command you typed.

GETTING HELP FROM MAN PAGES

By now, you should have a good idea about how to work your way around Terminal and how to work with files, but there is much, much more to UNIX than you'd possibly believe. There isn't enough space in this book to teach you how to become a UNIX-ninja, but you can learn as you go by using UNIX's built-in help documentation, which you access with the $ man (manual) command. man delivers text-based documentation on any command in UNIX. Entering the following, for example, displays information on the $ ls (list) command:

```
man ls
```

The man pages offer streams of information related to UNIX commands. For example, the ls man page gives you a brief description of the command, plus a list of the options available and the functions they perform.

To get information on commands you don't know, you use the following to get a complete list of commands:

man ?

You can even get a man page on the man command itself, by using this command:

man man

Using the man command enables you to learn much of what UNIX has to offer. However, if you want to learn more about UNIX, you should spend some time online researching the subject or buy a dedicated book.

PLAYING TETRIS IN TERMINAL

There are a few hidden games that you can play in Terminal, including the classic game Tetris. Here's how you open Tetris in Terminal:

1. Type **emacs** into Terminal and press Return.

2. Press Esc+x.

3. Type **tetris** and press Return.

4. You can exit **emacs** by pressing Ctrl+X and then Ctrl+C.

You control Tetris by using the arrow keys to rotate the blocks, and you press the spacebar to drop the blocks.

There are plenty of other games available in the **emacs** interface. You can find more by using this command:

ls /usr/share/emacs/

To start playing a game, you can press Esc+x in **emacs** and enter the name of the game.

LOGGING IN AS A SUPERUSER

When you use Terminal to manage and edit files in Mac OS X, you get the same rights as when using your User account in Finder. However, you can log in as a superuser by using the sudo command. A superuser account gives you pretty much unlimited access and enables you to change, modify, and move any file on the system.

▶ Having a superuser account is also known as having root access.

It's possible to gain superuser access in Mac OS X by creating a root account, but it's safer and faster to use Terminal and sudo. To login as a superuser, you type the following command:

```
sudo -s
```

The sudo command enables you to log in as another user, and the -s option enables you to enter your password and log in as a superuser.

The first time you log in as a superuser, UNIX displays a warning. You must enter your password before you can be logged in as a superuser. After you log in, Terminal displays a different user account, titled Bash-3.2#.

To leave superuser mode and return to your regular account, you type exit.

You can also use sudo directly with commands to execute a command with superuser privileges. For example, to remove a hidden and locked file—such as .CFUserTextEncoding—you type the following:

```
sudo rm .CFUserTextEncoding
```

You must enter your password to complete the command.

▶ Bash stands for Bourne Again Shell. It is named after an early UNIX command-line interpreter written by Stephen Bourne. The pound sign (#) indicates that you are in root mode.

▶ For safety reasons, you should leave superuser mode as soon as you finish whatever it is you've been doing as a superuser.

> **WARNING** Using a superuser account gives you pretty much unlimited ability to edit, change, remove, and generally screw up the file system in Mac OS X. You should use it carefully and only when necessary.

Using Terminal is fun once you know what you're doing, but the command-line interface isn't all that UNIX is about. You should also investigate UNIX applications with a graphical interface. These run in the X Window system, commonly known as *X11*.

RUNNING X11 PROGRAMS

X11 is a GUI that enables UNIX X11-based programs to run in Mac OS X. But Mac OS X is a GUI, so why run X11? Well, some UNIX programs run in X11 and are designed to run across UNIX and Linux distributions running on different computer systems, not just Apple Macs.

X11 is included on the Mac OS X installation disc but is not installed by default. To install it, you insert the installation CD, locate the folder called Optional Installs, and open the Optional Installs.mpkg installer. The Optional Installs program lists additional programs you can install (or reinstall) in Mac OS X. You open the Applications folder and select the X11 check box, as shown in Figure 22-4. Then click Continue to include X11 in Mac OS X.

▶ X11 runs as a program like Finder or any other application. The X11 program is installed in the Utilities folder.

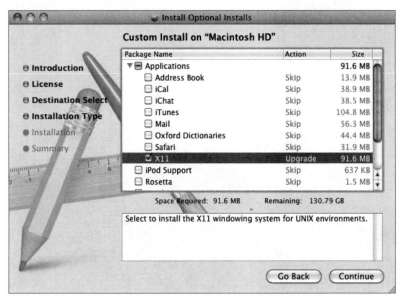

FIGURE 22-4: The Optional Installs programs on the Mac OS X installation disc.

X11 comes with a built-in command-line editor called Terminal, that you can access by choosing Applications ➔ Terminal. You can open a new Terminal window by pressing ⌘+N.

▶ The Terminal app is a command-line editor like Terminal in Mac OS X.

There are another two applications—xman and xlogo—present in the Applications menu. The xman program enables you to read UNIX man pages within a window environment, whereas xlogo displays a large X image within a window.

X11 includes 96 programs that you can open using Terminal. To open one of these apps, you simply open a new Terminal window and type in the name of the app. It then appears on the Desktop in an application window, like any regular Mac OS X application, as shown in Figure 22-5.

One key difference between X11 applications and Mac OS X applications is that you access them all through the X11 program, and they do not have independent menu bar items. (Instead, the X11 menu is always displayed.)

▶ Some X11 applications have their own menus, however.

Some interesting X11 applications include xcalc (calculator), xclock (a graphical clock), and xeyes (a set of eyes that follow the mouse pointer).

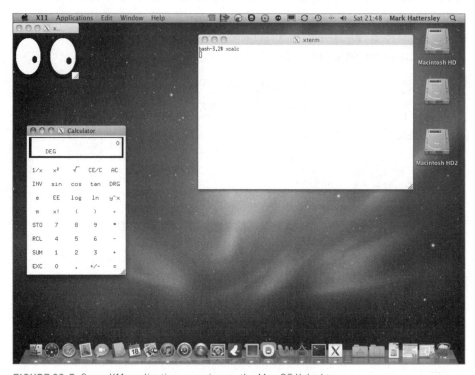

FIGURE 22-5: Some X11 applications running on the Mac OS X desktop.

You can get a list of all the applications included with X11 by using the following command:

```
ls /usr/X11/bin
```

You quit an application by clicking the red close button in the window or by quitting the Terminal window that you used to open the program.

It's also possible to add applications from X11 to the Application menu. For example, to add the xeyes application to X11, you follow these steps:

1. Choose Applications → Customize. This opens the X11 Application Menu window.

2. Click Add Item. A blank item is added to the menu list.

3. Click the new blank item and edit it. The Name field shows how the new item will be listed in the Applications menu. The Command item is the name of the application as you would enter it in Terminal.

4. You can also enter a shortcut combination to launch the app. Note that this combination will always be used in conjunction with the ⌘ key, even though you do not need to enter it specifically.

▶ You can also open XII applications by using the Terminal program provided with Mac OS X.

5. Click the red close button to close the X11 Applications menu.

6. You can now choose the program from the Applications menu.

The great thing about adding applications to the X11 Applications menu is that you no longer have to have a Terminal window open to use them.

> **TIP** You can get more information on any of the applications included with X11 by using **man**. You type **man xcalc** to get information on the xcalc application, for example.

While the applications that come with X11 are fun, they're unlikely to knock your socks off. But you can find much more professional offerings online. One of the most highly touted X11 applications is Gimp, which is an image editing suite that's similar in functionality to Adobe Photoshop.

You can download a copy of Gimp from http://darwingimp.sourceforge.net. It installs into the Applications folder just like any other Mac OS X program, although it opens via X11 when you double-click the icon.

You can look for other X11 applications online, and there are X11 programs like Fink (http://www.finkproject.org) that help you source and install X11 applications.

SUMMARY

Terminal's command-line interface is a real challenge to people who've only ever used the rich GUI in Mac OS X. But using UNIX can be extremely rewarding. UNIX is the engine that runs underneath the highly visual Mac GUI, and getting up to speed with it will vastly increase your understanding and ability to control the Mac operating system. We've only really scratched the surface here. When you have the hang of the Terminal command-line interface, you should investigate the man pages to get an understanding of what else is possible. Installing X11 is also rewarding because it opens up another world of applications that can be installed and run from within Mac OS X.

Installing Xcode and Programming Your Mac

At the heart of every computer lies programming, and I think it's a tragic shame to be a computer buff without attempting to create your own programs. Modern operating systems are so easy to use that many people don't bother with programming anymore. Instead, they use programs made by other people to be creative in other ways. There's nothing wrong with this, but on one level (especially the level that appeals to geeks), it's kind of missing the point: Programming is fun! It's much easier to start programming a Mac than you'd think—and Apple provides pretty much all you need on the installation disc. So head into Mac OS X and create your first programs!

INSTALLING THE DEVELOPER TOOLS

▶ Compared to the full version of Microsoft's Visual Studio Professional, Xcode is an amazing deal.

Programming on the Mac won't cost you a penny extra. Apple has built a complete programming environment called Xcode, and it's available for free to all Mac users. Xcode is an *integrated development environment* (IDE), which means it's a complete studio for writing, compiling, debugging, and building software applications.

What kind of applications can you create using Xcode? Just about anything that captures your fancy. You just need to know which programming language to use because Xcode supports several languages: C, C++, Objective-C, Objective-C++, Java, and AppleScript. The language of choice for most Apple developers is Objective-C, which is an object-oriented programming (OOP) language.

EXTENDING XCODE TO OTHER LANGUAGES

Xcode supports other languages, including Fortran, ADA, OCampl, and others. You can find out more information at **http://xcodeplugins.sourceforge.net**.

Installing Xcode

▶ Alternatively, you can download the latest version of Xcode from Apple's Developer Connection website (http://developer .apple.com).

Although Xcode is included with Mac OS X, it isn't installed by default with the operating system. Instead, you install it as an optional extra from the installation disc.

NOTE Xcode reports a size of zero for documentation during the install, but it downloads all the files (and keeps them updated) if you select the Documentation option. Otherwise, you need an online connection to access all the help documentation from within Xcode. On my Mac, the downloaded documentation folder is about 1.5GB.

Xcode installs in a folder called Developer at the root of your startup drive. This folder contains an Applications folder, which in turn contains Xcode and a collection of other applications to help you develop interfaces, web applications, audio, and so on.

Joining the Apple Developer Connection

Once you have Xcode installed on your Mac, you should also sign up for Apple Developer Connection, at http://developer.apple.com. It's free to join Apple Developer Connection, and once you sign up, you can download the latest version of Xcode, as well as documentation, sample code, development videos, and just about everything you need to get going as a coder.

There's also a series of three developer programs: Mac, iOS, and Safari. You need to pay annual fees to join the Mac Developer Program and iOS Developer Program. When you join the developer programs, you can download beta versions of upcoming software, including beta versions of both new Mac OS X and iOS software.

> You know beta often means unstable, right? Don't install beta software on your Mac or iPhone if you want to work on that device. Have separate test devices on hand for playing with betas.

WARNING   When you sign up with the Mac Developer Program or iOS Developer Program, be sure to read the agreement—especially the nondis- closure agreement (NDA). Apple has little patience with developers who talk publically about its beta software, and under no circumstances should you post screenshots of Apple beta software on the Internet.

Getting to Know the Xcode Interface

To start a new project, you select File ➜ New Project or click Create a New Xcode Project in the Welcome to Xcode window. The New Project window opens, with a series of templates for the kinds of program you can make, as shown in Figure 23-1. The sidebar divides templates into development environments, with options below each environment for specific kinds of programs, such as Application Plug-in, Frame- work & Library, and System Plug-in.

> The Mac OS X templates are included on the Mac OS X installation disc, but iOS templates require you to download the iOS software development kit (SDK) from Apple Developer Connection.

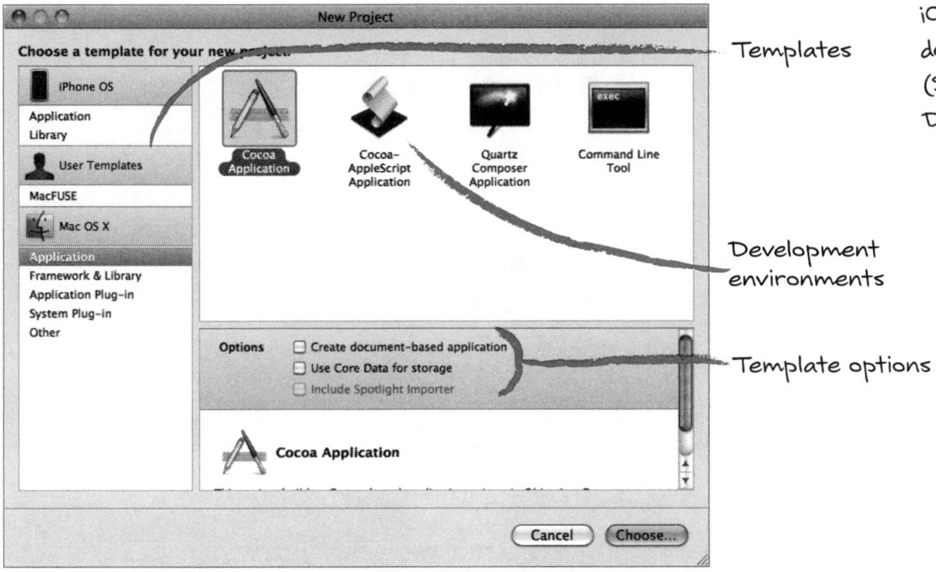

Templates

Development environments

Template options

FIGURE 23-1: The New Project window enables you to choose a template for your program.

▶ There may also be options (such as check boxes and pop-up menus) related to each type of application you choose.

The main window presents a further set of options for each selection in the sidebar. Choosing Application under the Mac OS X option, for example, gives you the following options: Cocoa Application, Cocoa-Applescript Application, Quartz Composer Application, and Command Line Tool.

The bottom half of the New Project window provides some information about the type of application, or program, that the template will help you develop. Select the appropriate template and click the Choose button to create an application.

> **TIP** If you're a beginner, you can choose Cocoa Application to learn how to create interface-based programs with windows or Command Line Tool to just work in a programming language.

Getting Help and Accessing Developer Documentation

▶ It's a bit like having a custom-built web browser, but Xcode downloads and stores most of the documents locally.

Apple provides comprehensive information related to Xcode and software development in general from within the Xcode environment itself. You can access Developer Documentation from Xcode at any point by using the Help menu, which provides several shortcuts to various documentation files (including quick start guides) from Apple. These appear in the Developer Documentation window, as shown in Figure 23-2.

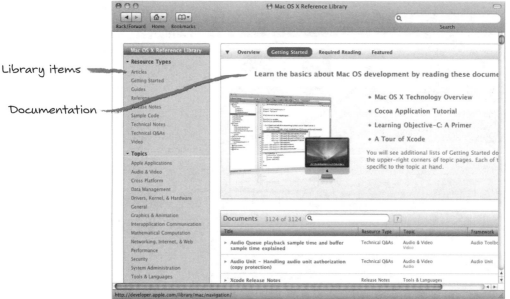

Library items

Documentation

FIGURE 23-2: The Developer Documentation window.

GETTING STARTED WITH PROGRAMMING

Xcode includes a lot of documentation to help you start programming, but much of it is aimed at high-end users. If you need help getting started, you might want to take a look at some of these resources:

▶ **"Learning Objective C: A Primer,"** http://developer.apple.com/library/mac/#referencelibrary/GettingStarted/Learning_Objective-C_A_Primer/index.html%23//apple_ref/doc/uid/TP40007594

▶ **"Introduction to the Objective-C Programming Language,"** http://developer.apple.com/library/mac/#documentation/Cocoa/Conceptual/ObjectiveC/Introduction/introObjectiveC.html

▶ *Objective-C for Dummies* by Neal Goldstein

▶ **"Stack Overflow,"** http://stackoverflow.com/questions/tagged/objective-c

Teaching you how to program from scratch is beyond the scope of this book, but this reading material will help you get started.

BUILDING A MAC OS X APPLICATION

It's actually much easier than you think to create a Mac OS X application. That is, it's easy to create an application that doesn't do very much.

In this section, you're going to use the Xcode interface along with the Interface Builder, as shown in Figure 23-3, to create an application that does nothing but print the words "Hello, world" in an otherwise empty window.

You follow these steps to get your Hello, World application up and running:

1. Choose File ➔ New Project or choose Create a New Xcode Project from the Welcome to Xcode window to open Xcode.

2 Click on Application underneath Mac OS X in the sidebar and choose Cocoa Application from the main window. Name your project HelloWorld and save it.

▶ There's a tradition in computing circles that the first program you learn, and use, in any new language should print "Hello, world" on the screen.

The applications menu   The main window

Library of
objects you
can add to
window

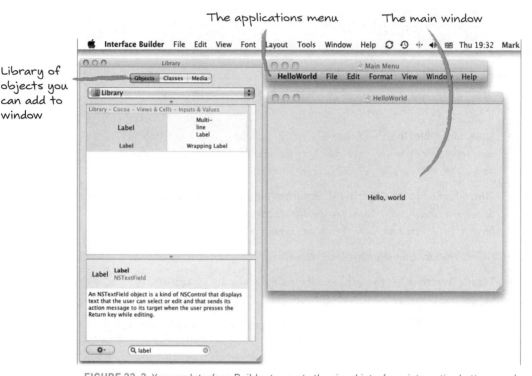

FIGURE 23-3: You use Interface Builder to create the visual interface, interactive buttons, and menu system of a program.

3. By default, your application is built with a single main window, which you can open in Interface Builder using the MainMenu.xib file. Double-click this file to open Interface Builder, revealing a series of windows used to build the application interface.

4. Drag a Label item from the Library to the HelloWorld window, as shown in Figure 23-3. Double-click the label and type `Hello, world`.

5. Save the changes to MainMenu.xib.

6. Return to Xcode and choose Build ➜ Build and Run.

The program compiles and then appears in the Dock (with a standard program icon), and it displays the window containing the Hello World text, as shown in Figure 23-4.

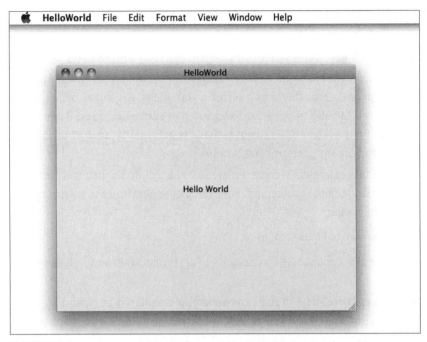

FIGURE 23-4: The new application, displaying the Hello World text.

This application may not do a great deal, but it shows how easy it is to create an application using the free Xcode environment.

A COMPLETE START

The Hello, World application has a lot of functionality, given that you haven't written a single line of code. It has a menu with the name of the program and a working About window. It also has File, Edit, Format, View, Window, and Help menu items, and they're all fully working, even though—like the application— they don't do much.

If you want to take Xcode further, you'll need to learn a programming language, typically C and then Objective-C. But learning these languages isn't an easy task, and you can use AppleScript and Automator to create applications much faster.

CREATING APPLICATIONS IN APPLESCRIPT

Unless you're a developer, you might find it tough to start out with Objective-C. If this describes you, you might want to investigate another language, called Apple-Script. AppleScript is a reasonably simply scripting language, developed by Apple and designed to control Mac OS X applications and automate common tasks. However, AppleScript also features some basic computational functionality, such as the ability to control program flow and perform calculations.

▶ In short, using AppleScript is a great way to program your computer without having to learn complicated computing processes.

Most AppleScript commands are written in reasonably plain English and com-mand programs using the tell command. For example, to get iTunes to start playing music, you type following:

```
tell application "iTunes" to play
```

After you type this command, you click Run to perform it right away. iTunes starts playing.

You can also get AppleScript to issue more complex commands by combining commands and using the end tell command to finish. The following script plays the Top 25 Most Played playlist at a volume level of 40 percent:

```
tell application "iTunes"
    set sound volume to 40
    play playlist "Top 25 Most Played"
end tell
```

You can also create applications directly from within AppleScript. When you have a script ready, you choose File → Save As and then choose File → Format → Application.

It's possible to create fairly simple scripts that quickly tell applications what to do. It's also possible to create fairly complex programs in AppleScript that use pro-gram flow and variables to perform intricate machinations.

SAYING HELLO IN APPLESCRIPT

You can get AppleScript to perform the Hello, World program by using the fol-lowing code:

```
tell application "Finder"
    display dialog "Hello, world"
end tell
```

This brings up a Mac OS X dialog window that displays the message "Hello, world."

The best way to learn AppleScript is to look at some specific resources. Here are some great places to get information:

▶ **DougsScripts (`http://dougscripts.com`):** This is a great collection of scripts, mostly focused on iTunes.

▶ **AppleScript Users mailing list (`http://lists.apple.com/mailman/listinfo/applescript-users`):** Apple has a selection of mailing lists for all kinds of AppleScript information.

▶ **MacScripter (`http://macscripter.net`):** This is a pretty good forum for Apple-Script users.

▶ *AppleScript (Developer Reference)* **by Mark Conway Munro:** This is a great book for developers who want to learn AppleScript and use it to create auto-mated programs.

▶ *Apple Automator with AppleScript Bible* **by Thomas Myer:** This book has incredibly deep coverage of Mac OS X automation that covers just about every task possible.

AppleScript is a lot easier to learn than Objective-C, but it's still fairly difficult to begin with (mostly because of its informal nature). But with a good reference guide and a bit of practice, you'll be amazed at its ability to transform the way you use your Mac.

> **TIP** A great technique is to simply look online for a script that does the sort of thing you're after. Many scripts have been written and placed online. You can cut and paste text from a website into AppleScript and edit it to your own needs.

QUICKLY CREATING APPLICATIONS IN AUTOMATOR

A final tool that you can use to create applications is a rather nifty program in Mac OS X called Automator. Automator is a lot like AppleScript, but without the scripting language. Instead, you drag and drop commands into a visual workflow.

Support for Automator by Apple is somewhat more extensive than support for AppleScript, although the independent developer community provides vibrant support for AppleScript.

▶ One key difference is that Automator supports Preview, which makes it better for adjusting images than AppleScript.

One key difference is that in Automator, *actions* are arranged by function rather than by application, as shown in Figure 23-5.

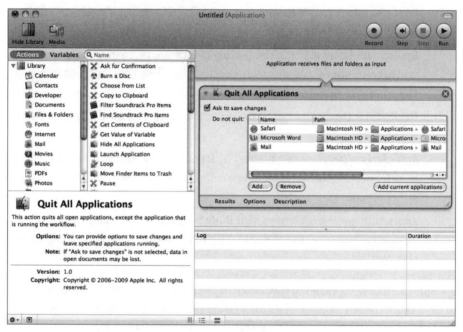

FIGURE 23-5: The Automator interface.

> ▶ A workflow is a series of steps that a process runs through from start to finish.

The Automator features sets of actions and variables in the sidebar, and another column to the right of it displays individual actions and variables. You drag these to the main window to create a workflow.

As with AppleScript and other programming languages, with Automator, you can use variables, although they are largely based on variables inside Mac OS X (system time, date, user name, and so on). You can create actions that depend on a specific set of variables.

Creating an application with Automator is really easy. You follow these steps to create a program that quits all the open applications except the ones you regularly use (in this example, Mail, Safari, and Microsoft Word):

1. Open Automator and select Application in the Choose a Template for your Workflow window. Click Choose.

2. Ensure that Actions is selected and click on Utilities in the Library.

3. Drag the Quit All Applications action from the list of actions to the workflow window.

4. Click Add and use the Open dialog to locate applications you don't want to quit. Alternatively, click Add Current Applications and then use Remove to get rid of unwanted programs.

5. Choose File ➜ Save As and give the application a name. Choose Application from the File Format pop-up menu and click Save.

The application is saved with an Automator icon. You can double-click the icon to launch and run the workflow, in this case quitting all open applications except the ones you identified.

It's incredibly easy to create simple applications using Automator, although, as with AppleScript, it can become complex when you start to add multiple actions together and involve variables. It's a lot easier to create applications in Automator than to program them in either Objective-C or AppleScript (although it has other limitations compared to both of these languages). However, if you're looking to add a personal, professional touch to Mac OS X, nothing does it quite like your own programs—and nothing creates them as quickly as Automator.

▶ When you create an Automator application, it will run the workflow and then immediately quit when it has finished.

▶ Plus there's just something really cool about building your own programs easily.

SUMMARY

It would be a real shame to own a modern computer as powerful as a Mac and never write your own computer program, so install Xcode and take a look at building your own programs in Objective-C. It's fair to say that Objective-C is a bit of a mindbender, though, and not everyone wants to learn a modern, object-oriented programming language just to get the operating system to do simple things. So Apple has kindly included not one but two environments for quick and easy program-making: Automator and AppleScript. Both have strengths (although I prefer Automator), and both enable you to quickly automate tasks and create programs. So next time you find yourself wishing Mac OS X did something just a little differently, why not create a program for it yourself? Just don't forget to share it with other Mac users.

Index